Sha'arei Teshuvah

Gates of Repentance

Rabbeinu Yonah

Hasidic

Rabbeinu Yonah Gerondi

SimchatChaim.com

There is no known book without mistakes. Therefore, I ask in every language of application if anyone has any questions, comments, clarifications, corrections, please send to: **simchatchaim@yahoo.com**

All material used in this section may not be used for commercial purposes, but only for study and teaching.

To get this book or books and information Email me at:

Sha'arei Teshuvah

Gates of Repentance

Rabbeinu Yonah

The contents of the book

Rabbeinu Yonah Gerondi

Hasidic Rabbeinu Yona

Rabbeinu Yona is the second central figure in the public and religious life of the Jews of Spain in the middle of the 13th century and the giant of the spirit of this glorious Judaism throughout the generations. For generations, he will be known as a man of great morals, and in his time, he was known mainly for his public work: a preacher, a brave fighter against corrupt leadership, and the head of a large yeshiva in Barcelona and Toledo, where he made many students who continued his path.

About the extent of his influence on Sephardic Jewry, we can quote him from the words of our Rabbi Chai Ben Asher [our Rabbi in his second life] about twenty-five years after the death of Rabbeinu Yona. When he chose from Rabbeinu Yona's commentary to tell the opening parables at the beginning of each Parsha - he wrote: "And from my commentary, one holy man speaks of great importance... He is a man of God, a pillar and corner of the Torah, the great rabbi Rabbeinu Yona, the late... How much more precious is his composition than gold and all pearls, Man Yahib lan Ma'apriya Demer and Melinan Einin [Who will bring us from the dust of the Lord, and we will fill our eyes]".

2

Rabbeinu Yona was his partner and friend, as well as his cousin and mother-in-law, of the Ramban, and their joint activity brought about a deep and far-reaching change in all Jewish life in Spain and the Talmud of the Torah in this country. One. This is what, for example, Rabbi Menachem Ha'Meiri writes in his introduction to Tractate Avot: "And in Catalonia, after Rabbi Alberceloni, we heard the great Rabbi Yona and the great RAMBA"N [Rabbi Moshe ber Nachman], whose wisdom was published in the world."

Up to this point in history, the Jewry of Spain was characterized almost from its first days, being a Jewry of the cave in general education and cultural circles. However, with the rise of the influence of Christianity in the country, we see a turning point in Spanish Judaism. The pinnacle of this turning point was brought about by the Ramba"n, but to a more prominent degree by Rabbeinu Yona, who brought to Spain the Prussian Hasidic spirit of the Ashkenaz Hasidic circle, a spirit of innocence and stickiness, zeal for the Torah and lofty moral standards of holiness and purity, and a rejection of external wisdom and considerable culture.

The main part of Rabbeinu Yona's publication is related to his moral teachings, "He who has not risen like him speaks in the fear of God to draw the hearts of men to the ways of Hasidism" [as Rabbi Shimon ben Rabbi Tzemach Duran says in the introduction to his commentary on the chapters of Avot].

This Torah is divided into three:

A. The next **direct** moral is expressed in his most famous book **"Sha'arei Tshuva"**. In this book, Rabbeinu Yona presented for the first time the moral problem as the vital concern of the entire public and not only as a concern of the elite "seekers of God". He presented public life as a subject for moral consideration and taught that the wholeness of the individual is not only found in the spheres between man and his creator, but to no less extent also in the spheres between man and his fellow man, and like communal public life in which all guarantee a mutual guarantee and bear personal responsibility for the actions of the common.

The book Shear Teshuva is part of a more comprehensive composition, which contained additional "gates" and some of them are mentioned in the Teshuva Gate - the Torah Gate, the Humility Gate, the Fear Gate, the Cruelty Gate, and the Labor Gate.

The great strength of the book is its direct, simple, and honest appeal to the common sense of the reader, a heartfelt appeal based on the foundations of simple religious logic and the familiar and convincing daily life experience of everyone. His way is to first bring verses from the Bible to prove the prohibition and voice its seriousness, then the articles of sages that belong to the matter, and finally he turns to the life experience of his readers, to draw their attention and

4

attention to the seriousness of their sin and to the relative ease with which they can return from their sin and make amends.

The structure of the book is like this:

The first gate: "In explanation of the answer and its main points".
The second gate: "Ways that a person will wake up in to return".
The third chapter: "The material of the commandments and warnings and the distribution of punishments", is the main part of the book, both in terms of quantity and quality.
And the fourth chapter: "In the distributions of atonement."

B. The second part of Rabbeinu Yona's moral theory is a wise literature whose moral take is like a direct result of the things but is not the focus of the direct reference, and within it should be listed the commentary to the book of Proverbs and the Tractate of the Fathers. The purpose of these explanations is a psychological analysis of the human soul and its essence, and they tend to instruct a person on how to utilize the powers of his soul correctly and how to control the positive forces over the negative forces.
C. The third part is Halacha literature addressed to the general public, which contains moral values and reverence for God: "Sefer Ha'Irah" and "Egret Teshuvah". These books are based on the understanding that a strict and meticulous observance of the mitzvot and the study of the Torah, Halacha,

and Aggada, are necessary and sufficient infrastructure for achieving piety and morality. Therefore, in these books, halakhic are presented in combination with words of awakening and directing attention to lesser-known practical aspects of the halachic issues raised in the book.

Sha'arei Teshuvah

Gates of Repentance

Rabbeinu Yonah

Chapter One

In explanation of repentance and its principles
Among the good things which God, may He be
blessed, has bestowed upon His creations is the path
which He prepared for them to ascend from the
baseness of their actions, to escape the trap of their
inequities, to hold their souls back from destruction
and to remove His anger from upon them. Because of
His goodness and uprightness, He has taught them
and warned them to return to Him when they sin
against Him - for He understands their nature, as it is
stated - Good[1] and upright is the Lord; therefore, He
shows sinners the way. Even if they greatly sin and
rebel and act like treacherous betrayers - He does not
close the doors of repentance to them, as it is stated -
Return[2], to Him to whom they have been so
shamefully false. It is also stated - Turn[3] back O
rebellious children I will heal your afflictions. We are
warned about repentance in several places in the
Torah. It is explained that repentance is accepted even
when the sinner repents because of his many troubles

---

[1] Psalms 25:8
[2] Isaiah 31:6
[3] Jeremiah 3:22

- how much more so will it be accepted if he returns because of fear or love of God - as it is stated - When[4] you are in distress because all these things have befallen you and, in the end, return to the Lord your God and obey Him. It is explained in the Torah that God will help those who repent beyond what their natural ability would allow; and that He renews a pure spirit within them, to reach great heights in His love - as it is stated - And[5] you return to the Lord your God, and you and your children heed His command with all your heart and soul, just as I enjoin upon you this day. Further, it is stated about the body of the matter - Then[6] the Lord, your God, will circumcise your heart and the hearts of your offspring. to acquire love for Him. And the Prophets and Writings constantly speak on the subject of repentance, such that the principles of repentance are all explained in their words, as will be explained.

Know that the punishment for the sinner who delays repenting of his sin will grow much heavier for him every day. For he knows that God's wrath has gone forth against him and that he has an escape route from it - that escape being repentance - yet he still remains rebellious and stays within his evil. Even though it is within his power to leave from within the disorder, he does not fear the anger nor the rage. Thus, his evil is great, see also Midrash[7] Kohelet which relates a

---

[4] Deuteronomy 4:30
[5] Deuteronomy 30:2
[6] Deuteronomy 30:6
[7] Kohelet Rabbah 7:15

parable illustrating this concept.

But delay of repentance is only found among the ignorant, who are sleeping - lounging. They do not turn to their hearts, and they have neither the knowledge nor the understanding to know that they should hurry, to escape for their lives. Some of them are led astray from God, Blessed be He, and they do not believe in punishment for sin. And our rabbis, may their memory be blessed, said - If[8] you saw a scholar transgress a prohibition at night, do not think badly of him the next day; for in truth, he has already repented.

And furthermore - reflect upon the evil of the one who delays repenting, as it is great. For if it were not that he had delayed - now when his impulse would confront him a second time and he have the opportunity to sin, he would recoil and sigh with a bitter heart, with anguish and worry; and his eye would weep with grief. He would [then] subdue his impulse, remember that the cup of bitterness had passed over him once and he would not drink it again. As it is stated - Tremble[9] and do not sin - its explanation is, tremble and fear and be troubled about your sinning, and do not sin again. For it mentioned their sin above in that chapter in Psalms, when it stated - You[10] sought falsehood Selah. And it's using the expression, **tremble**, confirms this explanation.

_____

[8] Berakhot 19a
[9] Psalms 4:8
[10] Psalms 4:3

As its usage is like in - Do[11] not tremble along the way. as it says - I[12] trembled where I stood. And their meaning is distress at something that passed and is still present. And it did not state in Psalms above, **Fear**, or **Flinch**. But when he delays from repenting - when the sin comes to his hands, he will fall into its trap like he fell at first. And his second iniquity will be very great and his evil will rise up in front of God. For at first, he did not think that the marauding impulse would come upon him. But after he saw the weakness of his power and that his impulse had overcome him and that it is more powerful than he; he should have seen that it is unbridled, and he should have sought to increase his fear of God, to bring down His fright upon his soul, to save it from the ambush of his impulse and to protect it from its iniquity. And King Solomon, peace be upon him, said - As[13] a dog returns to his vomit, so a fool repeats his folly. Its explanation is that a dog eats disgusting things; but when he vomits them, they are more disgusting, yet he returns to eat them. Such is the matter of a fool. For he will do a disgraceful act, but when he repeats it, it is even more disgraceful, as we explained.

Additionally, repentance is more difficult for one who repeats his sin; for the sin becomes as if it were permitted to him. And his sin is very weighty with regards to this, as it is stated - That[14] is how you spoke;

---

[11] Genesis 45:24
[12] Habakkuk 3:16
[13] Proverbs 26:11
[14] Jeremiah 3:5

you did wrong, and you were able. The meaning of, **you were able**, is that the evil deeds have become like that which is permitted to you, and like something within your ability and your authority - like the usage in the Torah - You[15] are not able to eat in your gates. for which the translation of Onkelos is - You do not have authority. And our Rabbis, may their memory be blessed, said in the Talmud - When[16] a person commits a transgression and repeats it, it becomes to him as if it were permitted. Additionally, our Rabbis, may their memory be blessed, said about a man who commits a transgression and repeats it - that from now on, if he thinks about doing that sin but is prevented from doing it by duress, his bad thought is joined with the act, it is counted as if he did it. And about him is it stated - I[17] am going to bring disaster upon this people, the outcome of their own thoughts.

And now understand - listen to this, for it is a great principle. It is true that there are righteous people who sometimes stumble into sin - like the matter that is stated - For[18] there is no man that is righteous on earth, who does good and does not sin. However, they conquer their impulses from in front of them. And if they do fall to sin once, they will not repeat it. [Rather] they will have it taken away from in front of them and repent. However, anyone who is not careful of a particular sin and does not take upon himself to

---

[15] Deuteronomy 12:17
[16] Yoma 86b
[17] Jeremiah 6:19
[18] Ecclesiastes 7:20

11

guard against it - even if it is from the light ones [and] even though he guards himself against all of the [other] transgressions of the Torah - the Sages of Israel call a habitual sinner **Mumar** [sinner] about one thing in the Talmud - He[19] is counted with the sinners, and his sin is too great to bear. For surely if a slave said to his master, I will do everything you tell me except for one thing, he has already broken his master's yoke from upon himself and will do what is proper in his own eyes. And this whole matter is stated - Cursed[20] be he who will not uphold the words of this Torah to do them. The explanation of the matter is that he does not accept upon himself to fulfill all of the words of the Torah, from beginning to end. And what indicates this is the phrase, who will not uphold… to do, and it did not state - who will not do them.

Furthermore, know that one who repeats one sin ten times - even though he guards himself against all of the other transgressions - is surely considered as if he transgressed different transgressions. And so did our Rabbis, may their memory be blessed, say in the Talmud that if they tell a **Nazirite** - Do[21] not drink wine, and he drinks, do not drink, and he drinks - at the end, he is lashed for each and every time - like one who eats a terminally **Tereifah** [sick animal], an impure animal, forbidden fat and blood.

---

[19] Chullin 4b
[20] Deuteronomy 27:26
[21] Makkot 21a

And we have surely seen that the iniquities of the generation have increased on account of this. For there are many people who do not take upon themselves to guard against specific sins. And they do not guard against them all the days of their lives, but these sins are rather like something permitted to them. And if they were only behaving like this with one sin, it would have been a bad disease upon their souls - as we explained. All the more when they behave so with many **negative** commandments, including weighty ones - such as unnecessary oaths, cursing one's fellow or oneself with God's name; mentioning God's name unnecessarily, in an impure place or with unclean hands; diverting one's eyes from the poor, evil speech, baseless hatred, pride, terrorizing others, staring at those sexually forbidden - and the neglect of Torah is equal to all of them together. And there are many like this - we have written some of them for the people of the generation, to remind them and to warn them. And likewise, is it fitting for all penitents to write in a scroll-book the things that they have stumbled upon, and the commandments in which their performance has fallen short; and to read from this book of memoirs every day.

And behold that there are many levels of repentance. It is true that you will find forgiveness for any repentance. However, the soul will only find complete purification - to be as if the iniquities never had been - when a person purifies his heart and prepares his spirit, as will be explained. And so is it written - Happy[22] is the man whom the Lord does not hold guilty, and in whose spirit, there is no deceit. And it is like the matter of a garment that needs washing: For a little washing will be effective to remove its soiling. However, it will only whiten according to the amount of washing. And so is it written there - Wash[23] me thoroughly of my iniquity. And the soul will be washed from iniquity according to how you wash its heart, as it is stated - Wash[24] your heart clean of wickedness, O Jerusalem. And our Rabbis, may their memory be blessed, said in the Talmud - Happy[25] is the man who fears the Lord. - When[26] he is still a man. This means to say that the most elevated repentance of a man is in the days of his youth - when he overcomes his impulse when his strength is still with him. However, any repentance is effective, as it is stated - You[27] return man to dust You said Return you mortals. And our Rabbis, may their memory be blessed, said in the Talmud - Until[28] the soul turns to dust.

Now we will explain the principles of repentance.

The first principle is regret:

His heart should understand that leaving God is bad

---

22 Psalms 32:2
23 Psalms 51:4
24 Jeremiah 4:14
25 Avodah Zarah 19a
26 Psalms 112:1
27 Psalms 90:3
28 Yerushalmi Chagigah 2:1

and bitter; and he should place into his heart that there is punishment, vengeance and repayment for iniquity, as it is stated - To[29] be My vengeance and repayment. And it is stated - Be[30] in fear of the sword, for your fury is iniquity worthy of the sword. And he should regret his bad deeds and say in his heart - What have I done? How did I not have fear of God in front of my eyes, and did not become afraid from the rebukes of iniquity and from the harsh judgments? For there are many aches waiting for the evildoer. I did not pity my body; and for a moment of pleasure, my eyes did not pity its being destroyed. I became like a man who robs and extorts, eats and is satiated; but who knows that after his eating and his drinking, the judge will grind his teeth with gravel - like the matter that is stated - But[31] later his mouth will be filled with gravel. And worse than this, I was cruel to the dear soul and I rendered it impure with the idols of my impulse. And what did it gain from all of its acquisitions, if they are bad in the eyes of its Master? And how did I trade a passing world for a world that exists for ever and ever? How have I become similar to animals? As I have gone after my impulse like a horse, like a mule that does not understand. And I have strayed from the way of the intellect. And behold the Creator blew a living soul into my nose - a wise heart and the benefit of intellect - in order to recognize Him and fear Him and to govern over the body and all of its actions, like it governs over the other animals that do not speak,

[29] Deuteronomy 32:35
[30] Job 19:29
[31] Proverbs 20:17

because it is precious in His eyes. And though I was created like this, it has become the opposite of this in me. Why am I alive? It is like the matter that is stated - A[32] man who strays from the path of the intellect will rest in the company of ghosts. Moreover, I have not even fulfilled the precept of the animal. Rather I have been lower than that. For the ox knows its master and the donkey the trough of its owner; whereas I have not known and not reflected. And I have sent my soul to be free from its master. So, I have tasted my nectar, but forgotten my end. And I have stolen and extorted and trampled upon the indigent. I have not remembered the day of death, upon which nothing will remain before my soul besides my corpse and my dirt. And this matter that we have explained is that which Jeremiah, peace be upon him, had spoken - No one regrets his wickedness and says - **What have I done**?

The second principle is leaving the sin:

That he should leave his evil ways and decide with all of his heart that he will not continue to return this way again. And if he did evil, he shall not do it any more, like the matter that is stated - Return[33] return from your evil ways. and likewise stated - Let[34] the wicked give up his ways. But know that in the case of one who sins by happenstance because he had a desire and his impulse overpowered him and attacked him,

---

[32] Proverbs 21:16
[33] Ezekiel 33:11
[34] Isaiah 55:17

whereas his ideas and senses did not rescue him when he encountered it; so they were not quick to rebuke him in the sea of desire, to dry it up - hence the impulse dragged him into its nets and he fell into its snares at that particular time and instant, at the time that the spirit of the evil impulse kicked him down, but not because of his [own] desire and will to find his iniquity and to do like this afterwards: The beginning of the repentance of this man is regret; to place sorrow into his heart about his sin, to have his soul be afflicted and bitter like wormwood. Afterwards, he should increase the fear of sin in his heart every day, and put the dread of God into his heart at all times, until his heart becomes steady in the trust of God. As if the impulse comes across him again - like it does from time to time - and his desire become fanned like the first case, his heart will not be seduced by it and he will abandon its path. This is as it is stated - But[35] one who confesses and abandons them will find mercy - it mentions **confesses** first, about the regret and the confession; and afterwards, **abandons**. However in the case of one who is constantly positioned on the path that is not good, and the man who treads on his sins every day and repeats them in his foolishness; and who runs after it many times in his race, loves his evil all the time, places the trap of his iniquity in front of his face - meaning his desire and impulse - and his craving is his occupation; he does not prevent himself from doing anything that he wants to do: For such a man, the beginning of his repentance is to abandon his evil way and thoughts,

---

[35] Proverbs 28:13

and to agree, resolve and accept upon himself to not continue sinning. Afterwards, he should regret and return to God, as it is stated - Let[36] the wicked give up his ways, the sinful man his plans; let him turn back to the Lord, and He will pardon him. And the parable for this is about one who holds a sherbet an impure crawling animal, and comes to immerse and become pure. For he must first leave the sherbets, and then immerse and become purified. But all the time that the sherbets is in his hand, his impurity is still with him and the immersion is ineffective. And behold that leaving the thoughts of sin is equivalent to throwing out the sherbets; and the regret of that which he sinned, the confession and the prayer are in place of the immersion. And when afflictions and aches come upon the evildoer for whom all of his plans are to continue with his crimes, he is first afflicted. And then he repents from the evil thoughts that he thought and cuts off the actions from his hands. And the parable for this is about a calf which they hit with a cow prod to direct his work on the furrows. So is one who is positioned on a path that is not good. He should take the chastisement first, to abandon the ways of death and to walk in a straight path - as it is written - I[37] can hear Ephraim lamenting - You have chastised me, and I am chastised like a calf that has not been broken. And it is further stated after it - Now[38] that I have turned back I am filled with remorse. This means to say - After you chastised me,

---

[36] Isaiah 55:7
[37] Jeremiah 31:18
[38] Jeremiah 31:19

and I was chastised and returned from my evil ways; I was filled with remorse afterwards and regretted what occurred with my iniquities. So, behold that all of this matter that we have explained has been clarified for you.

The third principle is grief:

His conscience should darken as he thinks about the great evil of one who rebels against his Maker. He should magnify the grief in his heart, experience a storm in his thoughts and sigh with a bitter heart. For it is possible for him to regret all the sins that he did and find them to be bad in his eyes, yet not fill his measure in this. For even the loss of a dinar or an **Isar** [a small coin] is difficult in the eyes of a man. However, if he lost all of his wealth in a bad way and was cleaned out of possessions, his soul would actually mourn and his sighing would be heavy. And likewise, is his pain infinite and his grief daily for many and frequent troubles. And more than about these is it fitting to be distressed and constantly sigh for one who rebelled against God, may He be blessed, was destructive, performed disgusting acts in front of Him; and who did not remember his Maker who created him ex nihilo, did kindness with him, placed His hand upon him at every instant and guards his spirit at all times - how could he have the temerity to bring anger in front of Him? And how were the eyes of the sinner shut from seeing; from having his heart understand? And one who understands and has eyes opened will inscribe these words onto his heart, so that they will enter the chambers of his spirit.

And the levels of repentance and their stature is based
on the greatness of the bitterness and the power of the
grief. And that is repentance that comes by way of the
purification of the soul and the purity of its intellect.
For according to his intellect and according to that
which he opens his eyes will be the grief of his
thoughts about his great poverty. As it is stated - For[39]
I will not always contend I will not be angry forever
nay - When spirits in front of Me cover themselves I
who create the souls. Its explanation is that according
to that which the spirit - which is in front of me -
covers itself and is distressed, and the souls which I
have made cover themselves; I will not contend and I
will not be angry. For how can I not have grace and
mercy upon the precious soul that is in front of Me?
Therefore, the sin will be light according to the
weightiness of the service of the sighing about it. For
grief comes from the purification of the highest soul.
And it is accepted through this more than it would be
accepted by many afflictions and aches of the body.
And the parable for this is that a king has mercy on
his attendants that were born in his household that are
close to him and from the respected nobles of the land
- and he gives them grace - more than on the distant
and smaller ones. And it states - I[40] who create the
souls. Due to their closeness to the higher ones, even
though the body and everything else are the work of
His hands. And like this is - The[41] tablets were God's
work. And our Rabbis, may their memory be blessed,

---

[39] Isaiah 57:16
[40] Isaiah 57:16
[41] Exodus 32:16

also said in the Talmud - There[42] are three partners in a man: His father, his mother and the Holy One, blessed be He. But because the father and mother have no partnership in the soul - therefore, it stated - I who create the souls, That the matter is as I have explained it, is shown from its stating - **when spirits in front of Me**.

And King David, peace be upon him, stated - O[43] Lord, all my desires are in front of You; my groaning is not hidden from You. Its explanation is that that all of my desire is revealed to You - that it is only for Your service. And You know that my sighing is not about matters of the world and finite things; but about my sins and the limits of my reach in Your service. And one of the supplicatory said, Examine His worth - My sighing is from Your fear - remove my sighing from me; I worried from the limits of my reach in Your service - remove my worries from me.

The fourth principle is pain in his actions:

as it is stated - Yet[44] even now - says the Lord - Turn back to Me with all your hearts, and with fasting, weeping, and lamenting. And they, may their memory be blessed, said the Talmud - The[45] heart and the eyes are the two intermediaries of sin. And so is it written -And[46] you shall not go astray after your hearts

---

[42] Kiddushin 30a
[43] Psalms 38:10
[44] Joel 2:12
[45] Yerushalmi Berakhot 1:4
[46] Numbers 15:39

and after your eyes. Hence with this will the sin of the intermediaries be atoned - with the measure of repentance according to the measure of the affliction. For the iniquity of the heart is atoned by its bitterness and sighing - with the brokenness with which it is broken, as it is stated - When[47] spirits in front of Me cover themselves. And it is also written - God[48] You will not despise a contrite and crushed heart. And the parable about this is from the impure vessels - when they are broken, they are purified, as it is stated - An[49] oven or stove shall be smashed. And the iniquity of the eyes is atoned by tears, as it is stated - My[50] eyes shed streams of water, because they do not obey Your Torah. It does not state - Because I do not obey Your Torah. But rather states - they do not obey; since they were what caused the sin - therefore, I shed streams of waters.

The fifth principle is worry:

As he will worry and fear from the punishment of his iniquities. For there are iniquities for which the repentance has the atonement depend upon cleansing afflictions, as it is stated - I[51] acknowledge my iniquity; I am fearful over my sin. The content of grief is about the past, whereas the content of worry is about the future. And he will also doubly worry - maybe he is falling short in his obligation of

[47] Isaiah 57:16
[48] Psalms 51:19
[49] Leviticus 11:35
[50] Psalms 119:136
[51] Psalms 38:19

repentance with pain, bitterness, fasting and crying. And even if he has multiplied the pain and multiplied the crying, he should crawl and fear - maybe corresponding to this had he multiplied his guilt; so that all of his affliction and having his soul cry in its fast did not fill his measure. And one who examines the greatness of the service to the Creator upon his creatures and that there is no end to the evil of one who rebels against His word will know that even with all of what he adds to his service and in the ways of repentance, is it not small? Behold it is like a little in his eyes. And King Solomon, peace be upon him, said - A[52] wise man is afraid and turns away from evil. And its explanation is that even though a wise man turns away from evil with all of the efforts of his ability, he should crawl and fear - maybe he did not complete his measure, and he was not careful according to the standard of what needs to be done. And like this is - Than[53] a rich man whose ways are crooked. Even though he is rich. And likewise did our Rabbis, may their memory be blessed, say in **Yilamdeinu** - Do[54] not explain it as A wise man is afraid and turns away from evil; but rather, A wise man turns away from evil and is afraid. And the end of the verse proves this - But[55] a fool rush and is confident. He states abut the traits of a fool, that they are the opposite of the traits of a wise man. For a fool rushes, but is nevertheless confident that iniquity and damage will not come to

---

[52] Proverbs 14:16
[53] Proverbs 28:6
[54] Tanchuma, Lech Lecha, 15
[55] Proverbs 14:16

him. Yet the angry person is given to sins and open to damages, as it is stated - A[56] hot-tempered man commits many offenses. And it is also stated - Like[57] an open city without walls is a man whose temper is uncurbed.

And the penitent should also worry lest his impulse overpower him. It is like they, may their memory be blessed, said - Do[58] not trust in yourself until the day of your death. All the more so, a man whose heart has already vanquished him. For it is fitting to guard oneself every instant from the ambushing impulse; and to add fear of God to himself every day. And it will then be a fortress when all of the breakers of the impulse that renew themselves in the future pass upon him.

And King Solomon, peace be upon him, spoke about the matter of repentance and specified this topic. And he surely opened his words and said - When[59] the righteous exult there is great glory, but when the wicked rise up, men will be sought. The explanation [of this] is that the righteous will exalt and honor people about all the good traits that are found with them; but the wicked seek peoples' blemishes and their mistakes, to put them down - even when they have already left these actions and returned in repentance. Afterwards he said - He[60] who covers up

---

56 Proverbs 29:22
57 Proverbs 25:28
58 Avot 2:4
59 Proverbs 28:12
60 Proverbs 28:13

his faults will not succeed but he who confesses and gives them up will find mercy. For even though a penitent should not reveal his iniquities to people - as is to be understood from that which is stated, but when the wicked rise up, men will be sought - He is obligated to confess them privately, like the matter that is stated - Then[61] I acknowledged my sin to You I did not cover up my guilt. And it is also stated - Lo[62] I will bring you to judgment for saying I have not sinned. But the Sages of Israel, may their memory blessed, explained in the Talmud - That[63] there are times when he who covers up his faults will not succeed - like with sins between a man and his fellow. As he does not attain atonement until he returns what was stolen, extorted or taken unjustly; and until he asks to be pardoned for that which he annoyed him, embarrassed him or spoke evil speech about him. Likewise, must he not cover up his sins between a man and the Omnipresent that have become known to people. For one who sins publicly desecrates God's name. [But Rashi, in the Talmud - Yom HaKippurim, understands it in a different way. See there]. So, he is obligated to grieve and mourn about it in front of people to sanctify God's name. And this is the meaning of that which is written - Now[64] that I have turned back, I am filled with remorse; now that I am made aware, I strike my thigh. The meaning of, I am filled with remorse. is regret and pain. For the essence

---

[61] Psalms 32:5
[62] Jeremiah 2:35
[63] Yoma 86b
[64] Jeremiah 31:19

of repentance is bitterness of the heart, as we have explained. And the meaning of, now that I am made aware, I strike my thigh, is after people have been made aware and my iniquities have been publicized, I mourned with actions that were visible to people. This is like - Strike[65] the thigh. and it is also stated - He[66] declares to men I have sinned I have perverted what was right.

But[67] he who confesses and gives them up will find mercy. The explanation is that even though there are three foundations of repentance - regret, confession and leaving the sin - and here it only appears like two, regret and confession are both included in - He who confesses. For one who confesses, regrets. But there is no repentance without these three - as one who regrets and confesses but does not leave the sin is like one who immerses with a sherbet in his hand. However, he who confesses and gives them up will find mercy - for he is a penitent. This is the case, even though there are many levels of repentance, as we have explained.

He said after this - Happy[68] is the man who is always afraid, but he who raises his heart falls into misfortune. Its explanation is, even though he confesses and gives them up, he should always be afraid that maybe he has not filled the required

---

[65] Ezekiel 21:17
[66] Job 33:27
[67] Proverbs 28:13
[68] Proverbs 28:14

measure of repentance. For it requires many levels, so he should increase his fortitude every day to attain these levels. He should also be afraid that maybe his impulse will return to him. So, he should guard against it every instant, always add fear of God to his soul and always pray to God to help him towards repentance and to save him from his impulse. But he who raises his heart falls into misfortune: One who says in his heart, I have filled my measure of repentance, and does not always make efforts to acquire higher levels of repentance and to add fear to his soul will be punished for this. For he is of a raised heart and does not recognize the deficiency of his spirit. And if he does not recognize the greatness of his obligation to refine his ways with great refinement, he will also not guard himself from his impulse, which always ambushes him. Hence, he will fall into the hands of his impulse.

The sixth principle is shame:

Like the matter that is stated - I[69] am ashamed and also humiliated, for I bear the disgrace of my youth. As behold that a sinner would be very ashamed to do transgressions in front of people; and he would be humiliated if people sensed and noted his transgressions. So how is it that he would not be ashamed in front of the Creator, may He be blessed? And this is only from the Holy One, blessed be He, being distant from his feelings. Hence, he is ashamed towards the creatures, but he is not ashamed towards

---

[69] Jeremiah 31:19

the Creator, may He be blessed. And our Rabbis, may their memory be blessed, said in the Talmud - That[70] at the time of Rabban Yochanan ben Zakkai's death, his students said to him, our teacher, bless us. He said to them, may it be His will that the fear of Heaven shall be upon you like the fear of flesh and blood. His students said - To that point and not beyond? He said to them, would it only be so! Know that when one commits a transgression, he says to himself, I hope that no man will see me.

And the highest level in this is that one would be humiliated by all of his iniquities in front of God, may He be blessed. And the content of humiliation is the feeling of shame and change in the radiance of his face, like the matter that is stated - Shame[71] covers my face. And you will see that in every place, humiliation is mentioned after shame - as it is more than shame: Be ashamed and humiliated - I[72] am ashamed and humiliated. And[73] when the sinner sees that God, may He be blessed, passes over his transgression, is patient with him, does not pay him back, does not do to him according to His sins and does not pay him back according to his iniquities, he has greater shame in his heart. For does not one who sinned against a king of flesh and blood and was treacherous to him, yet is forgiven by him, feel shame towards him? Accordingly, is it written - Thus[74] you shall remember

---

[70] Berakhot 28b
[71] Psalms 59:8
[72] Ezekiel 36:32
[73] Jeremiah 31:19
[74] Ezekiel 16:63

and feel shame... when I have forgiven you for all that you did. And our Rabbis, may their memory be blessed, said in the Talmud - That[75] someone who does something and is ashamed by it has all of his iniquities forgiven. And so do we find with Saul, who said - And[76] He no longer answers me, either by prophets or in dreams, but did not mention the **Urim and Thumim** [Meaning of these two words uncertain. They designate a kind of oracle]. For he was ashamed to mention them, since he killed [the inhabitants of] **Nov**, the city of priests. So, Samuel said to him - Tomorrow[77] your sons and you will be with me. - With me in my section of the world to come. And one acquires the level of shame by meditating to think about the greatness of God, and how evil is the one who rebels against His words; and in always remembering that God sees his deeds, examines his feelings and looks into his thoughts.

And the seventh principle is whole-hearted submission and lowliness:

For the one who knows his Creator knows how one who transgresses His words is crooked and lowly - so he is lowered in his worth, like the matter that is stated - For[78] whom a contemptible man is abhorrent. And it is also stated - What[79] then of one loathsome and foul man, who drinks wrongdoing like water. Also stated

---

[75] Berakhot 12b
[76] Samuel-A 28:15
[77] Samuel-A 28:19
[78] Psalms 15:4
[79] Job 15:16

- They[80] are called rejected silver. Therefore, he will be submissive and lowly in his own eyes. And when King David, peace be upon him, confessed after Nathan the prophet came to him, he said at the end of his words - True[81] sacrifice to God is a contrite spirit; God You will not despise a contrite and crushed heart - **A contrite spirit** is a lowly spirit. From this we have learned that submission is from the principles of repentance, since this psalm is wholly founded upon the principles of repentance. And with submission, a man is acceptable to God, as it is stated - To[82] the poor and broken-hearted. And it is stated about the matter of repentance, - The[83] GOD says Build up build up a highway Clear a road Remove all obstacles from the road of My people. For[84] thus said the One who high aloft Forever dwells whose name is holy I dwell on high, in holiness Yet with the contrite and the lowly in spirit Reviving the spirits of the lowly Reviving the hearts of the contrite. We learn also from here that submission is from the principles of repentance. And likewise does the entire remainder of this section speak about penitents - For[85] I will not always contend I will not be angry forever Nay I who make spirits flag Also create the breath of life. For[86] their sinful greed I was angry I struck them and turned away in My wrath Though stubborn they follow the way of

---

80 Jeremiah 6:30
81 Psalms 51:19
82 Isaiah 66:2
83 Isaiah 57:14
84 Isaiah 57:15
85 Isaiah 57:16
86 Isaiah 57:17

their hearts. I[87] note how they fare and will heal them I will guide them and mete out solace to them and to the mourners among them. Its explanation is, I see that their ways are grounded in submission, as it stated - Yet[88] with the contrite and the lowly in spirit. and with bitter-heartedness, as it stated - When[89] spirits in front of Me cover themselves. And I will heal them, as I will forgive his iniquity like in - I[90] will heal their affliction. And it stated - And[91] repent and save itself And I will guide them. I will help him to leave the sin, and give him strength against his impulse.

And know that there are many degrees of submission as will be explained in the Chapter on Humility no longer extant, with God's help. But the highest level that is necessary for the path of repentance is that one aggrandize Torah and enhance it and not claim any benefit for himself. For it will all be small in his eyes compared to what he is obligated to do for the service of God. Therefore, he will be submissive and serve with humility, and not desire honor for his honorable actions, nor glory for his glorious deeds. So, he will conceal them from his companions according to his ability.

And this matter of this principle of repentance is made clear by the words of the prophet, peace be

---

[87] Isaiah 57:18
[88] Isaiah 57:15
[89] Isaiah 57:16
[90] Hosea 14:5
[91] Isaiah 6:10

upon him, as it is stated - With[92] what shall I approach the Lord do homage to God on high. Its explanation is - **With what shall I approach the Lord** for all of his kindnesses - as he mentioned some of God's kindnesses above in this section, and with what will I **do homage to God on high**, for my many sins. And it mentions - **God on high**, to teach and make known to what extent it is fitting for one who rebelled against the One who is above everything, to do homage and submit. And it explained the matter afterwards - With[93] what shall I approach GOD Do homage to God on high Shall I approach with burnt offerings with calves a year old. Would[94] GOD be pleased with thousands of rams with myriads of streams of oil Shall I give my first-born for my transgression The fruit of my body for my sins. With which I should approach Him for his great kindnesses. Shall I give my firstborn for my transgression - To show my submission and my great subordination for my many sins, as I recognize the greatness of my transgression. For it would be fitting to give my firstborn as a sacrifice on account of my transgressions, for they are many and great. The fruit of my body for the sin of my soul - It mentioned **my firstborn** for the transgression, and the fruit of my body for the sin. For **Pesha** [transgression] is rebellion, as our Rabbis, may their memory be blessed, said in the Talmud - And[95] that is more than sin. And the answer was - You[96]

---

[92] Micah 6:6
[93] Micah 6:6-7
[94] Micah 6:6-7
[95] Yoma 36b
[96] Micah 6:8

have been told O mortal what is good and what GOD requires of you Only to do justice and to love goodness and to walk modestly with your God. For this is superior to burnt-offerings and meal-offerings with which to approach God for His kindnesses; **and to walk humbly with your God** - this is the essence of your submission and your subordination: To serve God with humility. For this shows your submission, that you do not desire honor for your honorable actions, nor for the virtues that the Maker does not [even] desire in His creations - for one should not glory in them - such as wealth and strength and types of wisdom, but rather only for understanding and knowing God, may He be blessed, as it is stated - Speak[97] thus - says GOD People's carcasses shall lie Like dung upon the fields Like sheaves behind the reaper With none to pick them up.

And the penitent is also obligated to submit, because he is obligated to remove from himself the traits that cause him to sin and to do rebellious deeds.

And pride causes several transgressions and amplifies the impulse of a man's heart against him, as it is stated - And[98] your heart grow haughty and you forget the Lord your God. And it is also stated - Haughty[99] looks, a proud heart the tillage of the evildoer's sin. Its explanation is: Pride is the tillage of evildoers, for the sins grow from it; as it was stated - **And your heart**

---

[97] Jeremiah 9:22
[98] Deuteronomy 8:14
[99] Proverbs 21:4

grows haughty and you forget. And it is also stated - The[100] wicked in his arrogance hounds the lowly. And it is further stated - That[101] speak haughtily against the righteous with arrogance. And it is also stated - Who[102] struck terror in the land of the living. And just like people make a tillage in the field in order to plant seeds and to harvest much produce, so do the evildoers make pride into a tillage in their hearts, and seed it with their evil thoughts to produce and to grow sins. Metaphorically speaking, these are the fruit of their thoughts - like the prophet stated - So[103] they conclude agreements and make covenants with false oaths and justice degenerates into poison weeds Breaking out on the furrows of the fields. And the explanation of **sin** is the tillage of the evildoers is the tillage of sin. And all mention of sin is actually plural, like is stated - The[104] guilt of Judah is inscribed with a stylus of iron Engraved with an adamant point on the tablet of their hearts and on the horns of their altars. Or alternatively, its explanation is **and sin**, like is stated - Sun[105] and moon stand still on high As Your arrows fly in brightness Your flashing spear in brilliance. which means, sun and moon. And the understanding is - beyond the fact that pride causes sins, the trait itself is a sin, as it is stated - Every[106] haughty person is an abomination to the Lord. And a

---

[100] Psalms 10:2
[101] Psalms 31:19
[102] Ezekiel 32:24
[103] Hosea 10:4
[104] Jeremiah 17:1
[105] Habakkuk 3:11
[106] Proverbs 16:5

proud person will be given over to his impulse; for God does not help him, since he is - **an abomination to the Lord**.

And the penitent is also obligated to be submissive and to fulfill and follow the path about which our Rabbis, may their memory be blessed, said - Be[107] of humble spirit before all men. And from this, he will acquire that he will not get angry at - or be exacting with - his fellows; and he will also not pay attention to everything that he hears and will forego his reckonings. And from this, all of his sins will be forewent to be atoned, as our Rabbis, may their memory be blessed, said in the Talmud - Whoever[108] forgoes his reckonings with others the heavenly court in turn forgoes all his sins. - Measure for measure. And this is a very glorious opening for hope. And it is stated - Let[109] him put his mouth to the dust there may yet be hope. Let[110] him offer his cheek to the smiter let him be surfeited with mockery.

The eighth principle is submission:

in his actions - such that one should be accustomed to giving a gentle response, as it is stated - A[111] gentle response allays wrath. For this is the way of lowliness, as it is stated - And[112] you shall speak from

---

[107] Avot 4:10
[108] Rosh Hashanah 17a
[109] Lamentations 3:29
[110] Lamentations 3:30
[111] Proverbs 15:1
[112] Isaiah 29:4

lower than the ground, your speech shall be humbler than the sod. The opposite of that which is stated about a rich man who is proud - The[113] rich man's answer is harsh. And he should not be occupied with the beauty of clothing and jewelry, as it is stated - And[114] now take off your finery. And it is stated about Ahab - He[115] fasted and lay in sackcloth and walked about subdued. And God, may He be blessed, said about this - Have[116] you seen how Ahab has submitted? And the matter of **walked about subdued**, is the opposite of the way of kings, who walk with many soldiers and the din of a troop. And he should always lower his eyes, like the matter that is stated - For[117] He saves those who lower their eyes. And signs of submission - like a gentle response, a soft voice and lowered eyes - remind him to have a submissive heart.

And the ninth principle is the breaking of physical desire:

One should put into his mind that desire causes harm to his soul - to sin and to be pulled after iniquity for worthless vanities. So, he should make a vow to protect the path of repentance: He should separate from pleasures and not be drawn after his desire - even with things that are permissible - and follow the

---

[113] Proverbs 18:23
[114] Exodus 33:5
[115] Kings-A 21:27
[116] Kings-A 21:29
[117] Job 22:29

path of asceticism. So, he should only eat to satiate his spirit and preserve his body, like the matter that is stated - The[118] righteous man eats to the satiation of his spirit. And he should not approach a woman except to fulfill the commandment of being fruitful and multiplying; or the commandment of the set time for his wife. For anytime that a man pursues desire, he is drawn after the effects of the physical and is distanced from the path of the reasoning soul; and then his impulse will overpower him, like the matter that is stated - And[119] Jeshurun waxed fat and rebelled. And it is also stated - Lest[120] being sated, I renounce. And they, may their memory be blessed, said in the Talmud - There[121] is a small limb in a man if he satiates it is hungry if he starves it, it is satiated.

And behold that the desire placed in the heart of man is the root of all of his actions. Therefore, if he refines the desire - instead of all the limbs serving it, he will draw them after the intellect. So, they will accompany him and serve him; and all of his actions will be proper, as it is stated - But[122] he is pure and straight in his actions. And it appears to me that he is understanding - **But he is pure**, as meaning to say, that he is pure from desire - **And straight in his actions** as all of his actions are assumed to be refined and straight. And that is something that can be learned from its context, as its opposite is written after it -

---

[118] Proverbs 13:28
[119] Deuteronomy 32:15
[120] Proverbs 30:9
[121] Sukkah 52b
[122] Proverbs 21:8

The[123] desire of the wicked is set upon evil. And it is
also stated - Desire[124] **Niheyeh** [here] is sweet to the
spirit. **Niheyeh** [here] is like broken, as its usage as it
is stated - I[125] was **Niheyeti** [broken] and languished.
It is stating that when a man breaks his desire - even
for things that are permissible - it renders his spirit
successful. So, this trait is sweet to it. For the intellect
raises its hand and is victorious. But[126] to turn away
from evil is abhorrent to the stupid. The[127] stupid who
do not break their desire but rather always pursue the
desires of people. When their desire confronts them
to do a sin or any bad thing, they will not veer from
it. And they are called stupid because of their pursuit
of pleasures - as it is stated - And[128] a stupid man will
swallow them. And it is stated - Ah[129] Those who
chase liquor from early in the morning and till late in
the evening Are inflamed by wine. Who[130] at their
banquets Have lyre and lute Timbrel flute and wine
but who never give a thought to the divine plan and
take no note Of GOD's design. And it is also stated -
But[131] the belly of the wicked is empty. And it is
further stated - And[132] I will strew dung upon your
faces, the dung of your festivals. And our Rabbis,

---

[123] Proverbs 21:10
[124] Proverbs 13:19
[125] Daniel 8:27
[126] Proverbs 13:19
[127] Proverbs 21:8
[128] Proverbs 21:20
[129] Isaiah 5:11
[130] Isaiah 5:12
[131] Proverbs 13:25
[132] Malachi 2:3

may their memory be blessed, said in the Talmud - These[133] are people for which all their days are like festivals. And it states - He[134] who isolates himself pursues his desires; he disdains all competence. Its explanation is, one who seeks to go after his desire and his will, will be isolated from any friend or countryman. As admirers and companions will distance themselves them from him, since the desires and measures of people are all different - the will of this one is not like the will of that one. However, if he will follow the path of the intellect, many friends will join themselves to him and his admirers will be many. And they said regarding ethics, one who insists upon his measures will have many against him. And it is possible to explain - **He who isolates himself pursues his desires**, about this matter itself: A man is isolated from every brother and friend, by the desire that he seeks. And since he seeks to go after his will - because of that, his companion's distance themselves from him. It is like the matter of - But[135] a poor man loses his friend. He[136] disdains all competence - One who follows his desires will not only sin in one thing. Rather he will disdain every thing in the Torah, since he will transgress all of it - like the wording - But[137] every fool disdains.

And there is another benefit to his breaking his physical desire - That if his desire asks him for

133 Shabbat 151b
134 Proverbs 18:1
135 Proverbs 19:4
136 Proverbs 18:1
137 Proverbs 20:3

something wicked and sinful, he will say to his heart, - Look, I do not fulfill my desire with the permissible so how could I reach my hand out for the forbidden?

And you will also find another big and great benefit in breaking desire: For he will reveal his true heart and goodly desire for repentance. As he is disgusted by the nature that caused him to sin. And through this, he will become acceptable to God, may He be blessed, and find favor in His eyes. And it is accordingly written - True[138] sacrifice to God is a contrite spirit God you will not despise a contrite and crushed heart. The contrite spirit is a lowly and submissive spirit; and a broken heart is speaking about the breaking of physical desire - for desire is placed into the heart, as it is stated - You[139] have granted him the desire of his heart. And this verse is stated in the psalm of repentance. And from its stating - You[140] will not despise a contrite and crushed heart. we learn that a penitent becomes acceptable to God, through the breaking of his physical desire, and that this is from the principles of repentance. And it is also stated about the matter of repentance - Reviving[141] the spirits of the lowly, reviving the hearts of the contrite.

And our Rabbis, may their memory be blessed, stated - Whoever[142] possesses these three things he is of the disciples of Abraham, our father... A good eye, a

---

[138] Psalms 51:19
[139] Psalms 21:3
[140] Psalms 51:19
[141] Isaiah 57:15
[142] Avot 5:19

humble spirit and a moderate appetite. And the meaning of a humble spirit is that he does not follow his physical desire even with permissible things. This is like we find that Abraham stated - Behold[143] I know what a beautiful woman you are - as he had not stared at her until that day, to contemplate the character of her beauty. And our Rabbis, may their memory be blessed, stated in the Talmud - About[144] that which is written - And[145] they remained in seclusion until the day they died, in living widowhood. That each day David would command that their heads be beautified and that perfumes be given to them to adorn them in order to provoke his desire and to [then] subdue it, when he would conquer his impulse for them, in order to atone for himself about the matter of Bathsheba.

The tenth principle is to improve one's actions with that which he was wanton:

If he stared at those sexually forbidden, he should accustom himself to lower his eyes. If he sinned with evil speech, he should occupy himself with Torah study. Likewise with all the limbs with which he sinned; he should attempt to fulfill the commandments with them. And so, our Rabbis, may their memory be blessed, said that the righteous ones become acceptable with the very thing with which they sin. And they also said in the Midrash - If[146] you

---

[143] Genesis 12:11
[144] Yerushalmi Sanhedrin 2:3
[145] Samuel-B 20:3
[146] Leviticus Rabbah 21:5

have done piles of sins, do piles and piles of commandments that correspond to them - Feet that ran to do evil shall run to the matter of a commandment; a false tongue, his palate should utter truth, he should open his mouth with wisdom and have the Torah of kindness on his tongue; hands that spilled blood, let him surely open his hand to his poor brothers; haughty eyes, let him be subdued and lower his eyes; a heart that seeks thoughts of injustice, let his heart mull words of Torah and the meditation of his heart be understanding; if he creates arguments between brothers, let him seek peace and pursue it.

And the eleventh principle is examining one's ways:

as it is stated - Let[147] us search and examine our ways, and turn back to the Lord. And he should do this for three reasons - The first is in order that he remembers all of the things about which he sinned and confess them all. For confession is one of the principles of atonement. And the second is in order for him to know how many iniquities and sins he has, and enhance his submission. And the third is that even though he takes on himself to leave the sin - he must know the things about which he sinned in order to make fences for them and to greatly safeguard his spirit from them; from the ambush of the impulse, since his spirit is prone to them, as they have become light in his eyes and his impulse has taken control over them. And behold that his soul is sick from his

---

[147] Lamentations 3:40

actions. And when a sick person begins healing, he needs to be careful about many matters, so that he will not have a relapse of his sickness.

The twelfth principle is that one needs to examine, know and recognize the greatness of the punishment for each one of his iniquities:

for which of them is there lashes, for which of them is there a liability for excision, for which of them is there a death penalty from the court - in order that he know the greatness of his iniquity when he confesses it, and cry bitterly about that which bitterly angered God. This is also in order that he will enhance his submission and in order that he will fear from his iniquities. For with weighty sins, repentance only suspends their atonement whereas afflictions absolve them. And so is it written - Look[148] at your deeds in the valley, consider what you have done! And this principle will be explained in the third chapter.

The thirteenth principle is that the light sins should be weighty in one's eyes from four angles:

The first is that he should not look at the smallness of a sin, but rather at the greatness of the One who commanded it. The second is that the impulse is in control over the light sins, and that may be a cause to do them constantly. And then they will also be considered like weighty ones - when the punishment of all of the times it is committed are combined. And

---

[148] Jeremiah 2:23

they compared it to a silk thread that is loose and weak; but when you combine it many, many times, it becomes a strong rope. And the third is that from his constantly doing the sin, it becomes like something permissible; and he will remove its yoke from upon him. So, he will not protect himself against it and he will be considered from those that remove the yoke and are heretics for one thing. And the fourth is that if he defeats the impulse with something small, he will defeat it tomorrow with something big - as our Rabbis, may their memory be blessed, said the Talmud - Anyone[149] who breaks vessels in anger should be in your eyes as if he worships idolatry. For this is the way of the evil impulse - Today it says to you thus, on the morrow, it tells you, 'Go worship an idol. And it is stated - Surely[150] if you do right There is uplift but if you do not do right Sin couches at the door Its urge is toward you Yet you can be its master. Its explanation in the verse - Why[151] has your face fallen. Is it not that if you do right, actions and repent to Me, **there is uplift** - like the usage in the verse - Then[152] free of blemish you will uplift your head. And it can be understood as an expression of forgiveness. But[153] if you do not do right sin couches at the door. - But if you do not repent from that which you sinned, it is not only this iniquity that will lay with you; but rather the impulse crouches at the door to make you sin in all that you do. And it will always defeat you,

[149] Shabbat 105b
[150] Genesis 4:7
[151] Genesis 4:6
[152] Job 11:15
[153] Genesis 4:7

since it defeated you and trapped you now and it also caught you, and you did not repent. And its urge is toward you, to lead you astray and it ambushes you at every instant. **Yet you can be its master**, if you want to overpower it. Therefore, you will be punished for the sin, since I gave you the ability to conquer your impulse.

And King Solomon, peace be upon him, said - He[154] who disdains a precept will be injured thereby and he who fears a commandment will be rewarded. He said this about one who disdains concern about light sins. For he will be injured from the angles that we mentioned. **And he who fears a commandment** - to make efforts not to negate fail to perform a commandment, like he fears from a weighty sin - **will be rewarded** - He is destined to receive the full reward for it. And our Rabbis, may their memory be blessed, said - And[155] be careful with a light commandment as with a weighty one. And they also said - For[156] the payment for performing a commandment is another commandment and the payment for committing a transgression is a transgression.

The fourteenth principle is confession:

as it is stated - And[157] he shall confess that wherein he

---

154 Proverbs 13:13
155 Avot 2:1
156 Avot 4:2
157 Leviticus 5:5

has sinned. And he must mention his iniquities and the iniquities of his fathers. For he is punished for them - if he holds on to the actions of his fathers. And likewise, is it written - and[158] they shall confess their iniquity and the iniquity of their fathers.

And the fifteenth principle is prayer:

A man should pray to God and request mercy to atone for all of his iniquities, as it is stated - Take[159] words with you and return to the Lord say to Him **Forgive all guilt and accept the good; and we will pay with the bulls of our lips** - this is the matter of confession. **Say to Him Forgive all guilt and accept what is good** - this is the matter of prayer. And its explanation is, **accept the good** - the good actions that we did. For they, may their memory be blessed, said in the Talmud - Sin[160] extinguishes the merit of a commandment. But at the time of repentance, the iniquities will be atoned; so, the merit of the commandment will arise, and its merit will shine. For before repentance, its light did not shine forth. And so, it is written - If[161] you are blameless and upright He will now awaken your merit for you and grant well-being to your righteous home. And our Rabbis, may their memory be blessed said in the Talmud - It[162] does not say - **If you were blameless and upright** but rather **If you are blameless and upright** - since

---

[158] Leviticus 26:40
[159] Hosea 14:3
[160] Sotah 21a
[161] Job 8:6
[162] Yerushalmi Rosh Hashanah 1:3

you have repented. He will now awaken your merit for you - now after the repentance that you have done, **He will now awaken** all of the righteousness that you had done before, and that which your home was wide open and you **planted a tamarisk** for lodging, as it is written - I[163] opened my doors to the road. But before your repentance, your righteousness did not protect you. However, after your repentance and when your iniquity was removed, He will awaken your merit for you and grant well-being to your righteous home. **And we will pay with the bulls of our lips** - our confession will be considered like the bulls of sin-offerings, for our acceptance in front of You. And it mentions bulls, because the bull sin-offering was inside the chamber and they would sprinkle from its blood on the curtain and on the golden incense altar.

And the penitent should also pray to God to erase his transgressions like a fog, and his sins like a cloud; and that He desire him, accept him and listen to him as if he had not sinned - like the matter that is written in the words of Elihu about a penitent after he has suffered afflictions - He[164] prays to God and is accepted by Him For it is likely for the iniquity to be forgiven and he be redeemed from all afflictions and from all decrees, but God still not desire him and not want to accept an offering from him. And it is the desire of the righteous from their successes, to incline God's will towards them and that He should desire them. And his will is for real everlasting life and for

---

[163] Job 31:32
[164] Job 33:26

the great light that includes all of the pleasant things
- like the matter that is stated - When[165] He is pleased
there is life. And it also stated - O[166] Lord God of hosts
restore us shine Your countenance that we may be
delivered. And our Rabbis, may their memory be
blessed said in the Midrash - We[167] have nothing
besides the shining of Your countenance. And that is
the matter of His desire - and we have already
mentioned this and explained it. Therefore, you will
see in the prayer of David at the time of his repentance
after he said - Wash[168] me thoroughly of my iniquity,
and purify me of my sin. That he prayed further about
the desire - that God's desire, may He be blessed - for
him to be like before the sin. So, he said - Do[169] not
cast me out of Your presence or take Your holy spirit
away from me. Afterwards he prayed and said - Let[170]
me again rejoice in Your salvation. That the miracles
of God and His salvation be found with him, and that
the spirit of God would come upon him as at first.
And afterwards he continued, and a generous spirit
sustain me. Its explanation is - behold I have been
lessened because of my transgressions and am not
fitting to be a prince, and for Your holy arm to be
revealed upon Me. And even if you have lifted
forgiven the iniquity of my sin, I am not worthy to be
beloved and acceptable as in earlier times. Yet sustain
me with a generous spirit; for there is no end to Your

---

[165] Psalms 30:6
[166] Psalms 80:20
[167] Midrash Tehillim 80
[168] Psalms 51:4
[169] Psalms 51:13
[170] Psalms 51:14

generosity and Your goodness. And the word, spirit, comes lacking a letter, bet in front of it, which would mean, with the spirit, like in the verse - Sustained[171] him grain and wine. Which is to be understood as if grain was preceded by a letter bet, meaning - With grain, etc. And Hosea, peace be upon him, said about this matter - I[172] will heal their affliction I will take them back in generous love. The matter of generous love is like the matter that David said - And a generous spirit sustains me.

And the penitent should also constantly pray to God that He help him towards repentance, as it is stated - Receive[173] me back let me return; for You O Lord are my God.

The sixteenth principle is the rectification of that which is twisted.

 in as much as one is able to rectify it - as the matter is stated - God[174] saw what they did how they were turning back from their evil ways. And it is stated - Let[175] everyone turn back from his evil ways and from the extortion that is their hands. For with things that are between a man and his fellow - such as robbery and extortion - his iniquity is not atoned until he returns what was robbed. And likewise, if he pained his fellow, harassed him, whitened his face from

---

[171] Genesis 27:37
[172] Hosea 14:5
[173] Jeremiah 31:18
[174] Jonah 3:10
[175] Jonah 3:8

embarrassment or spoke evil speech about him, he is not given atonement until he requests forgiveness from him. And likewise did our Rabbis, may their memory be blessed, say in the Talmud - That[176] even though he gave him the money of the embarrassment and the pain of the strike - the pain and the embarrassment of the strike are not forgiven until he requests forgiveness from him, as it is stated - Therefore[177], restore the man's wife - since he is a prophet he will intercede for you - to save your life.

And it is fitting for a penitent to do this before the confession, so that he can be accepted with his confession.

And at the time of his repentance, King David, peace be upon him, did this before the confession, as it is stated - Against[178] You alone have I sinned and done what is evil in Your sight so that You are just in Your sentence and right in Your judgment. The explanation of this is that I am only considered a sinner to you, and I need nothing besides your forgiveness; and if I sinned to a person, I have requested forgiveness from him and I have made amends with him. And similar to it is - I[179] shall stand guilty before my father forever. For this sin, I will be considered a sinner to my father forever, as he will never forgive me for it. And its translation By **Onkelos** is - And I will be a sinner to

---

[176] Bava Kamma 92a
[177] Genesis 20:7
[178] Psalms 51:6
[179] Genesis 44:32

father. Or alternatively the explanation in the verse in Psalms above is - **Against You alone have I sinned** - I have not sinned to a person and I have not said extra words about him, nor have I taken anything from a person; that I should require his forgiveness and return his stolen goods. So, my atonement is only dependent upon You. **So that You are just in Your sentence - and right in Your judgment** - in order to show Your charity and the greatness of Your forgiveness to the nations, on the day of Your speech and Your judgement at the time that You judged me. And the expression, **so that**, is to mean that the greatness of the sin is the reason to make known the greatness of Your charity in Your forgiveness. Therefore, the thing is compared to the head of sin, in order that God's kindness can be revealed - as well as His charity in His forgiveness - on the day of David's judgement. And like it is the usage of, so that as it is stated - Of[180] their silver and gold they have made themselves images so that it will be cut off. For their making the images is the reason for the cutting off of their silver and their gold - the thing was compared, as if they made the images in order that they would be cut off. Or its explanation in Psalms is, because of this, you will be justified in Your word about the judgement and the repayment meaning to say that he is justifying His judgement, may He be blessed. And likewise in Hosea - **So that it will be cut off** can be understood as, because of this will it be cut off.

And our Rabbis, may their memory be blessed,

---

[180] Hosea 8:4

explained - according to the first approach - in Midrash about this - There[181] is a relevant parable about a physician who examined a wound and said - **This is a great wound**. The patient said back to him, Was I not struck with a severe wound in order to show the sagacity of your healing and in order to show you your strength? And we will still add a teaching about this principle in the fourth chapter.

The seventeenth principle is to seek to do actions of kindness and truth.

As it is stated - Iniquity[182] is atoned by kindness and truth and evil is shunned through fear of the Lord. And now reflect upon the secret of this verse. For surely if the sinner has not repented to God, his sin will not be atoned by doing kindness - as it is stated - Who[183] shows no favor and takes no bribe. And our Rabbis, may their memory be blessed, explained - that[184] this means that He will not take the bribe of the fulfillment of a commandment to forgive and pass over iniquities. And they also said in the Talmud - Anyone[185] who states that the Holy One Blessed be He, is forgoing will have his life foregone. Rather He is slow to anger. But if they do not obey, he measures the punishment of their actions into their laps. Rather regarding that which King Solomon, peace be upon

---

181   Midrash Tehillim 51
182   Proverbs 16:6
183   Deuteronomy 10:17
184   Yalkut Shimoni on Nach 947
185   Bava Kamma 50a

him, said - Iniquity[186] is atoned by kindness and truth.
- he was speaking about a penitent. For there are sins
that repentance and Yom Kippur suspend, but
afflictions absolve, as will be explained in the fourth
chapter. But behold that kindness protects the sinner
from afflictions, since it also surely saves him from
death, as it is written - but **Tsedekah** [righteousness]
which can also mean - Charity[187] saves from death.
However, there is yet an iniquity - and that is the
iniquity of the desecration of God's name - which
repentance and afflictions suspend but death
absolves, as it is stated - This[188] iniquity shall never be
forgiven you until you die. But behold when a person
makes efforts to support the truth, follow it through,
be aroused by its words, present its light in the eyes
of people, strengthen the hands of the men of truth
and uplift their heads and to denigrate the circles of
falsehood and bring them to the dirt - behold, these
are the ways of sanctification of God's name, of
majesty and beauty to His faith and worship in the
world and of strength and splendor to the holiness of
his Torah. Therefore, in the increase of his actions to
sanctify God, to arouse the truth and to set it up and
assist it, he is forgiven the iniquity of the desecration
with his repentance - with his placement of the truth
across from the sin of the desecration, the measure of
his repentance corresponding to the measure of his
sin. This is the explanation of - **Iniquity is atoned by
kindness and truth**.

---

[186] Proverbs 16:6
[187] Proverbs 10:2
[188] Isaiah 22:14

The eighteenth principle is that his sin always be in front of him.

For it is fitting that the soul of the sinner always remember its content and not neglect forget them to the end of days. And he should not grab them away from his heart until his relief comes - like the matter that is stated - For[189] I recognize my transgressions and am ever conscious of my sin. And this principle will be explained in the third chapter.

The nineteenth principle is leaving the sin when it chances upon him and he is still at the height of his desire.

And our Rabbis, may their memory be blessed, said in the Talmud - Who[190] is the penitent whose repentance reaches the Throne of Glory? When he is tested and comes out clean at the same time in the same place and with the same woman. This is meaning to say, when the sin avails itself to him, he is at the height of his impulse and his might is in the muscles of his belly like the first moment when he sinned; but he conquered his impulse and escaped from the iniquity due to his fear of God and the greatness of his fright. But for the one to whom it has not availed itself in this manner, he should augment his fear of God on a daily basis all of his days. And when he has reinvigorated the strength of his fear enough to conquer his impulse with this strength and

---

[189] Psalms 51:5
[190] Yoma 86b

his power over the power of the desire - does not the Examiner of hearts understand and the Fashioner of his soul know that if a test would come to him and it be like the first situation, that he would save himself from his impulse? So, behold that in front of God he is on the highest level of repentance. And that which King Solomon, peace be upon him, said - Iniquity[191] is atoned by kindness and truth and evil is shunned through fear of the Lord. Its explanation is, and with fear of the Lord, to shun evil if it should chance upon him. And the word, shun, is an infinitive here; and the confirmation of this explanation is that it does not say, and shun which would make shun a command. And that which is stated - Shun[192] evil and do good. And - - Who[193] fears God and shuns evil. Its sense is that he should shun evil if it should chance upon him. For they do not say, shun the deed, but rather shun that which he comes close to doing. And our Rabbis, may their memory be blessed, said in the Talmud - If[194] one sits and does not transgress, he receives a reward as one who performs a commandment ... - it is speaking of a case where an opportunity to commit a sinful act presents itself to him and he is saved from it.

The twentieth principle is to cause the many to repent from iniquity to the extent of one's ability.

As it is stated - Repent[195] and make repent from all

---

[191] Proverbs 16:6
[192] Psalms 34:15
[193] Job 1:8
[194] Kiddushin 39b
[195] Ezekiel 18:30

your transgressions. We learn from this that it is from the principles of repentance. And it is stated - You[196] shall surely reprimand your countryman and not bear sin because of him. We learn from this] that if he does not rebuke him, he will be punished for the other's sins. And King David, peace be upon him, said in the psalm of repentance - I[197] will teach transgressors Your ways, that sinners may return to You.

Behold we have completed the explanation of the principles of repentance. And now pay attention to the things that obstruct repentance. This means to say that the repentance is difficult for one who removes his yoke and stumbles constantly in one of them. If you have constantly stumbled in one of them, be strong and of good courage to pour out your speech to God and to augment your prayer and supplication; gird your strength to fulfill every matter of the principles of repentance; and increase [your] understanding about them from the paths that will be explained in the fourth chapter - and you will find grace and be given mercy.

I will mention what our Rabbis spoke about this. Our Rabbis, may their memory be blessed, said - There are twenty-four things that obstruct repentance and these are them: Talebearing and evil speech:

One who is an angry person.

---

[196] Leviticus 19:17
[197] Psalms 51:15

One who has thoughts of evil.

One who befriends an evildoer.

One accustomed to eating from a meal that is not sufficient for its owners.

One who stares at those sexually forbidden.

One who shares stolen property with a thief.

One who says - I[198] **will sin and then I will repent** and they accordingly said in the Talmud - One[199] who says **I will sin and I will repent** - Heaven does not provide him the opportunity to repent ... **I will sin and Yom Kippur will atone for my sins** - Yom Kippur does not atone.

One who glorifies himself by the embarrassment of his neighbor.

One who separates from the community.

One who scorns his ancestors.

One who scorns his teachers.

One who curses the many.

One who obstructs the many from doing good acts.

_____

[198] Mishna Yoma 2:7
[199] Yoma 85b

One who sways his fellow from a proper path to an improper path.

One who uses the pledge of a poor person.

One who takes a bribe in order to sway judgement on others in court, one who finds a lost object but does not return it to its owner.

One who sees his son involved in wayward conduct and does not reprove him.

One who eats from the plunder of the poor, the orphans and the widows.

One who opposes the words of the Sages.

One who suspects proper people of forbidden acts. **One** who hates rebuke.

One who mocks the commandments.

Sha'arei Teshuvah

Gates of Repentance

Rabbeinu Yonah

Chapter Two

To instruct about the ways that arouse a person to repent to God Know that the paths of the causes by which a person is aroused to repent from his evil ways are six. And with each one of them, we have taught man's intellect how it is dissected for his understanding; so, let him give ear according to his preparation. And we will arouse the ear to understand them, to contemplate and know the precious principles - they are expounded and analyzed to all of their wants. But more than this, my son, be careful to repent and purify your soul each day - even without seeing a cause that arouses it or the events of the day striking your thoughts. For remember your Creator, and let the thought of Him be a restoration of the soul from the ways of the events of [those who are only] a clod of dirt. And so bare and prepare the bow of knowledge to straighten the refinements of your nature. And from the fear of God and love of Him, and from the shame of being before him, you will always increase virtue. Also be consistent in the purity of your hands, cut down the rebellious thoughts from your musings and feed the arms bearers of your soul - and with the remembrance of its Former, it will adorn its jewelry and be complete in its beauty, as it is written - It[1] is through the Lord that all the offspring of Israel Have vindication and praise. However, add strength to arouse your soul with these six causes which will be explained. And the one who does not grasp this virtue will surrender his uncircumcised heart from the way of the causes and from much seeing. And according to the paucity of the recognition of the way of a cause that arouses the heart of a man to repent - and according to his veering to the path of his own will - is it made known and verified that repentance is from the important soul.

The first path is that when a man encounters troubles, he will consult his heart and say [that] it is only his ways and his plots that have caused this to him, and that his sins have caused the pain to his soul. So, he repents to God; and He has mercy upon him, like the matter that is stated - And[2] many evils and troubles shall befall them and they shall say on that day **Surely it is because our God is not in our midst that these evils have befallen us**. But note that the custom among men is that if one sins to someone, and later at a time of trouble for him regrets it and submits to him because he needs him; such regret will be inferior in the eyes of his fellow - like the matter that Jephthah said - How[3] can you come to me now when you are in trouble? However, it is one of the kindnesses of God,

---

[1] Isaiah 45:25
[2] Deuteronomy 31:17
[3] Judges 11:7

may He be blessed, that He accepts repentance motivated by trouble and it is desirable in front of Him. And He will generously love the sinner when he returns to Him on the day of his rebuke and from amidst trouble, as it is stated - Return[4] O Israel to the ETERNAL your God For you have fallen because of your sin. Take[5] words with you and return to GOD Say Forgive all guilt and accept what is good Instead of bulls we will pay the offering of our lips. Assyria[6] shall not save us No more will we ride on steeds nor ever again will we call Our handiwork our god Since in You alone orphans find pity. I[7] will heal their affliction Generously will I take them back in love For My anger has turned away from them. And it is stated - For[8] whom the Lord loves, He rebukes, as a father the son whom he favors. But if the man does not repent from his evil on the day of evil, and the rebuked does not repent to the Rebuker, his iniquity grows and his punishment will be doubled. Do you not see that if a king rebukes someone who has sinned to him and he has not become chastised, the king will make his punishment harsher and be very hard on him. And it is written - And[9] if for all that you do not obey Me I will go on to discipline you. And it is also stated -But[10] the impious in heart become enraged they do not cry for help when He afflicts them. And

---

4   Hosea 14:2
5   Hosea 14:3
6   Hosea 14:4
7   Hosea 14:5
8   Proverbs 3:12
9   Leviticus 26:18
10   Job 36:13

if he does not know and does not contemplate that the events have found him because of sins, but rather says like the Philistines - It[11] was not His hand that struck us; it just happened to us by chance. There will be fury in front of Him for this, and his iniquity will grow. And the iniquity of this group will be greater than the sin of the first group. Therefore, it is written about the first group - I[12] will go on to discipline you. And it is written afterwards about the other group We mentioned - And[13] if you remain hostile toward Me and refuse to obey me I will go on smiting you sevenfold for your sins. For every group that is later in the section is more problematic than the one above it. So, it is written afterwards - And[14] if these things fail to discipline you for Me, and you remain hostile to Me. I[15] too will remain hostile to you: I in turn will smite you sevenfold for your sins. And afterwards, it is written - But[16] if despite this you disobey Me and remain hostile to Me. But[17] if despite this you disobey Me and remain hostile to Me. Its explanation is - You remain hostile to Me, because you will say - **It was just chance that it happened to us**. But when a man does not recognize his deeds and does not know that he has the iniquity in his hands from his sinning, he must examine his actions and search his ways, as the

---

[11] Samuel-A 6:9
[12] Leviticus 26:18
[13] Leviticus 26:21
[14] Leviticus 26:23
[15] Leviticus 26:24
[16] Leviticus 26:27-28
[17] Leviticus 26:27-28

matter is stated - Let[18] us search and examine our ways. But if he surely ignores his eyes and his ideas become foolish and deluded - From the expression in Scripture - The[19] nobles of Tanis have been foolish, the nobles of Memphis deluded, and he does not investigate his ways and does not know the acts of his hands and that which his fingers have done and says - **I have not sinned** - his sin is very weighty, as it is stated - lo[20] I will bring you to judgment for saying **I have not sinned**. And it is stated - It[21] blazed upon them all about, but they heeded not; it burned among them, but they gave it no thought. And it is stated - A[22] man's folly subverts his way, and his heart rages against the Lord.

Know and understand that the reproof of God, may He be blessed, is for the good of man. For if a man sins in front of Him and does evil in His eyes, God's reproof is upon him for two purposes: One is to atone for his sins and to remove the iniquity, as it is stated - Look[23] at my affliction and suffering, and forgive all my sins. So, with the sicknesses of the body, with which God has made him sick, is the sickness of the soul healed. For iniquity is the sickness of the soul, as it is stated - Heal[24] me, for I have sinned against You.

---

[18] Lamentations 3:40
[19] Isaiah 19:13
[20] Jeremiah 2:35
[21] Isaiah 42:25
[22] Proverbs 19:3
[23] Psalms 25:18
[24] Psalms 41:5

And it is also stated - And[25] none who lives there shall say **I am sick**. It shall be inhabited by folk whose sin has been forgiven. And the second is to remind him and have him repent from his evil ways, as it is written - Would[26] fear Me would take reproof. But if he does not receive the reproof and does not cease on account of the rebuke and does not circumcise the covering of his heart - woe is to him and woe to his soul. For he has suffered afflictions and bore his sin, but his iniquity was not atoned; but rather his punishment was doubled, as we explained.

But when a man accepts the reproof of God, improves his ways and his plans, it is fitting for him to rejoice about the afflictions - for they help him with lofty accomplishments. So, he should thank God, may He be elevated, for them. As it is stated - I[27] raise the cup of deliverance and invoke the name of the Lord. And it is also stated - The[28] bonds of death encompassed me the torments of **Sheol** [hell] overtook me I came upon trouble and sorrow. And[29] I invoked the name of the LORD O LORD save my life. And our Rabbis, may their memory be blessed, said in the **Sifrei** - Rabbi[30] Eliezer ben Ya'akov says - The whole time a person is dwelling in tranquility his iniquities are not atoned at all for him but through afflictions he becomes acceptable to the Omnipresent. And it is

---

[25] Isaiah 33:24
[26] Zephaniah 3:7
[27] Psalms 116:13
[28] Psalms 116:3
[29] Psalms 116:4
[30] Sifrei Devarim 6:5

stated - For[31] whom the Lord loves He rebukes as a father the son whom he favors. Its explanation is, like a father to a son, so too does God desire the one He rebukes and who accepts His reproof - in the same way a father desires his son after the rebukes. And it can also be explained, like a father rebukes the son that wants it; but he does not rebuke the sons about whom he has given up, and for which rebuke will not be effective. And it is stated about people that do not recognize the good of rebuke and its purpose - I[32] was their Redeemer yet they have plotted treason against Me. And it is also stated - I[33] braced I strengthened their arms and they plot evil against Me. And it is further stated - I[34] have pampered Ephraim taking them in My arms but they have ignored My healing care.

And one who trusts God should hold on during the vision of his distress; for the darkness will be the cause for the light - as it is written - Do[35] not rejoice over me O my enemy since I have fallen I rise again since I sit in darkness the Lord is my light. And our Rabbis, may their memory be blessed, said Midrash - If[36] I had not fallen I would not have risen If I had not sat in darkness the Lord would not have been my light. And every single person on the day of his trouble should put into his heart to understand and

---

[31] Proverbs 3:12
[32] Hosea 7:13
[33] Hosea 7:15
[34] Hosea 11:3
[35] Micah 7:8
[36] Midrash Tehillim 22

afflict himself, together with the repentance and
prayer - just like the community is obligated to fast
and afflict themselves at the time of their trouble, as
the Sages, may their memory be blessed, ordained.
And that fast day is chosen and is a day of acceptance.
And when the rebuke of God, may He be blessed,
comes to a man that is pure and straight, it becomes a
test, and enhances his reward in the world to come -
as it is stated - In[37] order to test you by hardships only
to benefit you in the end. And our Rabbis, may their
memory be blessed, said in the Talmud - If[38] one
searched his deeds at the time of his trouble sought
out and investigated, but did not find a sin - these are
certainly afflictions of love.

And included in this path that we mentioned is
repentance on the day of death, when the sinner sees
that his evil has finished him and hope is lost - as it is
written - At[39] death the hopes of a wicked man are lost.
When he confesses at that time and repents to God
with a full heart. And this repentance also is effective,
even though it does not reach the repentance of one
who repents with his full strength, as we have
discussed in the first chapter.

The second path is when the days of old age come and
the days of sagacity arrive - his strength fails and
diminishes, his impulse bows and he also remembers
that his end is near and understands his finish - so he

---

[37] Deuteronomy 8:16
[38] Berakhot 5a
[39] Proverbs 11:7

repents to God, and God has mercy upon him. But if he does not repent when the days of old age come, his punishment is redoubled and the animosity towards him is increased - as our Rabbis, may their memory be blessed, said in the Talmud - There[40] are three that the Holy One blessed be He hates - An arrogant pauper a wealthy person who denies monetary claims against him; and a lecherous old man. And it is stated - Strangers[41] have consumed his strength but he has taken no notice also grey hair is scattered over him but he has taken no notice. And it is a wonder and a surprise that a man stands at half of his days and see that the days are passing and lessening, that the destruction of the building has begun, that the state of his condition is dwindling and that he sees himself drying up - as the matter is stated - My[42] days are like a lengthening shadow I dry up like grass. How is it that he can seal his eyes from seeing and his heart from understanding, and not see that he is traveling to a place that is his permanent home, walking and going to it day and night?

But there are many people for which the light of repentance is obstructed. For since they are innocent and pure in their eyes, they do not avail themselves of the rectification of their actions - as it appears to them that they are already rectified, whereas they sin much to God. Is it not written - For[43] there is no righteous

---

[40] Pesachim 113b
[41] Hosea 7:9
[42] Psalms 102:12
[43] Ecclesiastes 7:20

man on earth who does what is best and doesn't sin? But since these people belittle iniquities, they do not feel or understand it; or when they are made known of their sins, it is afterwards forgotten from their hearts. And behold they are like a sick person who does not feel his sickness, so he does not think of a cure. So, his sickness constantly gets worse, until he is not able to be healed. And sometimes the reason for this is from their lack of understanding. For they do not go to seek God and do not want to know His ways. Therefore, they do not regularly visit the doors of the sages and the Torah students, like the matter is stated - The[44] scoffer dislikes being reproved; he will not resort to the wise.

And behold with people who are righteous and straight of heart, what constantly roars like a lion in their thoughts and growls like the sea is their sins, and their hands falling short from the service of God. For about the latter - when a person transgresses, his guilt grows as with weighty sins, like the matter that our Rabbis, may their memory be blessed, said in the Talmud - The[45] Holy One, blessed be He, forwent about prohibited sexual relations, but did not forego about the nullification of Torah wasting time that should be spent in Torah study. Especially since these people's main thoughts and actions are matters of their body and the vanities of their time, they have done much evil. But to the secret of fear, their souls should not come; and their glory should not be

---

44 Proverbs 15:12
45 Yerushalmi Chagigah 1:7

associated with the study of their consciences in the images of their hearts and chambers, and their images for fixed times within which they do not give a portion to Torah study among their occupations. And the calculation of their souls has been lost from within their hearts, for they are a nation that loses its counsel. And how much are they on the lowest level! And our Rabbis, may their memory be blessed, said - At[46] sixty old age, at seventy - fullness of years, at eighty - the age of strength, at ninety - a bent body, at one hundred - as good as dead and gone completely out of the world. And their intention, may their memory be blessed, with these words was to warn about repentance - that when a man reaches the days of old age, he should think about his end, if he did not merit to do so in the days of his youth. And since his time is close to coming, he should leave the matters of his body and his desires and rectify his soul. And when he reaches the days of fullness of years, he should add to the removal of involvement with the world from his heart. And according to the reduction of years left, he should reduce his occupation in the world. And he should constantly seclude himself to meditate about fear of God, to think about his soul, to refine his traits and to seek Torah and its commandments. And that which they said - At ninety a **Lasuach** [bent] body. is from the same usage as in - spill[47] his **Sicho** [prayer]. And it said - To[48] **Lasuach** [pray] in the field. As our Rabbis, may their memory be blessed, said the

---

[46] Avot 5:21
[47] Psalms 102:1
[48] Genesis 24:63

Talmud - Itzhak[49] established the afternoon prayers, as it is stated to **Lasuach** [pray] in the field. For after one reaches ninety years, it is fitting for him that all of his occupation should be with prayer and praises of God, and to speak about His wonders. And King Solomon, peace be upon him, spoke about the matter of the days of old age - that a person should not then be lazy about service to God, may He be blessed. And he said - Sow[50] your seed in the morning and don't hold back your hand in the evening, since you don't know which is going to succeed the one or the other or if both are equally good. He compared the days of childhood and youth to the morning and the days of old age to evening. And seed is metaphoric for children and for students, as our Rabbis, may their memory be blessed, said in the Talmud - If[51] he married a woman in his youth he should marry another one in his old age if he established students in his youth he should establish other students in his old age. For perhaps the children of old age will be more successful in Torah and in the commandments than the children of youth. And likewise, the students that he establishes in his old age may be more successful than the first ones. Or they could both be equally good. Afterwards, he stated - How[52] sweet is the light, what a delight for the eyes to behold the sun. Its explanation is that he went back to speaking about the days of old age which he compared to the evening.

---

[49] Berakhot 26b
[50] Ecclesiastes 11:6
[51] Yevamot 62b
[52] Ecclesiastes 11:7

And since an old man will not taste that which he eats and that which he drinks - like the words of **Barzilai**[53] **the Gileadite** - he stated that the old man should enjoy the light of the sun and not be disgusted by it. As disgust obstructs a person from his service to the Heavens. So, he should enjoy the light, when he compares it to the days of darkness that are coming - as it mentions in the verse below this - Even[54] if a man lives many years let him enjoy himself in all of them remembering how many the days of darkness are going to be the only future is nothingness. The explanation is that even if a person gets very old, let him not be a burden to himself. Rather he should rejoice in all of his years, so that he not loses one of his years and not rest from the service of the Creator. And he should remember the days of darkness, for they will be many. And then he will not be able to perform the service, like the matter that is stated - In[55] the pit who can acclaim You? And the righteous ones overcome their old age, gird their power and renew their strength for the service of God. It is as our Rabbis, may their memory be blessed, said in the Talmud - As[56] Torah scholars grow older wisdom is increased in them. And it is stated - In[57] old age they still produce fruit they are full of sap and freshness.

---

[53] Barzilai the Gileadite spies is a biblical character, his main mention is during the Absalom rebellion, when Barzilai is one of the people who supported King David and his men during their exile in Mahanai.

[54] Ecclesiastes 11:8

[55] Psalms 6:6

[56] Shabbat 152a

[57] Psalms 92:15

And he mentioned above - The[58] righteous bloom like a date-palm they thrive like a cedar in Lebanon. Planted[59] in the house of the LORD they flourish in the courts of our God. For the righteous are planted in the house of the Lord from their youth, and grow in the house of study from their young adulthood - like a date-palm that blossoms and like a cedar that grows in the Lebanon. And as our Rabbis, may their memory be blessed, likewise said in the Midrash - The[60] righteous bloom like a date-palm - these are the infants, in the way that it was stated - For[61] our sons are like saplings well-tended in their youth. And he stated after this about this thing, that they are not completely compared to trees. For trees will not give their strength when they age. But the righteous **in old age, they still produce fruit**. And King David, peace be upon him, also stated - And[62] even in hoary old age do not forsake me, God, until I proclaim Your strength to the next generation, your mighty acts, to all who are to come.

The third path is that when he hears reproof from the sages that are reprimanding him, he listens, submits, repents and accepts in his heart all the words of reprimand - and not subtract one thing from their words. And behold that man went out from darkness to a great light at that instant. For at the time that he listened and paid attention and his heart understood

---

58 Psalms 92:13
59 Psalms 92:14
60 Midrash Tehillim 92:14
61 Psalms 144:12
62 Psalms 71:18

and repented and accepted the words of the rebuker
on the day he heard them, and took upon himself to
do like everything that the holders of Torah instructed
him - from that day onward - to be careful as the
knowers of understanding of the times instructed him
- His repentance is effective and he is changed into a
different person. And from the time that he accepted
this in his heart, he acquired merit and reward for his
soul for all of the commandments and ethical acts.
And happy is he for justifying his soul in a short time.
And so, did our Rabbis, may their memory be well,
say - And[63] the Children of Israel went and did - and
did they do it right away? Did they not only do it on
the fourteenth of the month? Rather since they
accepted upon themselves to do it, the verse counts it
for them as if they did it immediately. And he said in
Avot of Rabbi Natan - Anyone[64] whose actions are
greater than his wisdom - his wisdom will endure, as
it is stated - We[65] shall do and we shall listen. The
explanation of the thing is that when a man accepts
upon himself with a faithful heart to keep and do
according to the Torah that he was taught and about
the law which those sitting upon judgement told him
- from that day, he has the reward for all of the
commandments that his ear heard and that he
understood, as well as for all of the things which his
ear has still not heard about. So, he wore
righteousness and acquired merit for all of what was
revealed to him and for all that was hidden from his

---

[63] Mekhilta d'Rabbi Yishmael, 12:28
[64] Avot d'Rabbi Natan 22
[65] Exodus 24:7

eyes. And after this, he should study from and
regularly attend the doors of those that reprimanded
him, and comprehend the teachings of all that teach
him. And it comes out that the actions of this man are
greater than his wisdom, since he did not know the
thing, but behold its reward for it is with him. And it
is like the matter that Israel said - We[66] shall do and
we shall listen. at Mount Sinai as they had the
acceptance of the deed upon themselves, precede the
listening. And in no other way it is possible for the
actions of a man to be greater than what he knows.

But the one who does not get aroused by the voice of
his rebukers will double his iniquities. For they
reprimanded him and he hardened his heart - as it is
stated - A[67] rebuke works on an intelligent man More
than one hundred blows on a fool. An[68] evil man seeks
only to rebel A ruthless messenger will be sent
against him. The explanation is that the evil man will
not submit to the voice of the rebukers. Rather he will
seek to rebel. And since he did not stop from the
words of the reprimanding angel, a cruel angel will
be sent against him - measure for measure. For
rebukers are called - **Malakhim** [angels], which
literally means messengers, as it is stated - But[69] they
mocked the messengers of God and disdained His
words and taunted His prophets. And King Solomon,
peace be upon him, also said - Discipline[70] seems bad

---

[66] Exodus 24:7
[67] Proverbs 17:10
[68] Proverbs 17:11
[69] Chronicles-B 36:16
[70] Proverbs 15:10

to him who forsakes the way he who spurns rebuke will die. Its explanation is that it is true that harsh rebuke is appropriate for one who has forsaken the way and transgresses the words of the Torah. However, there is hope that he will take the rebuke and repent from his evil way. But worse than him is one who hates rebuke. For he has no hope and rectification from harsh rebuke. Rather his one verdict is to die. For one who does a transgression - his desire overpowered him and the impulse pushed him. But it is likely that his soul is bitter about that which he was not stronger in the face of his impulse. And maybe he longs for reprimand and hopes for reproof. But one who hates reprimand has already abandoned his soul; and his hatred for reprimand will be a proof that he hates the words of God, may He be blessed.

King Solomon, peace be upon him, also said - What[71] brightens the eye gladdens the heart good news puts fat on the bones. He[72] whose ear heeds the discipline of life Lodges among the wise. And every wise-hearted person should know that it is not likely that King Solomon, peace be upon him, composed idle words like these in the middle of words of reproof and fear of God for nothing - since Scripture has already testified about him - He[73] was the wisest of all men. Rather this is the understanding of the thing - What[74]

[71] Proverbs 15:30
[72] Proverbs 15:31
[73] Kings-A 5:11
[74] Proverbs 15:30

brightens the eye gladdens the heart good news puts fat on the bones. The eye is a very esteemed organ, for they will see all the events that gladden the heart with it. But more esteemed than it is the ear, for they will hear good news, that puts fat on the bones, through it. For the ear has no feeling and it will not be fattened from the light of the eyes, unless it is a special enjoyment. And so did our Rabbis, may their memory be blessed, say in the Talmud - That[75] the ear is more esteemed than the other organs. For if one blinded his eye, he must pay for the value of his eye; but if he makes him deaf, he pays all of his value. And truly a person is obligated to serve, God, may He be blessed, with his limbs. And they were all formed for His service, as it is written - The[76] Lord made everything for His sake. Even with the esteemed limbs that He formed in him, is he obligated to serve their Maker. And the great punishment is even much greater if he prevents them from doing His commandments, he does not do the service with them and he does not pay back the good that is done through them. For with his esteemed senses, God gave him a great kindness; and He crowned him with beauty and glory through them. Therefore, he prefaced to mention one of the virtues of the ear in order for you to see the greatness of the obligation of its service. And afterwards, he explained that the service of the ear should be in listening to reprimand; and he said - He[77] whose ear heeds the discipline of

---

[75] Bava Kamma 85b
[76] Proverbs 16:4
[77] Proverbs 15:31

life Lodges among the wise. Its explanation is that it is fitting to dwell among the sages, since he can then listen to their reprimands. And our Rabbis, may their memory be blessed, said in the Midrash - If[78] a man falls from a roof and all of his limbs are broken, he needs a bandage and a plaster for every one of his limbs and his bones. And a sinner who has sinned with all of his limbs is considered as if he received a great wound on all of his limbs - from the sole of his foot to his crown, as it is stated - From[79] head to foot no spot is sound. But behold the Holy One, blessed be He, heals all of his limbs with one bandage. And that is the listening of the ear, as it is stated - Incline[80] your ear and come to Me hearken and you shall be revived.

The fourth path is that when a man meditates upon the Torah of God and reads the words of the Prophets and the Writings and understands the pleasantness of the reprimands and sees the warnings and the punishments - he trembles and prepares his heart to improve his ways and his plans and become acceptable to God, as it is stated - Yet[81] to such a one I look to the poor and broken-hearted who trembles about My word. And likewise, is it written about the matter of **Yoshiyahu** - And[82] when the king heard the words of the scroll of the Torah, he rent his clothes.

---

[78] Shemot Rabbah 27:9
[79] Isaiah 1:6
[80] Isaiah 55:3
[81] Isaiah 66:2
[82] Kings-B 22:11

And about the matter of Ezra is it stated - For[83] all the people were weeping as they listened to the words of the Torah. And the one that does not pay attention to the words of God will have his transgression become greater for him, like the matter that is stated - Yet[84] they showed no fear and did not tear their garments. And our Rabbis, may their memory be blessed, said in the Talmud - Anyone[85] who studies but does not uphold what he learned it would have been better that his placenta would have flipped itself on his face and he had not come out to the light of the world. And it is stated - The[86] many teachings I wrote for him have been treated as something alien. And it is also stated - How[87] can you say - **We are wise, and we possess the Torah of the Lord** assuredly for naught has the pen labored, for naught the scribe.

The fifth path is that on the ten days of repentance, the heart of one who fears the Lord will pine inside himself, knowing in his mind that all of his deeds are written in a book and that at that time, God brings all of His creation to judgement about all that is hidden - whether for the good or for the bad. For man is judged on Rosh Hashanah and his final verdict is sealed on Yom Kippur. And at a time that he knows that they will bring his case in front of a king of flesh and blood, does he not tremble greatly, seek counsel for himself and scurry industriously to find a way to

---

83 Nehemiah 8:9
84 Jeremiah 36:24
85 Yerushalmi Berakhot 1:1
86 Hosea 8:12
87 Jeremiah 8:8

escape? And it does not come to his spirit to turn to the right or to the left or to occupy himself with the rest of his business. And he will not break up and furrow his land nor turn through the vineyards. And on a day of distress, he will not falter from preparing his heart to escape like a deer from the hand of the hunter. Therefore, how foolish are those who go out to their labors and their work until the evening on the Days of Awe - days of judgement and verdict - and do not know what their verdict will be. Is it not that their hearts are preoccupied [even] about their sister on the day when she will be spoken for - as it is stated - What[88] shall we do for our sister when she is spoken for? And it is fitting for anyone that fears God to reduce his affairs, so that his ideas are at ease; to fix times during the day and night to seclude himself in his rooms, search his ways and investigate; to be early to the watches and occupy himself with the ways of repentance and the refinement of action; and to pour out speech, raise prayer and song and to lay down supplication. And this time is a time of good will, and prayer will be heard on it - like the matter that is stated - In[89] an hour of favor I answer you, and on a day of salvation I help you. And our Rabbis, may their memory be blessed, said in the Talmud - Seek[90] the Lord while He can be found these are the ten days between Rosh Hashanah and Yom Kippur. And it is a **positive** commandment from the Torah for a man to arouse his spirit to repent on Yom Kippur, as it is

---

[88] Song of Songs 8:8
[89] Isaiah 49:8
[90] Rosh Hashanah 18a

stated - Of[91] all your sins, you shall be pure before the Lord. Therefore, Scripture warned us that we should purify ourselves before God with our repentance; and He will atone for us on that day to purify us.

The sixth path is that he should prepare to meet his God every instant. Therefore, he should darken his conscience and prepare in righteousness to return his soul in purity to God who gave it to him. So, he should search his ways and his plans every day - record them in the mornings and examine them all the time. And our Rabbis, may their memory be blessed, said in the Talmud - Rabbi[92] Eliezer says - **Repent one day before your death**. His students asked him, our teacher, but does a person know the day on which he will die? He said to them, All the more so should one repent today, lest he die tomorrow and so, one will spend his entire life in a state of repentance. And it states - Let[93] your clothes always be white, and your head never lack oil. The whiteness of clothes is a metaphor for the cleanliness of the soul that has repented; and the oil is a metaphor for good deeds and a good name. And our Rabbis, may their memory be blessed, also said about this matter in the Midrash - There[94] is a relevant parable about the wife of a sailor who would adorn herself and paint her eyes while her husband was traveling on the seaways. So, her neighbors said to her, did not your husband go on a

---

[91] Leviticus 16:30
[92] Shabbat 153a
[93] Ecclesiastes 9:8
[94] Kohelet Rabbah 9:6

faraway journey? So, isn't this beautifying of yourself for naught? She said to them, my husband is a sailor. Maybe the sea wind will change and ease it for him to come quickly and he will find me - and behold I will be adorned. And when a person is at ease and tranquil, he should assess in his soul how his heart will worry, fear and tremble when the day of death comes to him - that he should be prepared to rise and give an accounting; and how he will give a confession with a crushed heart at the time of his death. So, the fear of heaven will be upon him.

And a person should always be performing new commandments - maybe the turn of his death has come, and he will otherwise not perform these commandments. And our Rabbis, may their memory be blessed, said in the Midrash - Anyone[95] who performs a commandment close to his death is as if he performed the entire Torah and was only lacking this commandment. And anyone who performs a transgression close to his death is as if he negated the whole Torah.

But there are people that do not sense the matter of death, to make provisions for the road and to rectify their actions; and they do not pay attention to the day of their death until it comes. So, they are compared to animals that do not sense the matter of death until the day of slaughter - as it is stated - Sheeplike[96] they head for the pit with death as their shepherd the upright

---

[95] Kohelet Rabbah 1:28
[96] Psalms 49:15

shall rule over them in the morning, and their form - from above him - shall waste away in the pit. Its explanation is - They lead their souls to the pit, since they don't sense the matter of their death until its sudden arrival. **With death as their shepherd** - the death of evildoers is not like the death of animals; the death of animals is once, but the death of the evildoers will shepherd them every day. That shepherd can be a verb in the continuous present is indicated from the wording - Shepherd[97] Bashan and Gilead. - And from the content of - Death's[98] first born consumes his tendons. For destruction and deterioration will cling to the soul of the evildoers at every instant, until it is destroyed, ends and is gone. Such[99] is the fate of those who are self-confident the end of those pleased with their own talk Selah. - It compared the time of the resurrection of the dead to the morning, when a man wakes up from his sleep; and like the matter that is stated - Many[100] of those that sleep in the dust of the earth will awake. For then the righteous will rule over the evildoers, as it is written - And[101] you shall trample the wicked to a pulp for they shall be dust beneath your feet. And our Rabbis, may their memory be blessed, said in the Talmud about the matter of the day of judgement for the resurrection of the dead - After[102] twelve months their bodies end, and their souls are burnt and become ashes under the feet of the

[97] Micah 7:14
[98] Job 18:13
[99] Psalms 49:14
[100] Daniel 12:2
[101] Malachi 3:21
[102] Rosh Hashanah 17a

righteous as is stated - **And you shall trample the wicked.** And it is written - Sheeplike[103] they head for **Sheol** [hell] with Death as their shepherd The upright shall rule over them at daybreak and their form shall waste away in Sheol till its nobility be gone. And their form **Tsuram** [jarring] shall waste away in the pit - **Tsuram** is like **Tsuratam** the conventional way of writing, their form. Likewise - Idols[104] ketvunam. Is understood as **ketvunatam.** And the soul is called the form of man. But there are some among those who speak about the soul that said, about the definition of the soul, that it is a contingent form. And the explanation of the matter is that the pit wears out the evildoer's soul. And it is - above **Zevul** [holy height] him - for the soul is from the higher beings. This is seen from the wording - From[105] Your **Zevul** [holy height]. And with his sins, the evildoer caused and brought about that his precious and elevated soul that is above him will be worn out by the pit below. And how difficult is death for the one who has not separated desires of the world from his soul until it is separated by death! And our Rabbis, may their memory be blessed, said in Mishna - Is[106] your will not to die? Die before you die. The explanation of the matter is that the one that wants that the day of his death be a gateway for him to eternal life should speak to his heart - since his end is to leave the ground and to leave the matters of the body, and in his end,

---

[103] Psalms 49:15
[104] Hosea 13:2
[105] Isaiah 63:15
[106] Derekh Erets

he will despise them and abandon them; he should leave them when he is still alive, and only use the ground for service to the Creator, may He be blessed. And then the day of death will be the beginning of life without end for him.

And know that the soul of the evildoer whose entire desire while alive is for the things of the body - the desire of which is separated from service to the Creator and is removed from its roots - will in his death descend to the ground, to the place of its desire. And its destiny will be - like the nature of the ground - to descend and not to arise. However, it will be brought up for justice and for trial and to see how it exchanged the above for the pit - like they bring up a stone to the hollow of a slingshot. But after they raise [the stone] up - by its nature - it comes down to the ground, when the stone comes back and falls down to the ground after its projection, as it is stated - The[107] life of my lord will be bound up in the bundle of life in the care of the Lord, your God but He will fling away the lives of your enemies as from the hollow of a sling. And our Rabbis, may their memory be blessed, said in Midrash Mishlei - Both[108] the souls of the righteous and the souls of the evildoers rise above and are judged there - The souls of the righteous are triumphant in their trial and hidden under the Throne of Glory, but the souls of evildoers, are eaten away to the ground, as it is stated, **but He will fling away the**

---

[107] Samuel-A 25:29
[108] Kohelet Rabbah 3:27

lives of your enemies. And it is stated - At[109] death
the hopes of a wicked man are lost. For there is no
hope for the soul of an evildoer to leave from the
darkness to the light, as it is stated - Yet[110] he must
join the company of his ancestors, who will never see
daylight again.

Behold it has been explained from the two verses that
we mentioned - as well as from the words of the
Sages, may their memory be blessed - that the soul of
the evildoers goes down to the pit. And it has also
been stated - For[111] an intelligent man the path of life
leads upward, in order to avoid the pit below. And it
has also been stated - Who[112] knows if the spirit of
men does rise upward and if a beast's spirit does sink
down into the earth? The explanation of this is who
can recognize the righteous ones and the evildoers in
this world? For there are evildoers whose actions are
in the dark, and people will not know it about them;
and there are righteous ones that fear the Heavens in
private, like the matter that is stated - And[113] walk
humbly. And he called the soul of an evildoer, the
soul of a beast, because it follows its physical desire
like a beast. And this is like the matter that is stated -
Who[114] do not yet know their right hand from their
left, and many beasts as well! But he called the
righteous ones, **the spirit of men** - like the matter that

---

[109] Proverbs 11:7
[110] Psalms 49:20
[111] Proverbs 15:24
[112] Ecclesiastes 3:21
[113] Micah 6:8
[114] Jonah 4:11

is stated - You[115] are men. And the explanation of the wording of the verse is like this: Who knows the spirit of men - which are the righteous ones - which goes above; for there are many righteous people that a person cannot determine in this world that they are truly righteous, and that their souls will arise above, like the matter that is stated - Man[116] sees only what is visible, but the Lord sees into the heart. And also, since there are many righteous ones whose fear of the Heavens is secret, and their righteousness is not known, and like the matter that is stated - And[117] walk humbly with your God. Who[118] knows if a man's lifebreath does rise upward and if a beast's breath does sink down into the earth? Is that there also many evildoers that a man would not recognize from their actions, like the matter that is stated - Who[119] do their work in dark places and say - **Who sees us who takes note of us**? And they, may their memory be blessed, likewise explained in Midrash Kohelet - That[120] the **spirit of men** is the righteous ones, **and the beast's spirit** is the evildoers. But a person cannot say that he is in doubt whether the soul of a man rise up; for behold it is written - And[121] the spirit returns to God who bestowed it. And also, how can he doubt whether the spirit of a beast descends below? Is the spirit of a beast not from the earth? So how could it rise? And it

---

[115] Ezekiel 34:31
[116] Samuel-A 16:7
[117] Micah 6:8
[118] Ecclesiastes 3:21
[119] Isaiah 29:15
[120] Kohelet Rabbah 3:21
[121] Ecclesiastes 12:7

is explained in the Torah that the soul of man is supernal. As it is written about the spirit of an animal that it is from the ground, as it is stated - Let[122] the earth bring forth living spirits according to their specie. But about the spirit of man, it is written - And[123] He blew into his nostrils a living soul. Therefore, the soul of man rises above with the death of the body; since all things return to their source, like the matter that is stated - And[124] the dust returns to the ground as it was, and the spirit returns to God who bestowed it. And it is stated about the soul of the righteous one - And[125] I will permit you to move about among these ones standing. Its explanation is among the angels that are standing and enduring - as it is stated - And[126] He made them stand forever. And it is also stated - Approached[127] one of the standings. And they, may their memory be blessed, said in the Talmud - The[128] souls of the righteous are hidden under the Throne of Glory, as it is stated - The[129] life of my lord will be bound up in the bundle of life.

And all men of heart will consider this world like a temporary dwelling; so, they will only use it for the service of the Creator, may He be blessed, and prepare provisions for their souls. For if a man lives

[122] Genesis 1:24
[123] Genesis 2:7
[124] Ecclesiastes 12:7
[125] Zechariah 3:7
[126] Psalms 148:6
[127] Daniel 7:16
[128] Shabbat 152b
[129] Samuel-A 25:29

many years - even if he lived twice a thousand years - since there is a number to his years, the number will end, and his end will be as if they had not been. But the world of repayment has no end, like the matter that is stated - For[130] a few more years will pass, and I shall go the way of no return. Even more so, since the days of man are like a passing shadow, like the matter that is stated - The[131] span of our life is seventy years or given the strength eighty years but the best of them are trouble and sorrow They pass by speedily and we are in darkness. And it is also stated - His[132] days are like a passing shadow. And our Rabbis, may their memory be blessed, said in the Midrash - Not[133] like the shadow of a tree or the shadow of a wall, but rather like the shadow of a flying and passing bird. It means to say a person is obligated to compare in his heart, this world to the shadow of a bird that if flying and passes over in a small instant - especially since a man does not know whether he is here today but, in the grave, tomorrow. And it would come out in his efforts today for tomorrow, that he has taken pains for a world that is not his. And our Rabbis, may their memory be blessed, said in the Talmud - Grieve[134] not about tomorrow's trouble, because you know not what a day may bring.

And King Solomon, peace be upon him, essentially composed the book of Ecclesiastes in order that man

---

[130] Job 16:22
[131] Psalms 90:10
[132] Psalms 144:4
[133] Kohelet Rabbah 1:3
[134] Sanhedrin 100b

put to his heart that the world is a vanity of vanities and that he only uses it for the service of the Creator, may He be elevated. And he made his intention known in his introduction and his conclusion: For he opened and said - Vanity[135] of vanities said Kohelet vanity of vanities - everything is vanity. And our Rabbis, may their memory be blessed, said in the Midrash - If[136] another man had said this we would have said - **Maybe he has not gathered two small coins in his entire days**. therefore, the world is considered like vanity in his eyes. However, it is appropriate for King Solomon - about whom it is written - The[137] king made silver as plentiful in Jerusalem as stones to say that the world is vanity of vanities. And he concluded his book and said - The[138] sum of the matter when all is said and done revere God and observe His commandments for this is all of man.

And whoever God, may He blessed, has graced with intelligence should place into his heart that God, may He be blessed, has sent him into this world to keep His watch, His statutes and His commandments. And he should only open his eyes to do his mission. And at the end of days - if he did his mission trust-worthily - he comes back with joy and with eternal gladness upon his head; like a servant that the king has sent to cross the sea, whose eyes and heart are only upon the

---

[135] Ecclesiastes 1:2
[136] Kohelet Rabbah 3:13
[137] Kings-A 1:27
[138] Ecclesiastes 12:13

matter of his agency until he returns to his master. And likewise did King Solomon, peace be upon him, say - That[139] you may put your trust in the Lord I let you know today yes you. Indeed[140] I wrote down for you a threefold lore Wise counsel. To[141] let you know truly reliable words That you may give a faithful reply to him who sent you.

And among the things for which a person is obligated to remember the day of death is in order that he not waste time and his hands not falter from the service of God, may He be blessed; that he remove sleep from his eyes to toil in Torah study and to contemplate fear of God, to refine the traits of his soul so as to reach levels of fear and love; and to think thoughts of how to enhance and beatify the commandments such that his soul should be a charm and a treasure - like the matter that is stated - He[142] whose heart is wise accepts commandments. For he will know and remember that the days are short - as our Rabbis, may their memory be blessed, said in the Mishna - The[143] day is short and the work is plentiful and the laborers are indolent, and the reward is great and the Master of the house is insistent.

But the one who does not always remember the day of his death is similar in his own eyes to one who has extra time and calm **Mitun** [patient] to reach his goal.

---

139 Proverbs 22:19-21
140 Proverbs 22:19-21
141 Proverbs 22:19-21
142 Proverbs 10:8
143 Avot 2:15

It appears to me that it is from the usage in Mishna], Be[144] **Matunim** [patient] in judgement. And in the Talmudwe read - **Matun**[145] [which can also mean two hundred] and **Matun** is equal to four hundred **Zuz** [Jewish silver coin] And our Rabbis, may their memory be blessed, said in the Mishna - More[146] precious is one hour in repentance and good deeds in this world than all the life of the world to come and more precious is one hour of the tranquility of the world to come than all the life of this world.

And likewise did King Solomon, peace be upon him, say - For[147] he who is connected with the living has hope even a live dog is better than a dead lion. Its explanation is that he praised life in this world with regards to repentance, performance of commandments, and attainment of spiritual virtues. And this is the hope that is found for those connected with the living. And the explanation of **even a live dog** is that even a lowly man that is alive can add to his spiritual virtues - which is not the case for a righteous sage that is dead. But in another place, he disgraced and condemned this world, regarding the attainment of pleasures and honor, and said - What[148] advantage is there for a man in all of his toil that he does beneath the sun? And he also said - Then[149] I accounted those who died long since more fortunate

---

144   Avot 1:1
145   Berkhot 20a
146   Avot 4:17
147   Kohelet 9:4
148   Kohelet 1:3
149   Kohelet 4:2

than those who are still living.

And our Rabbis, may their memory be blessed, said in the Mishna - Keep[150] your eye on three things, and you will not come to sin.... From where did you come? From a putrid drop. And to where are you going? To a place of dust, worms, and maggots. And before whom are you destined to give an account and a reckoning? Before the King of kings, the Holy One, blessed be He. The explanation of the content is [that] when you think of from where you came, your spirit will be humbled and you will hate pride. And when you remember where you are going, you will scorn the world, recognize that its superfluous luxuries are nothing and only be involved with it for the service of the Creator, may He be blessed. And when you put into your heart in front of whom you will be giving a reckoning, fear of the Heavens will be upon you. And our Rabbis, may their memory be blessed, said in the Midrash - And[151] God saw all that He had made and found it very good. - This[152] **very good** is death. For even death is good, so as to subdue spirits, that there be fear of God upon the hearts and that they not make this world into the main one. But there are people that do not give time to their souls to understand their ends, because of their preoccupation with acquisitions of the world - like the matter that is stated - Their[153] cord is moved and they die and not with

---

[150] Avot 3:1
[151] Genesis Rabbah 9:5
[152] Genesis 1:31
[153] Job 4:21

wisdom. Its explanation is, is not their **Yeteram** [cord] which can also be understood as their excess or advantage - their money - moved from them in their move; for behold they have no benefit from it when they die, yet it lost much good for them. For it caused them to die without wisdom, as they did not show wisdom to understand their end, to rectify their souls and prepare provisions for their journey, - like the matter that is stated - Were[154] they wise they would think upon this gain insight into their future.

And behold we shall conclude this topic with an esteemed statement of the Sages of Israel, may there memory be blessed, Hillel peace be upon him, used to say in the Mishna - If[155] I am not for myself who is for me? And if not now, when? The explanation of the content is that if a person does not arouse his soul, what effect can reproof have? For even if they enter his heart on the day that he hears them, the impulse will forget them and drive them out of his heart, like the matter of that which was stated - When[156] your goodness is like a morning cloud. And it is also stated - The[157] tongue of a righteous man is choice silver. But the heart of the wicked is of little worth **Kimeat** [almost]. Its explanation is that the reproof of a righteous man is pure without any dross, and his speech is chosen. But the heart of the evildoers that listen to his reproof is only for one instant. This is

---

[154] Deuteronomy 32:29
[155] Avot 1:14
[156] Hosea 6:4
[157] Proverbs 10:20

from the usage - Then[158] would I subdue their enemies instantly **Kimeat** [almost] - The meaning of which is, in an instant would I subdue their enemies. And only an understanding and refined heart is called a heart, as it is stated - He[159] who heeds reproof acquires heart. And it is stated - To[160] purchase wisdom, when he has no heart? Indeed, a man must arouse his heart when he hears reproof and place the things into his heart, to constantly think about them. And he should add teaching from his own heart and produce words. He should also meditate in the chambers of his spirit and repent, to turn the hand of the reproof upon himself and not just rely upon the rebuke of the rebuker. Otherwise. That rebuke will be like morning clouds, and for fleeting instants, until he takes the reproof upon himself and until he purifies himself. **But if I am for my own self only**, what am I?

Even when I am for myself and I reflect upon wisdom all the time, what am I? For the grasp of a man is short and weak. So even with the effort and the refinement, he will only attain a little of the virtues - see what I am and what my life is when I am not for myself, to make efforts to refine my soul. And the comparison here is to a field that is inferior. For with great toil and refinement, and with much work, it will bring out a small amount of seed. But if they do not toil in its refinement, it will not produce anything and no grass will grow in it besides thorns and brambles. However,

---

[158]   Psalms 81:15
[159]   Proverbs 15:32
[160]   Proverbs 17:16

there is benefit in sowing a superior field - even if he does not toil in working it. And our Rabbis, may their memory be blessed, said about this matter in the Midrash - That[161] which it is written - For[162] He knows our formation - there is a relevant metaphor of a king that gave a field to his servants and warned them to work it and guard it, and to bring him thirty kor from it each year. And they toiled on it and worked it well, but only bought five kor in front of the king. He said to them - **What have you done**? They said to him, our master, the king, the field that you gave us was inferior, and we worked it with all of our strength. But with all of the toil, it did not make more grain than this. **And if not now, when**? It is not appropriate for me to delay my efforts, a day or two, in refining my soul and fixing set times for Torah study. For if I say - I shall hope for leisure time and until I have enough money in my hands for my needs - behold the distractions of the world do not stop. As our Rabbis, may their memory be blessed, said in the Mishna - Say[163] not When I shall have leisure, I shall study lest you will not have leisure.

And the second reason - not to delay is after he gathers and brings in produce or other income, he will still long to gather. As our Rabbis, may their memory be blessed, said Midrash - A[164] man does not depart the world with half of what he desires in his hands. If

---

[161] Avot D' Rabbi Natan 16
[162] Psalms 103:14
[163] Avot 2:4
[164] Kohelet Rabbah 1:13

he has a hundred in his hands, he will desire to make two hundred; if his hands attained two hundred, he desires to make them four hundred. And so is it written - A[165] lover of money never has his fill of money.

And the third reason - is that the time decreases and the work is plentiful: The work of Torah study, refinement of the soul and attainment of the virtues - such as love, fear and cleaving. As they, may their memory be blessed, said - The[166] day is short, and the work is plentiful.

The fourth reason - is that when refinement of the soul is delayed, iniquity will happen and he will constantly stumble over transgressions.

The fifth reason - is that with the delay of the refinement of the soul, the impulse continually strengthens. So, it will be more difficult for him to refine his soul afterwards, as it is written - It[167] was all overgrown with thorns Its surface was covered with chickweed and its stone fence lay in ruins. And our Rabbis, may their memory be blessed, said that when the impulse is connected to transgression, it will become similar to the matter of heresy - and his hands will not attain his purification. And they said in the ethical teachings - **Habit about anything controls**.

---

[165] Ecclesiastes 5:9
[166] Avot 2:15
[167] Proverbs 24:31

The sixth reason - is that maybe his days will not be long and he will die before he completes the measure of his repentance. Therefore, Solomon warned - Let[168] your clothes always be white.

The seventh reason - is that with his delay in repentance, his iniquities will be old, and he will forget their anguish. So, he will not worry about them as he would have earlier.

The eighth reason - is that in his getting on in days and the weakening of the strength of the impulse, he will not receive the same reward for the repentance as it would be for the refinement of his heart during the days of his youth. And our Rabbis, may their memory be blessed, said in the Talmud[169] - Happy[170] is the man who fears the Lord. When he is still a man. And they also said in the Talmud - When[171] the thief is lacking what to steal he makes himself like a man of peace.

The ninth reason - is that during the days of his old age - with the absence of the power of emotion - he does not have the reserve of strength to create new paths in his heart, to arrange thoughts with which to fight his impulse, to attain virtues and to toil and strive in Torah and in his actions and in the worlds. As it is written - So[172] remember your Creator in the days of your youth before those days of sorrow come

---

[168] Ecclesiastes 9:8
[169] Avodah Zarah 19a
[170] Psalms 112:1
[171] Sanhedrin 22a
[172] Ecclesiastes 12:1

and those years arrive of which you will say **I have no pleasure in them**. Therefore, it is appropriate for a person to rush to save his soul, like the matter that is stated - I[173] have rushed and not delayed to keep Your commandments.

---

[173] Psalms 119:60

Sha'arei Teshuvah

Gates of Repentance

Rabbeinu Yonah

Chapter Three

We shall explain the severity of the **positive** commandments, and the warnings **negative** commandments, and different punishments for the penitent is warned to search his ways, and gauge how many iniquities and sins he has done. And after his search is done, he is warned to examine the magnitude of each sin - as it is stated - Let[1] us search and examine our ways. In order for him to know how much he is guilty for each sin that he sinned. For there is guilt that is big nought to reach the skies, and there is evil that corresponds to several big sins. For repentance is great according to investigations of the heart like these. As according to his knowledge of the greatness of the iniquity and its largeness will his heart trouble him. And he will then be able to subdue his uncircumcised heart, and his iniquities will then be atoned.

Moreover, the examination of the enormity of the iniquity will help to 'cover the mortification of his face' during his request for forgiveness, like the

---

[1] Lamentations 3:40

matter that is stated - O[2] my God, I am too ashamed and mortified to lift my face to You O my God. To wrap his soul in shame before God, may He be blessed, after the assurance of His forgiveness, like the matter that is stated, - In[3] order that you shall remember and feel shame and you shall be too abashed to open your mouth again when I have forgiven you for all that you did. and that the greatness of the kindness of the atonement be in front of his eyes, like the matter that is stated - For[4] Your kindness is in front of my eyes. And the parable for this is that if a slave sinned to his master and then comes to humble himself in front of him, the master's soul would not pay attention to him until after the slave knew of the weightiness of his sin. But if it appears to the slave like the sin is light, the master's rage against him would only grow. Therefore, the sinner is obligated to recognize the enormity of his sin and its punishment, like the matter that is stated - Behold[5] I have been a fool and I have erred so very much. Therefore, we need to teach the Children of Judah - for instruction and message - the weightiness of the punishments of each iniquity and of each sin. Hence the need for all these words of introduction. And another sublime, great and trenchant purpose is that I have surely seen most of the people thinking about several weighty transgressions that they are light; and about sins that carry the death penalty or

---

[2] Ezra 9:6
[3] Ezekiel 16:63
[4] Psalms 26:3
[5] Samuel-A 26:21

excision, that concern about them is just greater refinement or a measure of piety. So, they stumble without paying attention; and there is no rebuke, like the matter that is stated - Even[6] from yore your ears were not opened. Therefore, we need to warn them and to have their ears revealed about the weightiness of many sins, and that there are also many ways and angles to the light commandments that lead to decreed destruction and loss of the soul. And many of the evildoers would leave their paths if they will know the loss and damage that comes with it, when they hear about the greatness of the sin and the [punishment] which is decreed about it. This is so those that stumble will gird their power to conquer their desire. For how could they see the destruction of their souls and not react?

And the parable for this is about a man that wants to go to a city. And he is told that the path is confounded with thorns, snares and stumbling blocks. But because of his need for the place, he is not prevented from going. But if they would tell him that there is a lion on the path and a leopard constantly on it, he would then stop his feet from this path. Therefore King Solomon, peace be upon him, said - For[7] learning wisdom and reproof; for understanding. Its explanation is that proper action and abandonment of sins is called wisdom, like the matter that is stated - For[8] that is your wisdom and you're understanding.

---

[6] Isaiah 48:8

[7] Proverbs 1:2

[8] Deuteronomy 4:6

But after he learns and know the commandments and what are the sins, he needs to study the disgrace of the sins, and the damage and the loss that comes with them - in order to distance his soul from them; to reprimand himself by remembering the punishments and to reprove others. And this knowledge is called **Mussar** [reproof]. And it is pleasant for those that give rebuke to study this.

Now we will explain the levels of the positive and negative commandments and the allotment of the punishments

The first level is the severity of the words of the Scribes

We were obligated by the Torah to accept the ordinances of the prophets and the judges, to obey the words of sages and to be careful with their fences, as it is stated - You[9] must not deviate from the thing that they tell you either to the right or to the left. And even though we have also been warned by the Torah to be steadfast to do everything that they instructed us, nevertheless **positive** commandments directly from the Torah are more weighty than their words - since the essence of the thing is mentioned explicitly in the scroll of God's Torah, and God, may He be blessed, commanded it specifically. But there are ways and angles in which words of the Scribes are more weighty than the words of the Torah - like our Rabbis, may their memory be blessed, said in the Talmud -

---

[9] Deuteronomy 17:11

With[10] regards to the rulings of the rebellious elder there is greater stringency to the words of the Scribes than to the words of the Torah. For one who states - **There is no commandment to don tefillin** - to transgress the words of the Torah - is exempt. But one who says - **There are five compartments** - to add to the words of the Scribes - is liable. and in the Talmud - Anyone[11] who transgresses the words of the Scribes is liable for the death penalty.

And now, should you not know for what reason - one who transgresses against the words of the Sages is liable for the death penalty, more than one who transgresses most of the Torah's **positive** and **negative** commandments? And this is the understanding of the thing: It is because one who transgresses against the words of the Sages has had the temerity to do so since their commandments are light in his eyes; and not from his impulse overpowering him. Rather it is since his eyes have been dimmed from seeing the light of their words, so he does not follow the light of faith and does not pull the yoke of its decree upon himself. So, he does not toil to keep their statement, since it was not written in the Torah scroll. And he did not act like the one who transgresses the words of the Torah, about which his soul is bitter and taken away in front of him, such that he is afraid and frightened that his impulse moved him to sin. Therefore, there is a sentence of death for a person who knocked down something from all of

[10] Sanhedrin 88b
[11] Berakhot 4b

His good words their good words. And it is like he is
saying - **Let us remove their ropes**. And it is similar
to that which is written concerning the matter of the
elder who rebels against the words of the Sages -
Should[12] either party to the dispute act
presumptuously and disregard the priest charged with
serving there your God or the magistrate, that party
shall die Thus you will sweep out evil from Israel.

And the second reason is because this person is far
from repentance. Since the thing is not weighty to
him, he will constantly repeat it in his stupidity. And
in the sinner's stumbling upon it many times, this
light sin will have a greater punishment than that
which is heavy.

Our Rabbis, may their memory be blessed, also said
in the Talmud - That[13] the understanding of the verse
- For[14] your **Dodekha** [love] is better than wine. is that
the statements of the Scribes are more beloved than
the wine of the Torah. And we need to explain this
also: You should surely know that the fear of God is
the foundation of the commandments, as it is stated -
And[15] now O Israel what does the Lord your God ask
of you other than to fear the Lord your God. And
through this, God desires His creatures, as it is stated
- The[16] Lord desires those who fear Him. And the
ordinances of the Sages, and their decrees are the

12 Deuteronomy 17:12
13 Avodah Zarah 35a
14 Song of Songs 1:2
15 Deuteronomy 10:12
16 Psalms 147:11

foundation of fear of God. For it makes a fence and a separation, lest the hand of a man even touch a Torah prohibition. This is like the owner of a field that makes a fence for his field since it is precious in his eyes. For he is afraid lest people enter it and it become a place to send oxen and for sheep to trample, like the matter that is stated - You[17] shall keep My guarding. Make[18] a guarding for my guarding in the Talmud. And is much carefulness, the fence and the separation from the prohibition not from the essence of fear? And one who augments his carefulness will reach great reward, like the matter that is stated - Also[19] Your servant pays them heed in obeying them there is much reward. Therefore, they said that the statements of the Scribes are more beloved than the wine of the Torah. For their fences and decrees are from the foundations of fear of God. And the reward for the commandment of fear is great in comparison to many Torah commandments, as it is the foundation for them. And the example for this thing is that one who is careful not to isolate himself with a woman, from his fear lest he stumble into iniquity - and like our Rabbis, may their memory be blessed, decreed - is this not because the light of the fear of God, may He be blessed, shone upon his soul?

And behold we already introduced to you in the Chapter on Fear[20] that a person is obligated to

---

[17] Leviticus 18:30
[18] Yevamot 21a
[19] Psalms 19:12
[20] Sefer HaYirah

examine children and understand them and differentiate between the stubborn and crooked, and those that walk straight, for a sublime purpose that we have mentioned to you. And behold when you see gluttonous people belittling **Netilat Yadayim** [washing of the hands], when they come to eat bread, and they do not recite a blessing before they eat and after they eat, and disregard many like these of the words of the Sages and their ordinances, the fence of whom they breach - through this, you can distinguish; and through this, you can know and determine their ways; that they are evil and sinning greatly to God, and their end is to be permanently destroyed. And about them, they said in the Talmud that - One[21] who transgresses the words of the Sages is liable for the death penalty. For the impulse did not coerce these plotters to sin; nor did material forces and the desire for the physical coerce them to sin towards them. Rather this is nothing but a bad heart and the removal of the yoke of the Heavens from upon their necks. And behold they are like the masses from the group of criminals that say to God - **Go away from us**, and **We don't want to know Your ways**. Both these and the group that is not careful about gentile cheese and gentile cooking - since the words of the Sages are light in their eyes - are far from the true path. Even though they are also sinning to fill their bellies, behold they have disparaged the words of the Sages and broken the yoke of the Torah, and the teacher, and the fear. Also, about them is it said - One who transgress the words of the Sages is liable for the

---

[21] Eruvin 21b

death penalty. And the second reason for this is that since they know the holy people guards itself from all of these, they have separated themselves from our people and withdrawn from the ways of the community. And our Rabbis, may their memory be blessed, said in the Talmud - That[22] those that separate from the ways of the community go down to Gehinnom and are judged there for many generations. And know that the punishment of one who transgresses the words of the Sages was in the hands of the court to strike them with lashes of rebellion according to how the court saw fit to discipline them and punish them at that time - whether to have less than forty or to add to strike him more than that.

The second level is the severity of positive commandments

The foundation of the reward and the root of the recompense resulting from the service is found in the performance of **positive** commandments, as it is stated - He[23] who respects a commandment will be rewarded. And it is also stated - And[24] you shall come to see the difference between the righteous and the wicked between those who have served God and those who have not. And the service to God is with commandments that depend upon involve actions - whether there is nothing besides the **positive** commandment or whether there is also a **negative**

---

[22] Rosh Hashanah 17a
[23] Proverbs 13:13
[24] Malachi 3:18

commandment with them, such as - If[25] however there is a needy person among you one of your kin in any of your settlements in the land that your God is giving you do not harden your heart and shut your hand against your needy kin. which accompanies the **positive** commandment of charity. And the commandment of the service will be explained in the Gate of the Service no longer extant, with God's help. Nevertheless, there is a manner of reward for the one who is careful not to transgress a **negative** commandment that reaches [that] of one who does a commandment - such as if the opportunity for a sin comes to a man and he had a desire for a sexual prohibition, but he overcame his impulse - for this is from the essence of the fear of God, may He be blessed. And likewise, someone who had the opportunity to get rich by cheating and charging interest and there is no one to see and to know; yet he went with innocence and clean hands - his reward for this will be like one who plants righteousness and toils to do a **positive** commandment. And so, it is written - They[26] have done no wrong, but have followed His ways. And our Rabbis, may their memory be blessed, said in the Talmud - Since[27] they did not do wickedness they have **followed His ways**. And we have already discussed the explanation of this verse for you. And our Rabbis, may their memory be blessed, likewise said in the Talmud - If[28] one sits and

---

[25] Deuteronomy 15:7
[26] Psalms 119:3
[27] Yerushalmi Kiddushin 1:9
[28] Kiddushin 39b

does not transgress, he receives a reward as one who performs a commandment ... in a case where an opportunity to commit a sinful act presents itself to him and he is saved from it. And they also said in the Talmud - Those[29] who revere the Lord and esteem His name this is a case where an opportunity to commit a sinful act presents itself to him and he is saved from it. Even with this reward however, its essence and foundation is based in a **positive** commandment, since he suppressed his impulse with the fear of God, as it is stated - You[30] must fear the Lord, your God. And our Rabbis, may their memory be blessed, said in the Mishna - Be[31] careful with a light commandment as with a weighty one for you do not know the reward for the fulfillment of the commandments. Yet behold that what will be done to anyone who transgresses a **negative** commandment is explicit in the Torah; and it allocates punishments and statutes and a code for what to do to them. And the punishments are forty lashes, death and expiation at the hands of the Heavens and the four death penalties of the court. But the reward for the fulfillment of the commandments is not explicit in the Torah, so that people not prevent themselves from fulfilling the light commandments and involve themselves only in the weighty ones.

And they gave a parable about this matter of a king that said to his servants to plant every fine tree in his

---

[29] Berakhot 6a
[30] Deuteronomy 10:20
[31] Avot 2:1

109

garden. And he said that he would give them payment; but he did inform them of the payment for each type of tree, because the king desired that there would be nothing lacking in his orchard. Therefore, they planted many species of delightful saplings. But had the servants known the payment for the planting of each type of tree of the trees in the orchard, they would then have given all of their effort to the stems of the plantings for which the reward is greater than the other, in order to enhance their payment. The same is true with the matter of commandments. For God wanted to give merit to Israel with the fulfillment of all the commandments, to bequeath them eternal life and for all of the commandments together to be a charming wreath for their heads. For when they complete the measure of their work, their payment will be complete from Him. Did you not know that our Rabbis, may their memory be blessed, said in the Talmud - Anyone[32] who is only involved with Torah is similar to someone who has no God. Even though they said in the Mishna - The[33] reward for the study of Torah corresponds to all the commandments. And the reward of the light commandment is great and wondrous, such that it cannot be counted or measured. Do you not see with the commandment of sending away the mother bird - that has no toil and no large expenditure of money - it is stated about it - That[34] it may be well with you and that you may prolong your days. And our Rabbis, may their

---

[32] Avodah Zarah 17b
[33] Peah 1:1
[34] Deuteronomy 22:7

memory be blessed, said in the Talmud - Rabbi[35]
Yaakov says there is not a single light commandment
written in the Torah that the reward of, the
resurrection of the dead is not dependent upon - With
the sending of the mother bird from the nest, it is
stated - **That it may be well with you, and that you
may prolong your days ... that it may be well with
you** for the world where all is well, and **that your
days may be long** for the world that is entirely long.
And if that is what the Torah stated with a light
commandment that requires an expenditure of like an
Issar [small coin], all the more so with weighty
commandments.

And now we will speak about the matter of
punishment for the nullification of **positive**
commandments: Our Rabbis, may their memory be
blessed, said in the Talmud - That[36] if the court
warned someone to perform the commandment of the
sukkah or of the **LULAV** [palm branch] and he does
not do so, we strike. And they said in the Talmud -
That[37] men who have never placed tefillin on their
heads are called **rebellious Jews with their bodies**
and their punishment is more severe than one who
transgresses once against a sin for which he is liable
for excision. And they said that all whose sins are
greater than his merits and among his sins is the sin
of rebellious Jews with their bodies - for example, one
who has never worn tefillin or one who was involved

---

[35] Kiddushin 39b
[36] Ketuvot 86b
[37] Rosh Hashanah 17a

in transgressions such as forbidden sexual relations - descend and are judged in Gehinnom for twelve months. After twelve months, their body is finished; and their soul is burnt; and the wind spreads it under the soles of the feet of the righteous ones, as it is stated - And[38] you shall trample the wicked to a pulp for they shall be dust beneath your feet on the day that I am preparing said GOD of Hosts. And they said in the Talmud - That[39] one who is permissive in his eyes regarding **positive** commandments, such as one who belittles the intermediate days of the festival - which is from a **positive** commandment, as it is stated - You[40] shall observe the Feast of Unleavened Bread eating unleavened bread for seven days as I have commanded you at the set time in the month of **ABIB** [spring] for in it you went forth from Egypt and none shall appear before Me empty-handed. Has no portion in the world to come, even if possesses Torah and good deeds. And there is a general warning of a **negative** commandment, for all the **positive** commandments - as it is stated - Neither[41] add to it nor take away from it.

And the fulfillment of **positive** commandments is called, fear of Heaven; just like carefulness is understood as the **negative** commandments. For it is stated - You[42] shall rise before the aged and show deference to the old you shall fear your God I am the

---

[38] Malachi 3:21
[39] Sanhedrin 99a
[40] Exodus 23:15
[41] Deuteronomy 13:1
[42] Leviticus 19:32

Lord. And it is also stated - I[43] will teach you fear of the Lord. And after it is stated - Shun[44] evil and do good, seek peace and pursue it. We learn from this, that one who is not occupied with doing good and seeking peace annuls fear of Heaven. And he is from the evildoers, since he has no fear of God, as it is stated - And[45] it will not be well with the evildoer and he will not live long, because he does not fear God.

Among the **positive** commandments in the Torah are some of the weighty ones that the masses are not careful about - for example the mention of God's name in vain, as it is stated - You[46] shall fear the Lord, your God. And our Rabbis, may their memory be blessed, said in the Talmud - We[47] have been warned with this not to mention God's name in vain. And likewise acts of kindness, which is a **positive** commandment, as it is stated - And[48] make known to them the way they are to go. - That[49] is acts of kindness in the Talmud. And they said in the Talmud - Acts[50] of kindness are superior to charity since charity is given to the poor while acts of kindness are performed both for the poor and for the rich. Therefore, they said Mishna - The[51] world stands upon

---

43 Psalms 34:12
44 Psalms 34:15
45 Ecclesiastes 8:13
46 Deuteronomy 10:20
47 Temurah 4:1
48 Exodus 18:20
49 Bava Metzia 30b
50 Sukkah 49b
51 Avot 1:2

three things On the Torah on the service and on acts of kindness. And in the Talmud - Charity[52] can be performed only with one's money while acts of kindness can be performed both with his person and with his money. For a person is obligated to exert himself in seeking good for his people and to dedicate himself to the betterment of his fellow - whether poor or rich. And this is one of the main weighty commandments required of a person, as it is stated - He[53] has told you O man what is good and what the Lord requires of you only to do justice, and to love kindness. And likewise, to go beyond the law, as it is stated - And[54] the practices they are to follow. And our Rabbis, may their memory be blessed, said in the Talmud - This[55] is going beyond the letter of the law. And there are many ways in this matter, such that this commandment would be from the weighty ones. It is all according to the contents of the case - as our Rabbis, may their memory be blessed, said in the Talmud - Jerusalem[56] was destroyed only because they established their rulings on the basis of Torah law and did not go beyond the letter of the law.

And there are many people among the masses who think that the main loss and damage to the soul is only from sins that involve an action; and that there is no losing of the soul for a man that is pure from sinning actively and who did not walk in the way of

---

[52] Sukkah 49b
[53] Micah 6:8
[54] Exodus 18:20
[55] Bava Metzia 30b
[56] Bava Metzia 30b

transgressions, but rather only prevented himself from doing **positive** commandments and good deeds. Therefore, we are obligated to make discernment known to the ones of a mistaken spirit. For our Rabbis, may their memory be blessed, said in the Talmud - The[57] Holy One, blessed be He forewent idolatry. but He did not forego the sin of wasting time available for Torah study. And they said in **Sifrei** - Just[58] like the reward for Torah study is greater than that for all of the commandments in the Torah, so too is the punishment for wasting time for it greater than that for all of the sins. And they said in the Talmud - Because[59] he has despised the word of the Lord and has breached His commandment - Is[60] stated about anyone for whom it is possible to engage in Torah study and does not engage in it. And we have already mentioned all of these to you in the Gate of the Torah no longer extant.

And we find with the people of Sodom that they were very bad to God on several plains of corruption, such as theft, extortion, perversion of justice and forbidden sexual relations. Nevertheless, Scripture mentions that their souls were lost and destroyed by the sin of nullifying charity, as it is stated - Only[61] this was the sin of your sister Sodom: arrogance She and her daughters had plenty of bread and untroubled tranquility yet she did not support the poor and the

---

[57] Yerushalmi Chagigah 1:7
[58] Sifrei Devarim, Ekev
[59] Sanhedrin 99a
[60] Numbers 15:31
[61] Ezekiel 16:49

needy. And it is stated about the people that do not arrange their thoughts to constantly reflect on the fear of God - My[62] Sovereign said Because that people has approached Me with its mouth and honored Me with its lips but has kept its heart far from Me And its worship of Me has been A social obligation, learned by rote. Truly[63] I shall further baffle that people with bafflement upon bafflement and the wisdom of its wise shall fail and the prudence of its prudent shall vanish. And it is stated - You[64] will win, **O ETERNAL** One, if I make claim against You Yet I shall present charges against You Why does the way of the wicked prosper Why are the workers of treachery at ease. You[65] have planted them, and they have taken root They spread, they even bear fruit You are present in their mouths but far from their thoughts. And it is stated - Those[66] who keep far from You perish.

And know that depending on the greatness of the commandment will the punishment be great for the one who prevents himself from doing it, even though he does not do an act in breaching it - as we find with the commandment of the Passover offering and the commandment of circumcision, which are **positive** commandments but have excision as their punishment.

---

[62] Isaiah 29:13
[63] Isaiah 29:14
[64] Jeremiah 12:1
[65] Jeremiah 12:2
[66] Psalms 23:27

And know that there are sublime virtues given over in the **positive** commandments such as - The virtues of free choice, as it is stated - And[67] choose life. And the virtues of Torah study, as it is stated - And[68] you shall speak about them. And the virtues of walking in the ways of the Lord, as it is stated - And[69] you shall walk in His ways. And the virtues of contemplation of the greatness of the Lord, as it is stated - Know[70] therefore this day and keep in mind that the Lord alone is God in heaven above and on earth below there is no other. And David said - The[71] Lord looks down from heaven on mankind to find a man of understanding, a man who seeks God. And the virtues of remembrance of His kindnesses, as it is stated - Remember[72] the whole way. And it is also stated - And[73] you shall know that the Lord your God disciplines you just as a man disciplines his son. And David said - He[74] will contemplate the kindnesses of the Lord. And said - For[75] Your kindness is across from my eyes. And the virtues of holiness, as it is stated - And[76] you shall sanctify yourselves and you shall be holy. And the virtues of worship, as it is stated - And[77] He shall you

---

67 Deuteronomy 30:19
68 Deuteronomy 6:7
69 Deuteronomy 28:9
70 Deuteronomy 4:39
71 Psalms 14:2
72 Deuteronomy 8:2
73 Deuteronomy 8:6
74 Psalms 107:43
75 Psalms 26:3
76 Leviticus 11:44
77 Deuteronomy 10:20

worship. And the virtues of fear, as it is stated - And[78] you shall fear the Lord. and the virtues of love, as it is stated - And[79] you shall love the Lord your God. And the virtues of clinging, as it is stated - To[80] Him shall you cling. There are several levels to each of these as will be explained, with God's help. And man was created for the sake of these virtues, as it is stated - All[81] who are linked to My name, whom I have created for My glory. And what is the hope of a creation if it does not make the things for which it was created, the toil of his soul and his main occupation?

And behold the punishment for the nullification of a commandment is explained in the Torah, as it is stated - Cursed[82] is the one who does not fulfill the words of this Torah, to do them. It states - **to do them** - teaching that this is stated about the nullification of a commanded act.

And know that a creature is obligated to be a faithful agent and understanding servant in all of the cartful work of his Master. And a faithful worker will be quick at this craft and supervise the craft of his fellow workers. His eyes will be upon their ways, to see if they are faithful; and he will warn them and inform about the work they should do. For his desire and want is that the work of his Master be done without deceit. Therefore, he strengthens those doing the

---

[78] Deuteronomy 10:20
[79] Deuteronomy 6:5
[80] Deuteronomy 10:20
[81] Isaiah 43:7
[82] Deuteronomy 27:26

work to do it right. And our Rabbis, may their memory be blessed, said in the Talmud - Cursed[83] is the one who does not fulfill. - A[84] man who has studied, reviewed, taught others and fulfilled the Torah and the commandments, but has not strengthened others to do so is included in **who does not fulfill**.

And among the weighty **positive** commandments is not to have a trial in the courts of the idolater's gentiles, as it is stated - And[85] these are the judgments that you shall place in front of them. - **In front of them**, and not in front of the Canaanites. But rebels stumble in them. And we have already spoken about this transgression before.

And there is also a curse about the nullification of the fear of the father and the mother, which is a **positive** commandment - as it is stated - Cursed[86] be he who belittles his father or mother. The content of belittling is to disparage their honor and abrogate fearing them. As our Rabbis, may their memory be blessed, said in the Talmud - A[87] man must fear his mother and father. - What[88] is fear of the father? Not to sit in his place, not to contradict his words or determine an argument for him.

---

83 Yerushalmi Sotah 4:4
84 Deuteronomy 27:26
85 Exodus 21:1
86 Deuteronomy 27:16
87 Kiddushin 31b
88 Leviticus 19:3

And the commandment of **Tefillin** and the commandment of **Mezuzah** are **positive** commandments - but behold they are included in accepting the kingdom of the Heavens. For thus were they written in the section of **Shema Yisrael**. And from this, you can contemplate the punishment of one who nullifies these commandments, as he is breaking the yoke and removing the cords of God's authority. And we have already discussed these commandments. And about the commandment of **Tzitzit** [fringes], our Rabbis, may their memory be blessed, have said in the **Sifrei**[89] - that fringes adds to holiness, as it is stated - In[90] order that you shall be reminded to observe all My commandments and to be holy to your God. And even though the commandment of fringes is only for a garment that has four corners - and if one does not have a garment like this, he is not obligated to acquire one - nevertheless, our Rabbis, may their memory be blessed, said in the Talmud - That[91] he will surely be punished in times of trouble about the matter: That in his heart he did not desire the beauty of the commandment and its reward enough, to cause the matter of the obligation to apply to him and to get himself a garment that has four corners to make fringes on its corners.

And know that one who fears the word of God will be stringent and exacting and take himself in hand for

---

[89] Sifrei Bemidbar, Shelach
[90] Numbers 15:40
[91] Menachot 41a

120

light commandments, as he will for weighty commandments. For they will not focus on that which a certain commandment is light compared to the weighty ones. Rather they will focus on the One who warns about it, may He be blessed. And open your eyes well to see that this principle has been explained in the Torah. For about rising in front of an elder - just like the commandment of fearing one's father and one's mother and the observance of Shabbat - it is written - **I am the Lord**. And we have brought to this place many of the commandments about which the people found in this generation are short-handed in doing - the principle of each one is in this book, please take it to yourself and place it upon the tablet of your heart.

The third level is the negative commandment that is rectified by a positive commandment

Our Rabbis, may their memory be blessed, said in the Talmud - That[92] we do not give lashes for a **negative** commandment that is rectified by a **positive** commandment, for example - You[93] shall not take the mother from over the young. Is rectified by a **positive** commandment, as it is stated - You[94] shall surely send away. But even though they would not give lashes through the court in such a case, there were some with weighty punishments, such that it would reach the heavens and their judgement would be raised to the

---

[92] Chullin 141a
[93] Deuteronomy 22:6
[94] Deuteronomy 22:7

clouds. For example, theft - as it is stated - You[95] shall not rob. - Is[96] rectified by a **positive** commandment. as it is stated - and returned what he robbed. Yet they said in the Talmud - The[97] final judgement of the generation of the Flood was sealed only because of robbery, as it is stated - **The[98] end of all flesh has come in front of Me for the earth is filled with extortion**. And even though sexual immorality is weightier than robbery, it is the characteristic of the punishment of robbery to bring close its day and to quicken the future consequences to it. And they also said in the Midrash - If[99] you have a seah full of iniquities there is no prosecutor among all of them like robbery. And King Solomon, peace be upon him, said about treasures acquired from dishonesty and fraud - Treasures[100] acquired by a lying tongue are like driven vapor heading for death. The explanation is that treasuries acquired from dishonesty and fraud are vanishing vapor, for their end is destruction. And while they are still in his possession, they are his enemies and seek the life of their master and cause his death - like the matter that is stated - If[101] you have a seah full of iniquities, there is no prosecutor among all of them like robbery. You[102] have plotted shame

---

95 Leviticus 19:13
96 Leviticus 5:23
97 Sanhedrin 108a
98 Genesis 6:13
99 Vayikra Rabbah 33:2
100 Proverbs 21:6
101 Habakkuk 2:9
102 Habakkuk 2:10

for your own house and guilt for yourself. For[103] a stone shall cry out from the wall and a rafter shall answer it from the woodwork. And in the case of robbing the poor, one is liable for death at the hands of the Heavens on account of it, as it is stated - Do[104] not rob the wretched because he is wretched Do not crush the poor man in the gate. For[105] the LORD will take up their cause and despoil those who despoil them of life. Its explanation is **do not rob from the indigent** because **he is indigent** and has no one to help him; **and do not crush the poor man in the gate**, with shame and disgrace. And **in the gate**, is to say, in public. And it is like the matter that is stated - How[106] dare you crush My people and grind the faces of the poor? For the Lord will take up their cause, since they have no support, or someone to argue and take up their cause. And despoil those who despoil them of life - since the cry of the indigent has been brought to Him, He will not take money from you in place of the loot that you robbed, but rather God will remove your soul. And it is stated - For[107] what hope has the impious man when he is cut down when God takes away his life? And it is also stated - Such[108] is the fate of all who pursue unjust gain; It takes the life of its possessor. And one who torments and pains a widow or an orphan - whether with robbery, or fraud or shame or any type of pain - is liable for death at the

---

103 Habakkuk 2:11
104 Proverbs 22:22
105 Proverbs 22:23
106 Isaiah 3:15
107 Job 27:8
108 Proverbs 1:19

hands of the Heavens. And likewise, the judges who are able to rescue someone robbed from him who defrauded him, and do not judge [the case of an] orphan, have a death sentence upon them - as it is stated - You[109] communal leaders shall not ill-treat any widow or orphan. If[110] you do mistreat them, I will heed their outcry as soon as they cry out to Me. And[111] My anger shall blaze forth and I will put you to the sword and your own wives shall become widows and your children orphans. Its explanation is - And your wives shall become widows. corresponding to the oppression of the widow; and your children orphans, corresponding to the oppression of the orphan - measure for measure. And even though these punishments are not written about the following, one who pains any Israelite transgresses a **negative** commandment - as it is stated - A[112] man shall not **Tonu** [oppress] his kinsman. And our Rabbis, may their memory be blessed, said in the Talmud - The[113] verse is speaking about verbal oppression. And that is from the contents of pain and torment, like the usage - I[114] will make your **Monayich** [oppressors] eat their own flesh. And our Rabbis, may their memory be blessed, also said in the Talmud - All[115] the gates of prayer have been closed, except for the gates of one who is praying as a result of his oppression. And

---

109 Exodus 22:21
110 Exodus 22:22
111 Exodus 22:23
112 Leviticus 25:17
113 Bava Metzia 58b
114 Isaiah 49:26
115 Bava Metzia 59a

where Scripture was speaking about financial oppression, it mentioned buying and selling, as it is stated - When[116] you sell property to your kinsman. And they said in the Talmud - That[117] verbal oppression is greater than financial oppression, for this is upon his body and that is upon his money - and about the former it stated - But[118] you shall fear your God. But about the latter - but[119] you shall fear. Is not stated.

And with interest and usury, there is a **negative** commandment - as it is stated - Do[120] not exact from him usury or accrued interest but fear your God. And it is rectified by a **positive** commandment, as it is stated - Let[121] him live by your side as your kinsman. It is explanation is, if you have taken interest or usury from him, surely return it to your brother, in order that he may live with you. And his punishment is very weighty - so long as he does not fix that which is crooked, he does not come to the resurrection of the dead, as it is stated - He[122] has lent with usury or exacted accrued interest - shall he live; he shall not live. And our Rabbis, may their memory be blessed, explained in the Midrash - It[123] to be about the matter of the resurrection of the dead. And our Rabbis, may

---

[116] Leviticus 25:14
[117] Bava Metzia 58b
[118] Leviticus 25:17
[119] Leviticus 25:14
[120] Leviticus 25:36
[121] Leviticus 25:36
[122] Ezekiel 18:13
[123] Pirkei De'Rabbi Natan 33

their memory be blessed, said Midrash - Anyone[124] who has the iniquity of interest in his hands will not have an angel intervene teach merit on his behalf. And this is the understanding of that which, shall he live, is stated as an expression of question and wonder - is there an intervener that will say that his case is to live? All of them will answer, He shall not live.

The fourth level is a negative commandment that does not involve an action

Our Rabbis, may their memory be blessed, said in the Talmud - That[125] we do not give lashes for violating a **negative** commandment that does not involve an action. But it is explained in their words in the Talmud - May[126] their memory be blessed, that a **negative** commandment that does not involve an action is more weighty than a **negative** commandment that is rectified by a **positive** commandment. And among the **negative** commandments that do not involve an action, some of them are dependent upon the heart, some on the tongue, some on the closing of the hand not giving of one's money or possessions, and some on not doing an action. And there are likewise some transgressions that do not involve an action, but are dependent upon the sense of hearing or the sense of sight. And we have seen many people that have forgotten many of them. And there are some that know but are not

---

[124]   Exodus Rabbah 31:6
[125]   Sanhedrin 63a
[126]   Yoma 85b

careful about them, because they do not depend upon involve an action. For the transgressions that depend upon an action, such as the eating of forbidden fat, blood, a carcass or a torn animal **Tereifah** [sick animal] are not as accessible to violate as the ones done with thought or the tongue, or by rest from an action. Therefore, we have seen fit to mention some of them - to remind some of [the people], to remember; and those that do not know, to be forewarned. But we have not come to write about them at length, but rather only to hint to them, that they be a reminder for those repenting from rebellion. Among the **negative** commandments that are dependent on the heart are - Take[127] care lest you forget the Lord, your God. And in the Rabbis, may their memory be blessed, said in the Talmud - Wherever[128] it is stated in a verse **beware - lest** or **not**, this is surely a **negative** commandment. We are warned then with this to remember God, may He be blessed every instant. And a person is obligated to make efforts to always acquire for himself behaviors that are mandated by remembrance - such as fear, modesty, refinement of one's thoughts and strategies to acquire good traits - so that the holy seed will attain every fine behavior and be crowned through it from the remembrance of God, may He be blessed, just as it is stated - It[129] is through the Lord that all the offspring of Israel Have vindication and glory.

---

[127] Deuteronomy 8:11
[128] Sotah 5a
[129] Isaiah 45:25

Only[130] observe for yourself, and guard your soul diligently, lest you forget the matters that your eyes saw. And our Rabbis, may their memory be blessed, said in the Talmud - That[131] anyone who forgets even one matter from his studies violates two **negative** commandments. Is it possible even if his studies were too hard for him? Hence, we are taught to say - And[132] lest they depart from your heart. The verse is only speaking of one who causes them to depart from his heart, by being idle from Torah study and not constantly poring over it.

And[133] when your God has thrust them from your path say not to yourselves God has enabled us to possess this land because of our virtues it is rather because of the wickedness of those nations that God is dispossessing them before you. It[134] is not because of your virtues and your rectitude that you will be able to possess their country but it is because of their wickedness that your God is dispossessing those nations before you and in order to fulfill the oath that God made to your fathers Abraham Itzhak and Yaakov. We are warned with this not to imagine to ourselves that our success is from our righteousness and the rectitude of our hearts, but rather that we believe and know in our hearts that our success is from the kindness of the Most High and His great goodness - and like the matter that was said by our

---

[130] Deuteronomy 4:9
[131] Menachot 99b
[132] Deuteronomy 4:9
[133] Deuteronomy 9:4
[134] Deuteronomy 9:5

father, Yaakov - I[135] am unworthy of all the kindness and all the truth.

Do[136] not try the Lord your God. And we are warned with this that a man should not say, I will make a trial with my service of charity whether the Lord will make my way successful; and I will test through the properness of my actions, whether my gold and silver will grow. But the good man will not slacken from his toil in wisdom, knowledge and proper action when his path in the matter of his money and the rest of the goods of the body are not successful. And our Rabbis, may their memory be blessed, said in the Talmud in the Talmud - That[137] only with tithes of the storehouse is testing God permitted, as it is stated - Bring[138] the full tithe into the storehouse, and let there be food in My House, and thus put Me to the test. King Solomon, peace be upon him, said - Honor[139] the LORD with your wealth with the best of all your income. And[140] your barns will be filled with grain Your vats will burst with new wine. Its explanation is, if you do not have like this - to be filled with grain when you give from your wealth and from the first of all your produce - but you are rather seized by days of poverty - Do[141] not reject the discipline of the Lord.

---

135 Genesis 32:11
136 Deuteronomy 6:16
137 Taanit 9a
138 Malachi 3:10
139 Proverbs 3:9
140 Proverbs 3:10
141 Proverbs 3:11

and know that this is also for your good. For[142] whom the LORD loves He rebukes as a father the son whom he favors. To do good for him in his end; that the reward in this world and his honor be exchanged for the good that is hidden and continues forever.

Should[143] you say to yourselves These nations are more numerous than we how can we dispossess them. You need have no fear of them. You[144] have but to bear in mind what your God did to Pharaoh and all the Egyptians.

When[145] you an Israelite warrior take the field against your enemies and see horses and chariots forces larger than yours have no fear of them, for your God who brought you from the land of Egypt is with you. We were warned with this that if a person sees trouble nearby, the salvation of the Lord should be in his heart and he should trust in it - like the matter that is stated - His[146] salvation is near those who fear Him. and likewise, is it written - What[147] ails you that you fear man who must die.

Fear[148] no man, for judgment is God's. We were warned with this to believe that injury will not occur to us on account of righteous judgment, when we do

---

[142] Proverbs 3:12
[143] Deuteronomy 7:17
[144] Deuteronomy 7:18
[145] Deuteronomy 20:1
[146] Psalms 85:10
[147] Isaiah 51:12
[148] Deuteronomy 1:17

not show favoritism. It is like our Rabbis, may their memory be blessed, said in the Talmud - Agents[149] of a commandment will not be injured, not on their way to do it and not on their return. And this is the explanation of **for judgment is God's** - that injury caused by Him will not happen to you.

That[150] he will not act haughtily toward his brothers. We were warned with this to remove the trait of pride from our souls; and that the great not lord it over the small, but rather be of a lowly spirit. And pride is one of the weighty sins that lose and destroy the soul, as it is stated - Every[151] haughty person is an abomination to the Lord. And of what help is the procurement of his money, his great wealth and his lofty treasures in the heights? Behold, since he is loathsome and foul, the heights of his great splendor are lower than the pit. And even a wise man should not glory in anything besides the service of God, may He be blessed, and fear of Him, trust in Him, love of Him and clinging to Him - as it is stated - He[152] is your Glory and He is your God. And it is also stated - Thus[153] said GOD Let not the wise glory in their wisdom Let not the strong glory in their strength Let not the rich glory in their riches. But[154] only in this should one glory in being earnestly devoted to Me for I GOD act with kindness Justice and equity in the world for in these I delight

---

[149] Pesachim 5b
[150] Deuteronomy 17:20
[151] Proverbs 16:5
[152] Deuteronomy 10:21
[153] Jeremiah 9:22-23
[154] Jeremiah 9:22-23

declares GOD.

Give[155] to him readily and have no regrets when you give to him. We were warned with this to distance our souls from miserliness, but rather to be generous - like the matter that is stated - The[156] generous man is blessed. And it is not enough with the gifts of our hands, but we must rather plant the trait of generosity into our souls. Therefore, it warned and said - **and have no regrets**, after it is stated - **Give to him readily**.

Do[157] not harden your heart and shut your hand. We were warned with this to remove the trait of cruelty from our souls, and to plant delightful saplings in it - namely reliable mercy and kindnesses, as it is written - And[158] you shall walk in His ways. And because it is possible not to shut his hand and to grace the poor person, but not in the way of mercy - like the matter that is written - But[159] the mercies of the wicked are cruelty. Therefore, it is written - Do[160] not harden your heart. And the punishment for cruelty is bad and bitter, as will be explained in the Gate of Cruelty no longer extant, with God's help. And our Rabbis, may their memory be blessed, said in the Talmud - And[161] He will show you mercy and have compassion on you

---

[155] Deuteronomy 15:10
[156] Proverbs 22:9
[157] Deuteronomy 15:7
[158] Deuteronomy 28:9
[159] Proverbs 12:10
[160] Deuteronomy 15:7
[161] Shabbat 151b

and multiply you - Anyone[162] who has compassion for the creatures will receive compassion from Heaven, and anyone who does not have compassion for the creatures will not receive compassion from Heaven.

Show[163] him no pity or compassion, and do not shield him. We were warned with this to not have compassion nor to have mercy on those that cause people to sin and stumble. And our Rabbis, may their memory be blessed, said Midrash - Anyone[164] who becomes merciful upon the cruel will end up being cruel to the merciful.

You[165] shall not take vengeance or bear a grudge against your countrymen. Our Rabbis, may their memory be blessed, said - What[166] is revenge and what is bearing a grudge? Revenge is illustrated by the following example - One said to his fellow - Lend me your sickle, and he said - **No**. The next day he, the one who had refused to lend the sickle, said to the other person - Lend me your ax. If he said to him - I will not lend to you, just as you did not lend to me, that is revenge. he said back to him - I will not lend to you, just as you did not lend yours to me - that is revenge. And what is bearing a grudge? If one said to his fellow: Lend me your ax, and he said: No, and the next day he, the one who had refused to lend the ax, said to the other man - Lend me your robe; if the first

---

162 Deuteronomy 13:18
163 Deuteronomy 13:9
164 Midrash Tanchuma, Metzora 1
165 Leviticus 19:18
166 Yoma 23a

one said to him: Here it is, as I am not like you, who would not lend to me, that is bearing a grudge. Although he does not respond to his friend's inconsiderate behavior in kind, he still makes it known to his friend that he resents his inconsiderate behavior. This **Baraita** shows that the prohibition relates only to monetary matters, such as borrowing and lending. And the punishment for this is not for speaking, but rather for the grudge in the heart. And our Rabbis, may their memory be blessed, said in the Talmud - The[167] prohibition on bearing a grudge is for monetary matters, but it is permissible to keep words of pride or disgrace or seeking evil against him upon his heart. And our Rabbis, may their memory be blessed, said in the Talmud - Any[168] Torah scholar who when insulted does not avenge himself and bear a grudge like a snake is not considered a Torah scholar. But if they request forgiveness from him, he should forego his reckonings.

You[169] shall not hate your brother in your heart. We were warned with this to remove the trait of hatred from our souls. And it is a trait that brings many sins and causes several foul plots - such as evil speech which corresponds to several sins which are punished with a death penalty from the court, as will be explained; and like seeking the bad, and joy in calamity, causing injuries to one's fellow, talebearing, revenge and bearing a grudge. And it

---

[167] Yoma 23a
[168] Yoma 22b
[169] Leviticus 19:17

destroys much good for the soul, as will be explained
in the Gate of Hatred no longer extant. And see how
far the punishment of hatred reaches: For our Rabbis,
may their memory be blessed, said in the Talmud -
For[170] what reason was the Second Temple destroyed,
even though they were occupied with Torah study and
good deeds? Because of the causeless hatred that was
among them.

Be[171] on your guard against anything bad. They, may
their memory be blessed, explained in the Talmud -
A[172] person should not think impure thoughts by day
and thereby come to impurity by night. And even
though his thought is not to follow it up with action.
And it is something learned from its context. As after
it, it is written - If[173] anyone among you has been
rendered unclean by a nocturnal emission.

So[174] that you do not follow your heart and your eyes.
We were warned with this not to think to do a
transgression or upon any or and prohibition or sin -
like the matter that is stated - He[175] who thinks to do
evil. And not to think about words of heresy, lest one
stumble and be drawn after them. And when he places
upon his heart that God, may He be blessed, examines
the heart and investigates the kidneys understood as
the seat of wisdom, how can he dare to defile his heart

---

170 Yoma 9b
171 Deuteronomy 23:10
172 Ketuvot 46a
173 Numbers 15:39
174 Deuteronomy 23:11
175 Proverbs 24:8

and have a ruffian matter lodged upon it? And King Solomon, peace be upon him, said - The[176] schemes of folly are sin. He also said - Six[177] things the LORD hates Seven are an abomination to Him. A[178] haughty bearing A lying tongue Hands that shed innocent blood. A[179] mind that hatches evil plots Feet quick to run to evil.

Do[180] not bear a vain report. We were warned with this not to accept evil speech. And [it is] like the **Targum** [translation of **Onkelos**] says - Do not accept a false report.

You[181] shall not covet your neighbor's house. And[182] you shall not desire your neighbor's house. We were warned with this not to make evil plots to take the field or vineyard or anything of your our fellow, even if one gives their price. And we were warned about the thought of this evil thing, that we should not resolve in our thoughts to do it, as it is stated - **You shall not covet**. And if a person longs for his fellow to sell him a field or a vineyard or any of his possessions and the owner does not want to sell it - but if he pleads with him with many supplications, he will be embarrassed to answer him - it is forbidden to plead with him, as it is like coercion or duress. And

---

[176] Proverbs 24:9
[177] Proverbs 6:16
[178] Proverbs 6:17
[179] Proverbs 6:18
[180] Exodus 23:1
[181] Exodus 20:14
[182] Deuteronomy 5:18

one who covets to take any object and is a respected person - such that if he asked the question, they would not let his eminence down - it is forbidden to ask for any purchase or grant, unless he knows that the owner would give it to him with full agreement, and not regret giving it to him in his heart.

Among the **negative** commandments, that are dependent on the heart tongue are: Since[183] the Lord your God moves about in your camp to protect you and to deliver your enemies to you let your camp be holy let not anything unseemly be seen among you. They, may their memory be blessed, said in the Talmud - That[184] included in this prohibition is that when we speak words of the Torah of God, may He be blessed - and in our speaking in prayer in front of Him - our camp should be holy, and let not anything unseemly be seen among us. Therefore, we were commanded about this, to mention God's name in holiness and to engage in words of Torah and prayer in holiness; and not to mention God's name or words of Torah if he is naked or if there is a naked man across from him. And likewise, were we warned that the place be clean, as it is stated - You[185] shall dig a hole with it and cover up your excrement. And all the more so is he warned not to mention God's name if his hands are not clean. And if his hands touched something disgusting to him, he should wash them -

---

[183] Deuteronomy 23:15
[184] Berakhot 25b
[185] Deuteronomy 23:14

like the matter that is stated - I[186] wash my palms in cleanliness. And when one is walking on the path and he is in doubt if the path is clean, he should not mention God name, and he should not say words of Torah. And if there is something that is not clean behind him - such as excrement or a carcass or water used for soaking flax - one must move a distance of four ells away from where the odor ends; but in front of him, the distance is as far as his eye can see. And carefulness about this is one of the ways of fearing God, as it is stated - Concerning[187] those who revere the Lord and esteem His name. And our Rabbis, may their memory be blessed, said in the Talmud - For[188] he has shown contempt for the word of the Lord - This[189] is referring to one who says words of Torah in filthy alleyways. And our Rabbis, may their memory be blessed, said Midrash[190] - He[191] gives wisdom to the wise. Because the wise honor the Torah and occupy themselves with it in holiness. But if He had given it to the silly, they would have said words of Torah in filthy alleyways.

There are some **negative** commandments, that are dependent upon the tongue, for which we give lashes. For so did our Rabbis, may their memory be blessed, say in the Talmud - All[192] the warnings in the Torah -

---

[186] Psalms 26:6
[187] Malachi 3:16
[188] Berakhot 24b
[189] Numbers 15:31
[190] Kohelet Rabbah 1:17
[191] Daniel 2:21
[192] Makkot 16a

we do not give lashes for a **negative** commandment
that does not involve an action, except for one who
makes an oath or curses his fellow with God's name.
And even though there is no death penalty from the
court with a vain oath, its punishment at the hands of
the Heavens is more weighty than many sins that do
have a death penalty from the court. For making an
oath in vain profanes God's name - as it is stated -
You[193] shall not swear falsely by My name, profaning
the name of your God. And the punishment for
profaning the name is more elevated than that of all
of the sins. And it is not written like this about any of
the sins besides a false oath and idolatry, as it is stated
- Because[194] he gave of his offspring to Molech and so
defiled My sanctuary and profaned My holy name.
And it is stated in the warning about idolatry - You[195]
shall not bow down to them or serve them for I the
Lord your God am a jealous God. This means to say,
that He will not forgive the iniquity of idolatry in the
way of forgiveness for other sins - like the matter that
is written - Why[196] should I forgive you your children
have forsaken Me and sworn by no-gods. And
likewise, is it written in the warning for a false oath -
For[197] the Lord will not clear one who swears falsely
by His name. And the warning for a false oath is
written immediately after the warning of idolatry,
most certainly because the iniquity of profaning God,
may He be blessed, is found under the wings of a false

---

[193] Leviticus 19:12
[194] Leviticus 20:3
[195] Exodus 20:5
[196] Jeremiah 5:7
[197] Exodus 20:7

oath. And our Rabbis, may their memory be blessed, said regarding the matter of the verses - Keep[198] lies and false words far from me Give me neither poverty nor riches but provide me with my daily bread. Lest[199] being sated I renounce saying Who is the LORD Or being impoverished I take to theft and profane the name of my God. that the latter is harsher than the former - as it is stated - As[200] for you O House of Israel thus said the Sovereign GOD Go every last one of you and worship your fetishes and continue if you will not obey Me but do not profane My holy name anymore with your idolatrous gifts. It is meaning to say that the iniquity of the one who swears falsely in a court is more weighty than the punishment of one who worships idolatry in private, due to the profaning of the name involved in the former. And our Rabbis, may their memory be blessed, said in the Talmud - For[201] all of the other transgressions in the Torah, punishment is exacted only from the transgressor and his family; whereas here, punishment is exacted from him and from the entire world. And if the court obligates a man to make an oath but he knows that his mouth speaks falsely it would be a false oath, it is forbidden to even take the oath upon himself, saying, **I will swear** - in order to frighten his fellow - even though he does not plan to swear. For it is stated - You[202] shall not bear. And included in its meaning is not to accept agree to swear falsely. And likewise, did

---

[198] Proverbs 30:8
[199] Proverbs 30:9
[200] Ezekiel 20:39
[201] Shevuot 39a
[202] Exodus 20:7

they, may their memory be blessed, say in our Midrash[203] - And the **Targum** [translation of Onkelos] of - Do[204] not bear a vain report. is **do not accept**. And it is forbidden to make a needless oath, even if he is swearing about the truth, as it is stated - Do[205] not bear the name of God in vain - and its **Targum** is - **For nothing**. And likewise, is the iniquity of one who causes his fellow to swear for nothing, great - for example when his fellow owed him a hundred and he doubled it in his claim, in order that the law would come out that one who admits partially is obligated to make a Torah-based oath; or when he claims against his fellow for nothing and asks him for what he knows nothing about and makes him take a rabbinic oath of inducement. And our Rabbis said in the Talmud - that[206] this man is called a thief, as he is stealing his mind deceiving him. And about him is it stated - But[207] I have sent it forth declares the Lord of Hosts and the curse shall enter the house of the thief and the house of the one who swears falsely by My name, and it shall lodge inside their houses and shall consume them to the last timber and stone. And one who knows that if he takes an oath, people will suspect him about [the truth of] the oath, should restrain himself from [taking] the oath for the honor of the Heavens - even though the truth is with him.

---

203 Mekhilta d'Rabbi Yishmael, Yitro
204 Exodus 23:1
205 Exodus 20:7
206 Shevuot 39a
207 Zechariah 5:4

You[208] shall not curse powers, nor revile a chieftain among your people. You[209] shall not curse a deaf man. And we were warned with this not to curse any man of Israel with God's name or one of all of His appellations. And the reason the Torah mentions not to curse powers; a chieftain; and a deaf man, is to come to warn one not to curse a **Judge** - the power mentioned here, when he finds him guilty in the trial, nor a chieftain when he punishes him, to dispatch him for his transgression. And it was necessary to mention a deaf man, lest you say - If[210] a person incurs guilt When one has heard a public imprecation but although able to testify as having either seen or learned of the matter has not given information and thus is subject to punishment. And - You[211] shall not curse powers. is written at the end of **Parshat Mishpatim** [Statutes] to say that you should not curse a judge that judges with these statutes. But you may curse a judge that is not proper. And our Rabbis, may their memory be blessed, said in the Talmud - One[212] who curses his fellow or himself with God's name is lashed. And his punishment at the hand of the Heavens is very great, as it is stated - If[213] you fail to observe faithfully all the terms of this Teaching that are written in this book to reverence this honored and awesome Name your God. And[214] God will inflict

---

[208] Exodus 22:27
[209] Leviticus 19:14
[210] Leviticus 5:1
[211] Exodus 22:27
[212] Shevuot 36a
[213] Deuteronomy 28:58
[214] Deuteronomy 28:59

extraordinary plagues upon you and your offspring strange and lasting plagues, malignant and chronic diseases. And our Rabbis, may their memory be blessed, explained in the Talmud - The[215] topic of this verse as one who curses his fellow or himself with God's name.

And it is forbidden for a person to say that God should save him if the matter is true, when the thing is actually untrue. For he cursed himself with God's name by doing so - as the **negative** can be inferred from the **positive**.

Drink[216] no wine or other intoxicant you or your sons when you enter the Tent of Meeting that you may not die This is a law for all time throughout the ages. For[217] you must distinguish between the sacred and the profane and between the impure and the pure. And our Rabbis, may their memory be blessed, said in the Talmud - If[218] one drank a **Log** [quarter] of wine that was not mixed with water, he may not issue a ruling, but if he drink more than a quarter, he may not issue a ruling even though he mixed it with water.

A[219] man shall not oppress his countryman. The verse is speaking about verbal oppression, like we discussed above. And our Rabbis, may their memory

---

215 Temurah 3:2
216 Leviticus 10:9
217 Leviticus 10:10
218 Eruvin 64a
219 Leviticus 25:17

be blessed, said in the Talmud - If[220] one is a penitent another may not say to him **Remember your earlier deeds**, if one is the child of converts, another may not say to him, **Remember the deeds of your ancestors**. And that which is stated - You[221] shall not oppress a stranger or press him. is understood as - **You shall not oppress** him verbally; **Or press him** with money. And the Torah warned in several places about oppression of the convert, for he forgot his own people and the house of his father, and came to seek refuge under the wings of the Divine Presence - like the matter that is stated - How[222] you left your father and mother and the land of your birth and came to a people you had not known before. And it is stated - May[223] the Lord reward your deeds may you have a full recompense from the Lord, the God of Israel under whose wings you have sought refuge. And there is a relevant parable about a gazelle that comes to a flock, and crouches with the sheep there. So, the owner of the flock had compassion on it - since it left a broad pasture to stand in a narrow place.

You[224] shall not follow the many to do bad. We were warned with this not to verbally strengthen the hands of sinners, and not join with those that conspire to do injustice - like the matter that is stated - You[225] must not call conspiracy, all that people call conspiracy.

---

[220] Bava Metzia 58b
[221] Exodus 22:20
[222] Ruth 2:11
[223] Ruth 2:12
[224] Exodus 23:2
[225] Isaiah 8:12

And it is forbidden to make an association with an evildoer for matters of the world, as it is stated - As[226] you have made an association with Ahaziah, the Lord will break up your work. And it is also stated - Do[227] not envy a lawless man, or associate with any of his ways. And our Rabbis, may their memory be blessed, said in Midrash - Do[228] not befriend an evildoer even for the matter of a commandment. And there are many paths of death found in the association with evildoers; and we have already spoken about this iniquity and the severity of its punishment.

You[229] shall not place a stumbling block before the blind. And we were warned with this not to give a ruling to the Israelites which is not like the doctrine and not like the **Halakha** [law]. And our Rabbis, may their memory be blessed, said in the Mishna - Be[230] deliberate in judgement. And the ones who are impatient to understand and give a ruling will not save their souls from putting a stumbling block before the blind; and their sin is very heavy, as it is written - They[231] neither know nor understand, they go about in darkness all the foundations of the earth totter. And they also said in the Mishna - Be[232] careful in study, for an error in study counts as deliberate sin. And our

[226] Chronicles-B 20:37
[227] Proverbs 3:31
[228] Avot DeRabbi Natan 9:4
[229] Leviticus 19:14
[230] Avot 1:1
[231] Psalms 82:5
[232] Avot 4:13

Rabbis, may their memory be blessed, said in the Talmud[233] - For[234] she has cast down many wounded. this is referring to a Torah scholar who has not yet attained the ability to issue rulings, and yet issues rulings. **And a mighty host are all her slain**; this is referring to a Torah scholar who has attained the ability to issue rulings, but does not issue rulings.

We are also warned by this verse to give proper advice when we advise one of our people, and not to make him stumble with boorish advice; and not to advise one's fellow for one's own advantage.

And a man is obligated to think thoughts that will bring up proper and coherent advice for this fellow. And this is one of the main types of acts of lovingkindness, as it is stated - Oil[235] and incense gladden the heart, and the sweetness of a friend is better than one's own counsel.

Do[236] not go talebearing among your people. And our Rabbis, may their memory be blessed, said in the Talmud - That[237] included in this **negative** commandment is not to put out a bad name for any of our people. And the punishment for doing this is very stringent, as will be explained in the level of those liable for the death penalty. And our Rabbis, may their memory be blessed, also said in the Talmud -

---

[233] Sotah 22a
[234] Proverbs 7:26
[235] Proverbs 27:9
[236] Leviticus 19:16
[237] Ketuvot 46a

That[238] Do not go **Rakhil** [talebearing] is a prohibition to the judge, that he should not be soft to **Rakh-La** this one and harsh to that one.

Make[239] no mention of the names of other gods - A person should not say to his fellow - Wait for me by idol so and so.

You[240] shall not grant them grace. It[241] is forbidden for a person to say - how handsome this non-Jew is. Our Rabbis, may their memory be blessed, explained in the Talmud - it[242] as do not give grace to the seven Canaanite nations.

And[243] not be like Korach and like his community. And our Rabbis, may their memory be blessed, said in the Talmud - Anyone[244] who perpetuates a dispute violates a **negative** commandment, as it is stated **and not be like Korach and like his community**. But it is permissible to say evil speech about disputatious people, as it is stated - But[245] he did not invite me your servant or the priest **Zadok** or **Benaiah** son of Jehoiada or your servant Solomon.

One who does not perpetuate a dispute against those

---

238 Ketuvot 46a
239 Exodus 23:13
240 Deuteronomy 7:2
241 Rasi on Deuteronomy 7:2
242 Avodah Zarah 19a
243 Numbers 17:5
244 Sanhedrin 110a
245 Kings-A 1:26

who stand on a path that is not good, and those that haul in iniquity, is surely punished for their transgressions in all their sins of the actual sinners; and also transgresses a **negative** commandment - as it is stated - You[246] shall not hate your kinsfolk in your heart Reprove your kin but incur no guilt on their account. And it is stated - You[247] have sinned more O Israel than in the days of Gibeah there they stand shall they not be overtaken as at Gibeah by a war upon scoundrels. Its explanation is that if that generation of Hosea was standing there, they would not have overtaken those in Gibeah in war, to destroy the evil, as that generation had overcome the evildoers of that time in war. The understanding of **there they stand** is, if they stood there. And likewise - And[248] leave his father. Is, if he left. This is meaning to say, that their sin was of the type of sin of Gibeah. However, the earlier generation was better than these, since they gathered and stood with their lives to destroy the evil. And it is stated - **Curse**[249] **Meroz** said the angel of the Lord **Bitterly curse its inhabitants** because they came not to the aid of the Lord to the aid of the Lord among the warriors. And it is stated - Do[250] not fear in front of a man. And anyone who is for God, may He be blessed, should give over his life for the sanctification of God, as it is stated - Whoever[251] is for the Lord come to me and all the Levites gathered to

---

[246] Leviticus 19:17
[247] Hosea 10:9
[248] Genesis 44:22
[249] Judges 5:23
[250] Deuteronomy 1:17
[251] Exodus 32:26

him. And it is also stated - When[252] Phinehas son of Eleazar son of Aaron the priest saw this he left the assembly and taking a spear in his hand. And it is an obligation on all that fear God - even if he is one that loves pureness of heart - to arouse zealotry when he sees that behold, the officers and the prefects are in trespass, as it is stated - And[253] it was the hand of the officers and prefects who were in this trespass first.

But[254] as for your brothers of the Children of Israel, no one shall rule ruthlessly over the other. A man may not subjugate his fellow. And if his fear is upon them or they are embarrassed to violate his word, he should not command them to do [anything at all], except from their own will and for their benefit - even to heat up a jug of water or to go on an errand to the town square to buy as much as a loaf of bread. But it is permitted to command anything he wants to a man who does not behave properly.

You[255] shall not profane My holy name. This is among the sins for which one is liable for excision, as will be explained. And know that, is not the greatest damage and destruction found among the souls of the masses on the lips of the tongue? For they mention God's name for nothing, and they also mention it without reverence. And about this matter did our Rabbis explain in the Midrash - That[256] which it is written -

---

[252] Numbers 25:7
[253] Ezra 9:2
[254] Leviticus 25:46
[255] Leviticus 22:32
[256] Leviticus Rabbah 27

Israel[257] did not know. And they are also not exacting about the cleanliness of the place and cleanliness of their palms.

And when people are not careful with their tongues about the honor of Torah scholars - whether in front of them or not in front of them - they turn into those categorized as **Apikorsim** [heretics] who do not have a share in the world to come. And likewise, is not the destruction of the four groups, see in the Talmud - From[258] the sin of their mouth and the word of their lips? It is all like it will be explained in this chapter. Therefore, it is written - Death[259] and life are in the power of the tongue.

Observe and see the iniquity of the tongue and the severity of its transgression: For the punishment of one who curses his father and mother is more severe than one who strikes them. As the sentence of the one that curses is stoning - which is the most stringent of the court's death penalties - whereas the sentence of the one who strikes them is strangulation.

And many are also ensnared and trapped in profaning their glorious senses - the sense of seeing and the sense of hearing. And it is stated about the sense of seeing - So[260] that you do not follow your heart and eyes. We were commanded with this that a man

---

257 Isaiah 1:3
258 Sota 42a
259 Proverbs 18:21
260 Numbers 15:39

should not stare at a married woman or at other sexual prohibitions, lest he be ensnared by them.

And among the sins that are dependent on the sight of seeing is that of raised eyes. For it is caused by pride, as it is stated - I[261] cannot endure one of raised eyes and a thick heart.

And among the words of our Rabbis about the sense of hearing is in the Talmud - A[262] person should not allow his ears to hear idle matters, because they are the first of the limbs burned. And about the one that audits a mouth that speaks vulgarity, it is stated - The[263] mouth of strange women is a deep pit. One who is of the fearers of God and of the penitents should pay attention to all of this, in order to save his soul from the flame. And we have already written fine words about this matter in the Gates of Precautions of Caution no longer extant.

Among the **negative** commandments dependent upon the shutting of the hand and the one who prevents himself from an act is - If[264] however there is a needy person among you one of your kin in any of your settlements in the land that your God is giving you do not harden your heart and shut your hand against your needy kin. Rather[265] you must open your hand and

---

[261] Psalms 101:5
[262] Ketuvot 5b
[263] Proverbs 22:14
[264] Deuteronomy 15:7
[265] Deuteronomy 15:8

lend whatever is sufficient to meet the need. Beware[266] lest you harbor the base thought the seventh year the year of remission is approaching so that you are mean and give nothing to your needy kin who will cry out to God against you and you will incur guilt. We have learned from this that one who refrains from lending to a poor person violates two **negative** commandments. And they are **Beware**, and **Lest**. So, if at the time that the seventh year is approaching, we are warned not to prevent ourselves from loaning because of the fear of the matter of the year of remission, certainly is it so at a time when he will not lose the loaner's debt - for the sin of one who shuts his hand from lending will become greater. And from the greatness of this iniquity, the verse called the thought of stinginess from lending, **Devar B'eliaal** [base thought]. And our Rabbis, may their memory be blessed, said in the Talmud - Regarding[267] anyone who averts his eyes from the obligation to give charity, it is as if he engages in idol worship. It is written here - Beware[268] lest you harbor the base thought the seventh year the year of remission is approaching so that you are mean and give nothing to your needy kin who will cry out to God against you, and you will incur guilt. And it is written there - That[269] some scoundrels from among you have gone and subverted the inhabitants of their town saying Come let us worship other gods whom you have not

---

266 Deuteronomy 15:9
267 Ketuvot 68a
268 Deuteronomy 15:9
269 Deuteronomy 13:14

experienced. - And our Rabbis, may their memory be blessed, said in the Midrash - That[270] a miser is called base. And so, is it written - Please[271] my lord pays no attention to that wretched fellow Nabal For he is just what his name says His name means boor and he is a boor Your handmaid did not see the young men whom my lord sent. Because he was stingy, since he said to King David's servants - Should[272] I then take my bread and my water and the meat that I slaughtered for my own shearers and give them to men who come from I don't know where. And our Rabbis, may their memory be blessed, said in the Talmud - Greater[273] is one who lends to a poor person than one who gives charity.

You[274] shall not abuse your neighbor. And the explanation is that this is also from the **negative** commandments] that are dependent upon the shutting of the hand. For the verse is speaking about abusing the wage of a wage-worker, such that the employer prevents himself from paying him his wage. And likewise, that which **Rabbenu Yonah** brings the verse - **The wicked man**, after this is because it is from this type in which one prevents himself from paying the debt. And King David, peace be upon him, said - The[275] wicked man borrows and does not repay.

---

[270] Yalkut Shmuel 28:134
[271] Samuel-A 25:25
[272] Samuel-A 25:11
[273] Shabbat 63a
[274] Leviticus 19:13
[275] Psalms 37:21

You[276] shall not leave over the wages of a laborer with you until morning. You[277] must pay him his wages on the same day, before the sun sets. It is the same for the rent of an animal, the wage of a person or of vessels - one transgresses - **You shall not leave over**. Even with contracting, one transgresses, in the Talmud - You[278] shall not leave over.

You[279] must not leave over his corpse on the stake overnight. One who leaves over his dead relative overnight transgresses a **negative** commandment, unless he leaves him over for the sake of his honor.

You[280] may not be indifferent. We were warned with this not to be negligent from saving the wealth of our fellows - whether movable property or lands - as our Rabbis, may their memory be blessed, said in the Talmud - And[281] so too shall you do with anything that your brother loses to include the loss of land. For example, if there was water streaming and coming there, he is obligated to block it. And also, were we warned with this verse to make efforts to rescue our neighbors, and to save our fellows at the time of their troubles. And it is likewise written - You[282] may not stand over your neighbor's blood. And Solomon said

---

276 Leviticus 19:13
277 Deuteronomy 24:15
278 Bava Metzia 101b
279 Deuteronomy 21:23
280 Deuteronomy 22:3
281 Bava Metzia 31a
282 Leviticus 19:16

- If[283] you showed yourself slack in time of trouble and wanting in strength. Its explanation is that if you have the ability to save with counsel or with effort, but you show yourself as if you do not have the strength, your strength will be reduced - measure for measure. And it is stated afterwards - If[284] you say we knew nothing of it surely He who fathoms hearts will discern the truth He who watches over your life will know it and He will pay each man as he deserves. Behold one who prevents himself from the salvation of others and from giving counsel to help, the Holy One, blessed be He, will consider it like his act. It appears to me that his intention in explaining the verse is that even though the iniquity of preventing himself is passive, nevertheless it will be counted for him as if he had actively done evil to his fellow. For that evil that came to his fellow in a place where he could have been saved through the sinner, is considered for the one that prevented himself from saving the other as if he was active and did it. And this is the understanding of its being considered like his act.

And it is good and very correct that there be volunteers from the people in each and every city, to be ready and prepared for any matter of rescue, when an Israelite man or woman is found in trouble. And behold we became obligated to exert ourselves for his missing ox or sheep, to be with us - now what fineness and greatness to do for its owners - until our brother

---

[283] Proverbs 24:10
[284] Proverbs 24:12

requests it; and it is written - And[285] take the wretched poor into your home.

You[286] shall surely reprimand your countryman and not bear sin because of him. We were warned with this not to incur sin from the sin of our fellow, in our preventing ourselves from rebuking them. And if one-man sins when his sin is completely revealed and they did not rebuke him with a rod of reprimands, the whole congregation is punished. And it is accordingly written - When[287] Achan son of Zerah violated the proscription anger struck the whole community of Israel he was not the only one who perished for that sin. And it is stated - But[288] with overt acts it is for us and our children forever. And even the nations of the world said - Let[289] us cast lots and find out on whose account this misfortune has come upon us. And certainly, with Israel, who are responsible for one another.

And in order to be saved from this punishment, it is a proper thing to choose men of truth and to identify men of valor from all of the people; and to place them as the heads of supervision over every marketplace and lot of their dwelling places - in order to supervise their neighbors and to reprimand them for any matter of rebellion and destroy the evil that they find.

---

285 Isaiah 58:7
286 Leviticus 19:17
287 Joshua 22:20
288 Deuteronomy 29:28
289 Jonah 1:7

When[290] you make a vow to the Lord, your God do not delay fulfilling it. Behold there is a punishment for the delay of vows and charity, even though one pays them later. And if someone vows to give charity to the poor, he is obligated to pay it immediately. And if by way of forgetfulness, a delay of the vow happens to him, this too will surely be punished. For since he knows that forgetfulness is found with people, he should have remembered his vows and constantly put them into his heart, so that he would not forget them - like the matter that is stated - It[291] is a snare for a man to pledge a sacred gift rashly and to give thought to his vows only after they have been made. Therefore, his punishment for his negligence is severe, as it is stated - Don't[292] let your mouth bring your flesh to sin and don't plead before the messenger that it was an error but fear God else God may be angered by your talk and destroy the work of your hands. Its explanation is - Don't let your mouth bring your flesh to sin. Why do you vow, if you are not careful with your vows and bring guilt upon yourself? And we have already explained this verse in the Gates of Precautions of Caution no longer extant. And our Rabbis, may their memory be blessed, have said about the iniquity of unfulfilled vows in the Talmud - That[293]children die as a result, as it is stated - And[294] destroy the work of your hands. The verse is also explained to be about the matter of evil speech, that

---

[290] Deuteronomy 23:22
[291] Proverbs 20:25
[292] Ecclesiastes 5:5
[293] Shabbat 32b
[294] Ecclesiastes 5:5

one is punished for negligence with it - even if he does not intend to disgrace his fellow. And likewise did our Rabbis, may their memory be blessed, say in the **Sifrei** - and Rashi cites it in his commentary on the Torah concerning Miriam - and this is its language - Miriam[295] and Aaron spoke against Moshe because of the Cushite woman he had taken into his household as his wife He took a Cushite woman. As[296] the cloud withdrew from the Tent there was Miriam stricken with snow-white scales When Aaron turned toward Miriam he saw that she was stricken with scales. And it concludes in the **Sifrei** - But rather for praise on account of the commandment of being fruitful and multiplying. And behold we were commanded not to make vows, as it is stated - Whereas[297] you incur no guilt if you refrain from vowing. And our Rabbis expounded from this in the Talmud - That[298] if one does vow, he incurs guilt. For a vow is a stumbling block for the one who vows, lest he profane his word or delay fulfilling it. Rather a righteous man is gracious and gives without his vowing. It is hence forbidden to vow except for when he calls out from distress. For then he should make a vow, like the matter that is written - And[299] Yaakov then made a vow saying If God remains with me protecting me on this journey that I am making and giving me bread to eat and clothing to wear. And likewise in the gathering together of the heads of the people - the

---

295 Numbers 12:1
296 Numbers 12:10
297 Deuteronomy 23:23
298 Nedarim 77b
299 Genesis 28:20

Tribes of Israel - They should make vows to strengthen weakened hands. It appears to me that his intention in that which he wrote - To strengthen weakened hands, is meaning to say that it energizes the rest of the people whose hands are weakened in the trait of volunteering, since they are not used to it. And through his vowing publicly in front of many people, their hearts are elevated to volunteer as well. And so is it written - King[300] David said to the entire assemblage God has chosen my son Solomon alone an untried lad although the work to be done is vast for the temple is not for a man but for the LORD God. I[301] have spared no effort to lay up for the House of my God gold for golden objects silver for silver copper for copper iron for iron wood for wooden onyx-stone and inlay-stone, stone of antimony and variegated colors every kind of precious stone and much marble. Besides[302] out of my solicitude for the House of my God I gave over my private hoard of gold and silver to the House of my God in addition to all that I laid aside for the holy House. 3,000[303] gold talents of Ophir gold and 7,000 talents of refined silver for covering the walls of the houses. Gold[304] for golden objects, silver for silver for all the work into the hands of craftsmen Now who is going to make a freewill offering and devote himself today to the LORD. The[305] officers of the clans and the officers of the

---

[300] Chronicles-A 29:1
[301] Chronicles-A 29:2
[302] Chronicles-A 29:3
[303] Chronicles-A 29:4
[304] Chronicles-A 29:5
[305] Chronicles-A 29:6

tribes of Israel and the captains of thousands and
hundreds and the supervisors of the king's work made
freewill offerings. Giving[306] for the work of the House
of God 5,000 talents of gold, 10,000 darics 10,000
talents of silver 18,000 talents of copper, 100,000
talents of iron. Whoever[307] had stones in his
possession gave them to the treasury of the House of
the LORD in the charge of Jehiel the Gershonite.
The[308] people rejoiced over the freewill offerings they
made for with a whole heart they made freewill
offerings to the LORD King David also rejoiced very
much.

**The fifth level is a negative commandment that
involves an action**

Our Rabbis, may their memory be blessed, said in the
Talmud - We[309] give lashes for a **negative**
commandment that involves an action. And the
number of lashes is forty minus one. And our Rabbis,
may their memory be blessed, said in the Talmud -
That[310] lashes come instead of the death penalty. And
they said in the Talmud - Someone[311] who was lashed
and repeats the sin, we put into **Kippah** [jail]. And it
is an obligation upon the reprimanders to investigate
the ways of the people and to know what they are
stumbling in. Since there are many **negative**

[306] Chronicles-A 29:7
[307] Chronicles-A 29:8
[308] Chronicles-A 29:9
[309] Makkot 13b
[310] Sanhedrin 10a
[311] Sanhedrin 81b

commandments - even though they observe many of the **negative** commandments, they also negate many of them. For example, they keep most of the prohibitions of work on Shabbat - but there are types of work that part of the people is not careful about, since they are not known to them. And their mistakes are attributed to themselves, since they did not lodge among the sages and seek Torah from their mouths. Hence, they transgressed the practices and will be punished, as it is stated - But[312] when the evildoer is spared, he learns not righteousness. And there are rebels that stumble in them; for they did not become accustomed to them in their youth, in the houses of their fathers, to be careful about them. And they inherited the ways of the fathers, and did not listen to the voice of their teachers. Hence these are doing these sins wantonly.

And likewise, all of the people are careful about the blood of the soul and the blood of exudate; but some of them are not careful about the preparation of salting, to remove the blood from the meat according to the law. And there are very many like these [examples], without knowledge and without reprimand. And it is like it is stated - For[313] lack of vision a people become wild.

And there are some **negative** commandments that some of the masses do not keep the main **negative** commandment, such as wounding and hitting. For

---

[312] Isaiah 26:10
[313] Proverbs 29:18

one that hits his fellow violates two **negative** commandments, as it is stated - You[314] shall strike him forty you shall not add lest you add. And many transgress these **negative** commandments by hitting their wives. And our Rabbis, may their memory be blessed, said in the Talmud - Anyone[315] who raises his hand to strike another, even if he does not strike him, is called wicked - as it is stated - And[316] he said to the wicked one. Why should you strike your friend? **Why did you strike**, is not stated, but rather, 'should you strike. And Job said - If[317] I raised my hand against the fatherless. And our Rabbis, may their memory be blessed, said in the Talmud - That[318] Rav Huna would cut off the hand of the striker. He would say - And[319] the high arm shall be broken.

And likewise with destruction of the beard, as it is stated - And[320] you shall not destroy the side-growth of your beard.

And there are people that do not refrain from wearing a garment that is of a forbidden mixture of fabrics. For they sew a wool garment with a linen thread or make a linen rim for the edge of a woolen garment.

---

314 Deuteronomy 25:3
315 Sanhedrin 58b
316 Exodus 2:13
317 Job 31:21
318 Sanhedrin 58b
319 Job 38:15
320 Leviticus 19:27

No[321] man shall approach anyone of his own flesh. Any approaching of the flesh is forbidden, such as touching the hands of a married woman. And its explanation in the continuation of the verse **to uncover nakedness**, is because approaching leads to nakedness forbidden intercourse. And should you say in your heart - Where is it found in Scripture that the Torah made a fence, that you should say that it forbade the touching of hands, that it should be a sin - we will answer you this word in the Midrash - Behold[322] the commandment of the Nazirite in which one's main separation is lest he forget the Lawmaker or be fooled by a spirit of licentiousness, and yet the Torah forbade him from consuming everything that is from the vine of wine. And all of that is as a fence to distance him from drinking wine. And likewise did our Rabbis say in the.

And[323] do not place a stumbling block in front of the blind. Our Rabbis said in the Talmud - That[324] we were warned with this that a man should not strike his grown son, lest it be a snare and a stumbling block for the son's tongue and to hit his father. And likewise, were we warned with this not to bring about any stumbling block for the iniquity of an Israelite or even a gentile, such that he not gives a cup of wine to a Nazarite or a limb from a living animal also to a Noahide, and also not extend to him that which is

---

[321] Leviticus 18:6
[322] Exodus Rabbah 16:2
[323] Leviticus 19:14
[324] Moed Katan 17a

forbidden to him, nor to cause him to stumble upon one of the things about which the Noahides were forbidden.

You[325] must not destroy its trees, wielding the ax against them. For we were warned with this not to cut down any fruit tree - even to build fortifications with it, so long as one finds enough fruitless trees for his needs. And we were also warned with this not to throw money around for no reason - even the value of a **Perutah** [small coin]. And our Rabbis said in the Talmud - One[326] who rends his garments excessively over his dead relative is lashed. And all the more so, one who breaks vessels in his anger, as he has done two evils - destroying his wealth; and letting his anger be in control, to make him transgress matters of the Torah. As from now on, he will have a struggle with the impulse of anger, to make him transgress his religion - like the matter that is written - A[327] hot-tempered man commits many offenses. And we have already let you know that which our Rabbis, may their memory be blessed, said in the Talmud - One[328] who rends his garments in his anger or who breaks his vessels in his anger or who scatters his money in his anger should be like an idol worshipper in your eyes as that is the craft of the evil inclination. Today it tells him do this and tomorrow it tells him do that, until eventually when he no longer controls himself it tells

---

[325] Deuteronomy 20:19
[326] Bava Kamma 91b
[327] Proverbs 29:22
[328] Shabbat 105b

him worship idols and he goes and worships idols Rabbi Avin said What verse alludes to this There shall not be a strange god within you and you shall not bow to a foreign god. And our Rabbis, may their memory be blessed, said in the Talmud - A[329] man should not pour out water from his well when others need it. We were even warned not to waste the body, by giving it over to dangers or torturing the body to consume it needlessly with fasts from his distress and anger, and not to mourn more than is necessary for his dead relative. But regarding one who grieves and mourns over his iniquities - about him is it stated - I[330] note how they fare and will heal them; I will guide them and mete out solace to them and to the mourners among them. And it is stated - But[331] for your souls' blood I will require a reckoning. And our Rabbis, may their memory be blessed, said in the Talmud - From[332] the hand of your souls That is from yourself will I require your blood.

Three[333] years it shall be **Arelim** [forbidden] for you, not to be eaten. Orlah is applicable outside of the Land of Israel and it is forbidden in benefit. And anything that is forbidden in benefit is forbidden to give to a gentile. And the fourth-year vineyard is forbidden in benefit, when not redeemed. And we may not redeem it until its fruits have reached the season of the tithes. So, when is the season of the

---

[329] Yevamot 44a
[330] Isaiah 57:18
[331] Genesis 9:5
[332] Bava Kamma 91b
[333] Leviticus 19:23

tithes? From the time that the fruits have been completed, like the matter that our Rabbis, may their memory be blessed, learned - From[334] when are the fruits obligated in tithes?

Therefore[335] the Children of Israel do not eat the **Gid HaNashei** [sciatic tendon]. The **Gid HaNashei** [sciatic tendon] is forbidden in benefit, so it is forbidden to give it to one's Canaanite slave or maidservant. And it is forbidden to send a thigh as a gift to a Canaanite with the sciatic tendon inside it. And likewise does Rosh bring in the name of **Rabbeinu Yonah** at the beginning of the chapter entitled **Gid HaNashei** [sciatic tendon] in the discussion of a man sending a thigh to a Canaanite. But we do not establish the law to be like him in this, but rather like the opinion of Rambam - that the sciatic tendon is permissible in benefit, so one may send a thigh to a Canaanite with the sciatic tendon inside it. And it is explained in Tur and Shulchan Arukh[336].

You[337] shall not steal; you shall not deal deceitfully or falsely. Our Rabbis said in the Talmud - You[338] shall not steal in order to aggravate - that one should not say - **I will steal vessel x**, in order that he will be pained and I will make him aggravated **Nakot**, [like]

334 Maasrot 1:2
335 Genesis 32:33
336 Yoreh Deah 65
337 Leviticus 19:11
338 Bava Metzia 61b

the usage - Then[339] you shall recall your evil ways and your base conduct and you shall loathe yourselves for your iniquities and your abhorrent practices. Be careful in watching his vessels and give it back to him afterwards. And it is likewise forbidden to take vessels from the house of one's fellow in the way of theft, to use them and then return them to him. And[340] one may not steal what is his from behind the thief - so that he will not appear to be a thief.

You[341] shall not practice divination or soothsaying. **You shall not practice divination** - such as those that divine with weasels and birds. It is if his bread fell from his mouth or a gazelle crossed his path, and he said it is a sign that his journey will not be successful - so he leaves his journey because of this. And that which is similar to this, such that he follows the augurs, whether to do something or to refrain from the action. You[342] shall not practice **Teonenu** [soothsaying]. is an expression of **Onot** [times] and hours. That he says - Day **X** is good to begin work, hour **Y** is bad for leaving. And one should also not listen to the astrologers. But rather one's heart should trust in the Lord, the God of the heavens and the God of the earth. Therefore, it is written about this matter - You[343] must be wholehearted with the Lord your God. We have learned from this that the diviners and the augurs are lacking trust. And these plots and

---

[339] Ezekiel 36:31
[340] Sifra, Kedoshim, Section 2:2
[341] Leviticus 19:26
[342] Leviticus 19:26
[343] Deuteronomy 18:13

divining's are the acts of the Land of Canaan, as it is
stated - For[344] those nations that you are about to
dispossess do indeed resort to soothsayers and
augurs; to you, however the Lord your God has not
assigned the like.

You[345] shall do no unrighteousness in judgment.
Behold, afterward it states, you shall not favor the
poor or show deference to the rich; judge your
countryman fairly. So, what is, **judgement** stated at
the beginning of the verse? Our Rabbis, may their
memory be blessed, said in the Midrash[346] that this is
referring to length, weight and capacity - It is to teach
us that a measurer is called a judge, and if he falsifies
in measurement it is as if the perverts justice; and he
is called wrong... revolting, rejected and abominable,
and he brings about five things like one who perverts
justice - He defiles the Land, he profanes the Name,
he drives out the Divine Presence, he causes Israel to
fall by the sword, and he exiles them from their land.
And it appears to me that there is a lacuna here - and
it is accordingly found below - You[347] shall not falsify
measures of length weight or capacity. You[348] shall
have an honest balance honest weights an honest
ephah and an honest Hin I God am your God who
freed you from the land of Egypt. **Measures of length**
- that is measuring of land; **Weight** - like its meaning;
Or capacity - that is a liquid and a dry measure;

344 Deuteronomy 18:14
345 Leviticus 19:15
346 Sifra, Kedoshim, Chapter 8:5
347 Leviticus 19:35
348 Leviticus 19:36

Honest weights - masses to weigh across from them; **An ephah** is a dry measure; **A Hin** - is a liquid measure; **I am the God your God who freed you, you from the land of Egypt**. - in Egypt, I distinguished between the drop of a firstborn and the drop that was not a firstborn, so I am credible to punish the one who hides his weights in salt, in order to fool the creatures who are not aware of them.

You[349] shall not act towards him as a creditor. We were warned with this not to distress the borrower. And the creditor may not pass in front of him when he knows that the borrower does not have with what to pay him back. For he torments him and weakens his spirit with this. And our Rabbis, may their memory be blessed, said in the Talmud - Behold[350] it is as if he is judging him with two punishments, as it is stated - You[351] have let men ride over us; we have endured fire and water.

If[352] you lend money to My people to the poor among you do not act toward them as a creditor exact no interest from them. You shall not put usury upon him - this is a **negative** commandment for the witnesses - as the creditor, the borrower and the witnesses all transgress a **negative** commandment. Therefore, it states - you shall not **Tasimun** [put], in plural, after it stated - You shall not   act   singular towards him as a

---

[349] Exodus 22:24
[350] Bava Metzia 78b
[351] Psalms 66:12
[352] Exodus 22:24

creditor - Since it is a warning to the witnesses.

There[353] must be no blemish in it. We were warned with this not to introduce a blemish into a firstborn - even in our times.

You[354] shall not plow with an ox and an ass together. We were warned with this not to plow - nor to tread - with two species, when they are joined with a yoke or with a rope. And the law is the same for driving them when they are joined. And the reason that it only spoke about plowing is that the verse mentioned the common case. And it is even forbidden to drive them with one's voice. And it is forbidden to drive together two mules, if one is the daughter of a female horse and one is the daughter of a female donkey. And it is forbidden to drive a mule with either a horse or a donkey.

And[355] a figured stone you shall not set in your land. We were warned with this not to bow down on a floor of stones in the synagogue or in any other place, except for the Temple.

You[356] shall not make yourselves abominable. We were warned with this not to eat fish or a grasshopper until they die. And likewise, should one not drink from the horn of a bloodletter that he uses for his

---

[353] Leviticus 22:21
[354] Deuteronomy 22:21
[355] Leviticus 26:1
[356] Leviticus 11:43

craft. One who delays his bodily needs also transgresses on account of the Talmud - You[357] shall not make yourselves abominable.

Do[358] not degrade your daughter and make her a harlot, lest the land fall into harlotry and the land be filled with depravity. Our Rabbis explained in the Talmud that this verse comes to warn that a man not give over his single daughter for intercourse that is not for the sake of **Kiddushin** [marriage]. Lest[359] the land fall into harlotry - for if you do this, the land will be untrue and give its fruit elsewhere, and not in your land. And likewise, does it state - And[360] when showers were withheld and the late rains did not come your face had the brazenness of a harlot.

And behold you have seen the greatness of the punishment of one who designates a single woman as a harlot for himself. For it is stated about this - Lest[361] the land fall into harlotry and the land be filled with depravity. That is besides the great evil stumbling block that is found for those having intercourse with a single woman - for she is ashamed to immerse in the waters of a river or a mikveh to purify herself from the impurity of her menstruation, lest a rumor of her harlotry become public. Therefore, she will usually remain in menstruation; her impurity in the bottom of her skirts, she does not think of her end. Our Rabbis

---

357 Makkot 16b
358 Leviticus 19:29
359 Sanhedrin 76a
360 Jeremiah 3:3
361 Leviticus 19:29

also said in the Talmud - Do[362] not degrade your daughter and make her a harlot - behold this is a **negative** commandment that a man not marry off his daughter to an old man.

You[363] shall not eat any corpse. Our Rabbis, may their memory be blessed, said in the Talmud - Anything[364] that is disqualified during slaughter is a **Neveilah** [corpse]. And it is goodly for the reprimands to warn the people, so that they should be careful about the law of slaughtering and all of its details, to fulfill its dictates. And for all of its laws, they should choose a **Schochet** [slaughterer] who fears sin, since a large number of Israelites are dependent upon him for the proper execution of the commandments of slaughter and examination. And though it is true that our Rabbis, may their memory be blessed, said in the Talmud - Most[365] of those found around slaughter are experts. There are places without concern and without reprimand. There, most of the people found around slaughter are not understanding experts. And we have also seen scandal in some of them. For many of the experts have distanced themselves from these places out of fear of sin; and the heart of those that do not fear, does not understand how to be exacting in the examination of the knife. For one has to focus his heart very, very much in its examination. Do you not see that a man may check two or three times and not

---

362 Sanhedrin 76a
363 Deuteronomy 14:21
364 Chullin 32a
365 Chullin 3b

feel a small nick that would render the knife improper, but find it afterwards when he set his heart to it in the end? So [this shows] that the sense of touch is according to the focus of the heart. This is besides that a man that has no fear will err in the examination of the marks and the rest of the ways and angles that are clearly revealed to anyone who knows the doctrine and the law.

And[366] you shall not take a bribe - even on condition to have the innocent be innocent and the guilty be guilty, and even if the two parties to the argument have agreed to give him a wage together. Thus did our Rabbis, may their memory be blessed, say in the Talmud - Regarding[367] one who takes a wage to judge his decisions are null. But they are permitted to give him the wage of the loss he incurred, in that they disturbed him from his regular activities - if the loss is recognizable and fixed, and it is known to people. And this is so long as one of them does not give more than his fellow towards the wage of the loss.

Our Rabbis, may their memory be blessed, said in the Talmud - And[368] you shall not take a bribe - even a bribe of words. As if one of them said words of a flatterer to him, he must withdraw himself from that case. And if he brings him a present when he comes to be judged in front of him, he should not take it from his hand. And even if he preceded and gave him a gift

---

[366] Exodus 23:8
[367] Ketuvot 105a
[368] Ketuvot 105b

in front of him to take from him before he received his summons, this judge has already been disqualified from judging him.

You[369] shall celebrate a sacred occasion on the first day and a sacred occasion on the seventh day no work at all shall be done on them only what every person is to eat that alone may be prepared for you. Our Rabbis said in the Talmud - From[370] transporting being permitted for the sake of food for people, it was also permitted not for its sake - so long as it is for the sake of the day. And it is like the matter that they said in the Talmud - We[371] transport a Torah scroll on a holiday to read it on that day. But it is forbidden to transport for the needs of weekdays - only for the needs of the holiday. And many of the people sin by transporting a key for their containers into the public domain on the holiday, even though there is no food that can be eaten on the holiday in the container.

A[372] man shall not wear a woman's clothing. This is a **negative** commandment against removing underarm and pubic hairs.

So[373] that you do not bring bloodguilt in your house. This is a **negative** commandment against placing a bad dog or a rickety ladder inside one's home.

---

[369] Exodus 12:16
[370] Beitzah 5a
[371] Beitzah 12a
[372] Deuteronomy 22:5
[373] Deuteronomy 22:8

You[374] must not work your firstling ox or shear your firstling sheep. The law of the firstborn is practiced both in the Land of Israel and outside the Land. And a firstling that is mixed in a hundred or even a thousand other animals render all of them prohibited in benefit.

You[375] shall not do like this to the Lord, your God. This is a **negative** commandment against erasing God's name.

And[376] you shall not follow their practices. And we were warned with this to distance ourselves from all the ways of the emoratas. And among them are incantations, and amulets that are not from an expert for healing.

And[377] you shall eat no bread or parched grain or fresh ears until that very day. And until the day it becomes permitted, the new grain is forbidden by the Torah also outside of the Land.

We have written some of the things about which many people err unknowingly, for their ears had not been exposed to them; and some of the things they knew were forbidden, but did know the severity of the prohibition. And we mentioned some of these things so that the people will not err in them laying down.

---

[374] Deuteronomy 15:19
[375] Deuteronomy 12:4
[376] Leviticus 18:3
[377] Leviticus 23:14

The wise man will hear this and add more teaching, to warn the people about the things like this that happen to them. And the understanding ones will note their mention, and so, shine with the shine of heaven.

And the sixth level is the sins that come with a death penalty at the hands of the Heavens

The difference between this death penalty and **Karet** [excision] is that the liability for the death penalty is upon him, but not upon his progeny; whereas with the punishment of excision, he and his progeny are excised. Nevertheless, our Rabbis, may their memory be blessed, have said in the Talmud - That[378] regarding one matter, in one aspect, death at the hands of the Heavens exceeds the severity of excision. For the one who is liable for death at the hands of the Heavens has death in his apertures, and the animals of his livestock die - His cow eats dust and dies; his chicken eats from the Dung heap and dies. And so, death clings to him until it finishes him off.

And some of those liable for a death penalty at the hands of the Heavens were enumerated in the Mishnah, such as one who eats untitled foods - and that is grain that was not prepared by the separation of the priestly tithe and the tithe from it. And this commandment is practiced only in the Land of Israel. And another example is an impure priest that eats pure priestly tithe or a non-priest that ate the priestly tithe.

[378] Pesachim 32b

And there are some of them that our Rabbis, may their memory be blessed, explained in the Talmud and in the Midrash, and most of them can be learned from the verse itself. For example, one who afflicts a widow or an orphan, as it is stated - You[379] communal leaders shall not ill-treat any widow or orphan. If[380] you do mistreat them I will heed their outcry as soon as they cry out to Me. And[381] My anger shall blaze forth and I will put you to the sword and your own wives shall become widows and your children orphans. And our Rabbis, may their memory be blessed, said in the Midrash - It[382] is one if they cry out or they do not cry out. This is meaning to say that when one who afflicts the widow or orphan is punished, it is the same doctrine whether the afflicted surely cries out under his hand or is surely silent. But when the orphan cries out to God, may He be blessed, the punishment comes quickly.

Likewise, stealing from the poor person, as it is stated - Do[383] not rob the wretched because he is wretched Do not crush the poor man in the gate. For[384] the LORD will take up their cause and despoil those who despoil them of life. And we have already explained this in the third level. And our Rabbis, may their memory be blessed, said in the Talmud - That[385] one

---

[379] Exodus 22:21
[380] Exodus 22:22
[381] Exodus 22:23
[382] Mekhilta D'Rabbi Yishmael, Mishpatim 18
[383] Proverbs 22:22
[384] Proverbs 22:23
[385] Bava Kamma 119a

who steals from a poor person is as if he takes his life, as it is stated - Such[386] is the fate of all who pursue unjust gain; it takes the life of its possessor. Sometimes it deprives him of his livelihood - even with the theft of less than the value of a **Perutah** [very small coin]. Therefore, it is considered like bloodguilt for that person: If he stole the value of a **Perutah**, he has spilled blood.

Likewise, one who put out a bad name on someone else, as it is stated - And[387] those who spread such calumnies about the land died of plague in front of the Lord. And our Rabbis, may their memory be blessed, said in the Talmud - That[388] if the punishment for one who puts out a bad name on the land is death, all the more so for one who puts out a bad name on a fellow Israelite - who is obligated in Torah and the commandments. And it is stated - And[389] they shall fine him a hundred shekels of silver and give it to the girl's father for that householder has defamed a virgin in Israel Moreover she shall remain his wife he shall never have the right to divorce her. Behold, the verse did not mention his sin about having tried to take the life of the woman, and causing her to be killed in court with false witnesses that he brought about her fabricated harlotry; yet it mentioned the iniquity of putting out a bad name! For it is a greater iniquity than one seeking to squelch a life, as the pain of the

---

386 Proverbs 1:19
387 Numbers 14:37
388 Arakhin 15a
389 Deuteronomy 22:19

shame is more bitter than death. And so did our Rabbis, may their memory be blessed, say that he is liable lashes and [a fine] for putting out a bad name, not for having sought to kill her. And our Rabbis, may their memory be blessed, said in the Talmud - That[390] one who puts out a bad name with words about a blemish in the family is never able to atone. For it is not enough for him to get pardoned by those still alive, as he caused the shame and disgrace of their forebears that gave him birth. And we will still add more to its explanation when we explain the severity of the four death penalties of the court.

And one who plays with children and masturbates whether with the hand or the foot is liable. And our Rabbis, may their memory be blessed, said in the Talmud - That[391] his punishment is like the punishment of the generation of the flood, that had corrupted their ways. And likewise, one who does like the act of Er and Onan - to thresh the penis inside the vagina and winnow outside, to destroy the seed - is liable, as it is stated - And[392] what he did was displeasing to the Lord, and He killed him as well. And it is stated about those that waste seed - You[393] who inflame yourselves Among the terebinths Under every verdant tree Who slaughter children in the wadis Among the clefts of the rocks.

---

[390] Yerushalmi Bava Kamma 8:7
[391] Niddah 13b
[392] Genesis 38:10
[393] Isaiah 57:5

And a Torah scholar that does not act modestly is liable, because he distances the Torah from the love of the creatures. And our Rabbis, may their memory be blessed, said in the Talmud - About[394] this is it stated - All[395] who hate me love death. The explanation of haters is, those that cause hate - as they cause the creatures to hate the Torah. And our Rabbis, may their memory be blessed, said in the Talmud - When[396] a man reads Torah, studies Mishnah... and he speaks pleasantly with other people, is pleasant with them in his business transactions in the marketplace and gives and takes faithfully - what do people say about him? Fortunate is his father and his mother who taught him Torah ... woe to the people who have not studied Torah. So-and-so who was taught Torah - see how beautiful are his ways, how proper are his deeds. About him does the verse state - You[397] are My servant, Israel, in whom I will be glorified. But when a man reads Torah, studies Mishnah... but he does not speak pleasantly with other people, is not pleasant with them in his business transactions in the marketplace and does not give and take faithfully - what do people say about him? Woe to so-and-so who studied Torah, woe to his teacher and to his father who taught him Torah. So-and-so who studied Torah - see how ugly are his deeds, and how corrupted are his ways. About him, the verse states - But[398] when they came to those nations they caused My holy name

---

[394] Shabbat 114a
[395] Proverbs 8:36
[396] Yoma 86a
[397] Isaiah 49:3
[398] Ezekiel 36:20

to be profaned in that it was said of them These are
GOD's people yet they had to leave their land.

Our Rabbis, may their memory be blessed, said in the
Midrash - Anyone[399] who has a **Beit Midrash** [study
hall] in his city but does not go there is liable.

And one who rivals his rabbi's yeshiva is liable.

And one who issues a legal ruling in front of his
teacher is liable. And our Rabbis, may their memory
be blessed, said in the Talmud - That[400] when **Nadav**
and **Abihou** brought a foreign fire, they did not die
for the sin of bringing it, since their intention was for
the sake of a commandment: They said - Behold it is
written in the Torah - And[401] the sons of Aaron the
priest shall put fire on the altar - although fire
descends from Heaven, it is nonetheless a
commandment to also bring ordinary fire. Rather
their punishment was because they issued a legal
ruling in front of Moses, their teacher.

Our Rabbis, may their memory be blessed, said in the
Mishna - Pestilence[402] comes to the world for sins
punishable by death according to the Torah, but
which have not been referred to the court, and for
neglect of the law regarding the fruits of the
sabbatical year. And they also said in the Mishna -

---

[399] Derekh Eretz Rabbah 11:13
[400] Eruvin 63a
[401] Leviticus 1:7
[402] Avot 5:8

At[403] four times pestilence increases - In the fourth year, in the seventh year, at the conclusion of the seventh year and at the conclusion of the **Sukkot** [Feast of Tabernacles] in every year. In the fourth year, on account of the tithe of the poor which is due in the third year; in the seventh year, on account of the tithe of the poor which is due in the sixth year; at the conclusion of the seventh year, on account of the produce of the seventh year; and at the conclusion of the Feast in every year, for robbing the gifts to the poor. We have seen from this that there is death at the hands of the Heavens for robbing the gifts of the poor. And from this, know and examine the severity of one who makes vows of charity but does not fulfill them. Also, one who shuts his hand from his poor brother and turns away from his flesh is similar to these - for since he has already been obligated to give these sums by the Torah, behold he is like someone robbing the gifts of the poor.

The seventh level is the severity of excision

The punishment that one is liable when the consequence of the sin's wanton transgression is excision; when inadvertent, is for one to bring a sin-offering. And so did our Rabbis, may their memory be blessed, say in the Talmud - That[404] a person is only liable to bring a sin-offering for something the punishment of which, when done wantonly, is

---

[403] Avot 5:9
[404] Keritot 2a

excision. This is like the matter that is stated - They[405] shall bear their guilt they shall die childless. And there are two categories of those liable for excision:

The first category is composed of the ones excised only from this world: For example, one who has sexual relations with his sister, the sister of his father, the sister of his mother, the sister of his wife or the sister of his brother after he divorces her or after the death of her husband. And likewise, one who has sexual relations with the wife of his father's brother or with the wife of the mother's brother; one who eats forbidden fat or blood; who eats **Chamets** [leaven] at Passover; one who does forbidden work on Yom Kippur; one who did not eat from a Passover offering; and one who has sexual relations with a menstruant.

The second category is composed of the ones excised from this world and from the next world - For example, one who worships idolatry; one who sins publicly; one who disgraces Torah, such as if he disgraces its students or those that love God, may He be blessed; and those that rescind the covenant on their flesh circumcision. And we will explain the content of these groups more fully in the eleventh level.

And there are times when the merit of someone who is liable for excision lasts him two or three generations. And the delay in the death of evildoers is to pay their reward in this world, and so to destroy

---

[405] Leviticus 20:20

them in the world to come. For it is stated - But[406] who instantly repays with destruction those who hate Him - never slow with those who hate Him, but repaying them instantly. And the thing is explained in the words of King David, peace be upon him - A[407] brutish man cannot know a fool cannot understand this. Though[408] the wicked sprout like grass though all evildoers blossom it is only that they may be destroyed forever. And likewise did Asaf, peace be upon him, say - For[409] I envied the wanton I saw the wicked at ease. Death[410] has no pangs for them their body is healthy. Until I entered God's sanctuary and reflected on their fate. Its explanation is that vengeance upon the evildoers is at their end, as it is stated - For[411] there is no future for the evil man; the lamp of the wicked goes out.

And our Rabbis, may their memory be blessed, said in the Midrash - Rabbi[412] Yoshiyahu said - For three things does the Holy One, blessed be He, delay punishment of evildoers in this world - Lest they repent; because they have done a commandment, such that the Holy One, blessed be, will pay them back in this world; or lest righteous children will come out from them - like we have found when He showed favor to Achaz, such that Hezekiah came out

---

[406] Deuteronomy 7:10
[407] Psalms 92:7
[408] Psalms 92:8
[409] Psalms 73:3
[410] Psalms 73:4
[411] Proverbs 24:20
[412] Kohelet Rabbah 7:32

of him; as well as Amon, from whom Yoshiyahu came out; as well as Shimi, from whom Mordechai came.

And part of the content of excision is the shortening of years; like the matter that is stated - But[413] the years of the wicked will be shortened. But there is a difference in the matter of the shortening of the years between death at the hands of the Heavens and excision. For in the case of excision, the death of the person is before fifty years, whereas in the case of death, it is before sixty - like those that died in the desert. This is meaning to say, that one about whom it was decreed to live for seventy or eighty years, but became liable for death at the hands of the Heavens, will die at less than sixty years. However, there are righteous ones the decree for which is to have less days than sixty years, as they said in the Talmud - One[414] who dies at fifty-two years, this is the death of Samuel of Rama. And it is stated - Do[415] not let the group of Kohathite clans be cut off from the Levites. And our Rabbis, may their memory be blessed, expounded in the Talmud - From[416] this that excision is before fifty years. Its explanation is, let not an accident be how you cause the tribe of the **Kohatites** [Levi family] to be cut off from the service of the Levites. For if you do not guard them - that they should not come to see when the holy vessels are

---

[413] Proverbs 10:27
[414] Taanit 5b
[415] Numbers 4:18
[416] Yerushalmi Bikkurim 2:1

covered - they shall be excised from the service of the Levites, and will die before they are fifty years; as it is stated - But[417] at the age of fifty they shall retire from the work force and shall serve no more.

And among those liable for excision are those that cause a bad trap and corruption for one's offspring, besides that the end of the offspring is to be excised. And that is one who has sexual relations with a menstruant. Such a one is tearing up evil seed; for there will be a strip of brazenness upon the child's forehead while he is still alive. It is as our Rabbis, may their memory be blessed, said in the Midrash, Brazen[418] faced - is that not the son of a menstruant woman? And the iniquities of the son will be upon the bones of the father. For he caused his soul to be a sinner from the womb. And woe is the evil of the evildoer, for it corrupts him; and his soul and his wife's soul will surely be excised. And his ruffian seed will be completely cut off. And behold that the woman is in menstrual impurity even if she is pure from [having] her flow and counted seven clean days - as is her statute - so long as she has not immersed in a source of water, a river or a spring that has forty seah. And the numerical **Gematria** [equivalent] of the thing is walking **Leat** [slowly].

---

[417] Numbers 8:25
[418] Kallah Rabbati 2

And the eighth level is the four death penalties of the court:

And they are stoning, burning, killing and strangulation. Stoning is more severe than burning; burning than killing, which is with a **Decapitation** [sword]; and killing than strangulation. And from the sins punished by stoning - A[419] man who has sexual relations with the wife of his father, with his daughter-in-law or with a male; a **Baal Ov Or Yidaoni** [types of fortune tellers]; one who profanes the Shabbat; one who curses his father or mother; a man who has sexual relations with a betrothed maiden; one who entices others to idolatry; a sorcerer; a rebellious son; and - more severe than all of them - one who blasphemes or worships idolatry.

By burning - A[420] man who has sexual relations with a woman and her daughter, with the daughter of his wife, with the daughter of his son, with the daughter of his daughter, with his mother-in-law, with the mother of his mother-in-law and with the mother of his father-in-law.

By the sword - A[421] murderer and the people of a condemned city.

By strangulation - One[422] who strikes his father or his mother; one who abducts an Israelite; a rebellious

---

[419] Sanhedrin 53a
[420] Sanhedrin 75a
[421] Sanhedrin 76b
[422] Sanhedrin 84b

elder according to the court; a false prophet; one who prophesies in the name of idol worship; and one who has sexual relations with a married woman.

Our Rabbis, may their memory be blessed, said in the Talmud - From[423] the day that the Temple was destroyed, although the four death penalties of the court have ceased, ...the principle of the four death penalties of the court has not ceased - One who is liable for stoning, either he falls from a roof or an animal tramples him. One who is liable for burning, either he falls into a fire or a snake bites him as a snakebite causes a burning sensation. One who is liable for killing, robbers come upon him and execute him. One who is liable for strangling either drowns in a river or dies of **Bisronekhi** [diphtheria].

And the law of a man who has sexual relations with a maidservant is similar to those liable for the death penalties of the court in two ways. For our Rabbis, may their memory be blessed, said in the Talmud - One[424] who has intercourse with an Egyptian woman, zealots may accost him, like the matter which is written - He[425] followed the Israelite man into the chamber and stabbed both of them, the Israelite man and the woman, through the belly. Then the plague against the Israelites was checked. And this matter is more severe than the death penalties of the court, for they do not put to death, except with witnesses and a

---

[423] Sanhedrin 37b
[424] Sanhedrin 81b
[425] Numbers 25:8

warning and by the decision of the Talmud - Sanhedrin, which is not the case here.

And besides these, the evildoer discussed profaned the holy ones of God, whom He loved, and had intercourse with the daughter of a foreign god. And every foreign son he fathers will be a snare and a trap and a reminder of the iniquity - the father will carry the iniquity of the son. And he betrayed God, for he bore foreign children.

And secondly, the Heavens will reveal his iniquity and the earth will oppose him. For his sin will maintain his decline. And behold he will be similar to those liable for the death penalties of the court after the destruction of the Temple, such that they are judged from the Heavens - that they will die in their rebellion and not die like every other person, as we have explained. And it is stated - May[426] the Lord leave he who does this without anyone awake or coherent in the tents of Yaakov. And our Rabbis explained in the Talmud - Awake[427] among the Sages, or **coherent** among the disciples.

And our Rabbis, may their memory be blessed, said in Mishna - Seven[428] kinds of punishment come to the world for seven categories of transgression: When some of them give tithes, and others do not give tithes, a famine from drought comes some go hungry,

---

[426] Malachi 2:12
[427] Shabbat 55b
[428] Avot 5:8

and others are satisfied. When they have all decided
not to give tithes, a famine from tumult and drought
comes; [When they have, in addition, decided] not to
set apart the dough-offering, an all-consuming famine
comes. Pestilence comes to the world for sins
punishable by death according to the Torah, but
which have not been referred to the court, and for
neglect of the law regarding the fruits of the
sabbatical year. The sword comes to the world for the
delay of judgment, and for the perversion of
judgment, and because of those who teach the Torah
not in accordance with the accepted law. Wild[429]
beasts come to the world for swearing in vain, and for
the profanation of the Name. Exile comes to the world
for idolatry, for sexual sins and for bloodshed, and for
[transgressing the commandment of] the [year of the]
release of the land. At four times pestilence increases:
in the fourth year, in the seventh year and at the
conclusion of the seventh year, and at the conclusion
of the Feast [of Tabernacles] in every year. In the
fourth year, on account of the tithe of the poor which
is due in the third year. In the seventh year, on
account of the tithe of the poor which is due in the
sixth year; At the conclusion of the seventh year, on
account of the produce of the seventh year; And at the
conclusion of the Feast [of Tabernacles] in every
year, for robbing the gifts to the poor.

And among the things that are pleasant for the
reprimands to watch and testify about the people, are
to keep in view the fate of the lawless concerning the

---

[429] Avot 5:9

laws of the Shabbat - regarding the main and derivative categories of forbidden work. For many of them have vanished from the eyes of the masses. And there is no one speaking up and no one making it heard.

And the ninth level

Is the severity of the sins for which one is killed rather than transgressing them: Our Rabbis, may their memory be blessed, said in the Talmud - With[430] regard to all transgressions in the Torah, if a person is told - **Transgress and you will not be killed**, he may transgress and not be killed, ...as it is stated - You[431] shall keep My statutes and My judgments which a person shall do and he shall live by them and live by them and not to die by them. Except for idol worship, forbidden sexual relations, and bloodshed. For if a person tells him about one of these three, **Transgress and you will not be killed**, he must let himself be killed and not transgress - even when they tell him to do the transgression in private; whereas with other sins, such a law would only apply in public, as it is stated - That[432] I may be sanctified in the midst of the Israelite people.

And regarding these three transgressions, even the punishment for their lighter side is more stringent than several weighty transgressions. And our Rabbis,

---

430 Sanhedrin 74a
431 Leviticus 18:5
432 Leviticus 22:32

may their memory be blessed, called the lighter side of a transgression, the dust of the transgression. And they said in the Talmud - One[433] may heal oneself from a disease that brings a mortal danger with anything except for wood of an **Asheira** [a tree designated for idolatry] - such that if they say to him, bring leaves from an **Asheira** and you will be healed by them, he should allow himself to die and not be healed by them. And even though one who benefits from the wood of an **Asheira** is not worshiping idolatry - since it is the dust of idolatry, he should let himself die and not be healed by it. For he would be strengthening the hands of the worshipers of the **Asheira**, lest they would say - The **Asheira** saved him.

And likewise with forbidden sexual relations - for example, if a man desired a married woman and they said to him - Your healing will not be accomplished until she stands in front of you naked - or that she should talk with him - he should let himself die and not breach the fence around the prohibition of a married woman. And from this, you can recognize the weightiness of touching the hand of a married woman.

And behold the dust of murder is whitening someone **else's face** [embarrassing someone]. Since his face turns white and the ruddy appearance leaves it, it is similar to the draining of blood caused by murder. And so did our Rabbis, may their memory be blessed,

---

[433] Pesachim 25a

say in the Talmud - And[434] secondly because the pain of the embarrassment is more bitter than death. Therefore, our Rabbis, may their memory be blessed, said in the Talmud - Really[435] it is preferable for a person to make himself fall into a fiery furnace, and not whiten the face of his fellow in public. But they did not say this about other weighty transgressions. Indeed, they compared the dust of murder to actual murder: And just like they said that he must let himself be killed and not murder; they likewise said that he should make himself fall into a fiery furnace, and not whiten the face of his fellow in public. And they learned this from the matter of Tamar, as it is stated - As[436] she was being brought out she sent this message to her father-in-law It is by the man to whom these belong that I'm pregnant and she added Examine these whose seal and cord and staff are these. Behold even though she was being taken out to be burned to death, she did not reveal that she was pregnant from Yehudah, so as not to whiten his face.

And they also said in the Talmud - Anyone[437] who descends to Gehinnom eventually ascends, except for three who descend and do not ascend - One who whitens the face of his fellow in public; one who calls his fellow a derogatory name; and one who has sexual relations with a married woman. Behold that they compared one who whitens the face of his fellow in

---

434 Bava Metzia 58b
435 Ketuvot 67b
436 Genesis 38:25
437 Bava Metzia 58b

public and one who calls his fellow a derogatory name - in that he also whitens his face - to one who has sexual relations with a married woman, which is from the transgressions for which one should die and not transgress.

And they also said in the Talmud - One[438] who whitens the face of his fellow in public has no share in the world to come. And that which they did not say this about a murderer - that he has no share in the world to come the explanation is that since **whitening** [the face] is a derivative of murder - as he said above, that it is the dust of murder - murder should be no worse than **whitening** [the face] in this context; yet they did not say that he has no share in the world to come - it is because one who whitens the face of his fellow does not recognize the greatness of the sin. So, his soul is not bitter towards himself about this iniquity, as is a murderer. Therefore, he is far from repentance.

And our Rabbis, may their memory be blessed, said in the Talmud about Shabbat - That[439] it corresponds to all of the other commandments. And our Rabbis, may their memory be blessed, also said in the Talmud - That[440] one who worships idolatry or publicly profanes Shabbat is one who denies the whole entire Torah; so, his slaughter renders an animal a carcass, and he makes wine forbidden by touching it.

---

[438] Bava Metzia 59a
[439] Yerushalmi Nedarim 3:14
[440] Chullin 5a

The tenth level is the severity of the transgressions for which those who do them have no share in the world to come: All creatures are created for God's glory, as it is stated - All[441] who are linked to My name, whom I have created, formed, and made for My glory. Hence it is logically understood that one who profanes God's name and disgraces His word will lose his hope. For it is not enough that he does not fulfill that which is expected from him from the essence of his creation - to glorify God and to sanctify Him - but he rather puts out his hands to do the inverse and the opposite, and to profane His holy name. And so is it written - But[442] the person whether citizen or stranger who acts defiantly reviles God that person shall be cut off from among the people. Because[443] it was the word of God that was spurned and God's commandment that was violated that person shall be cut off and bears the guilt. For death does not atone for him, and he has no share in the world to come. Therefore, it mentions, **he bears his iniquity** in this matter - for it does not mention this in other excisions. And the explanation of **who acts defiantly literally, with a high hand**, is such that he publicly does sins known to people. And likewise, one who removes the yoke of the kingdom of the Heavens - and even privately, because he too is doing it defiantly. And the content of one who removes the yoke is, for example, one who is defiant in eating carcasses or forbidden fat or blood, or to profane

---

[441] Isaiah 43:7
[442] Numbers 15:30
[443] Numbers 15:31

holidays - even though he does not transgress the
other commandments. Since he removed the yoke of
one **negative** commandment from upon himself, he
has already rebelled against God, may He be blessed.
It is true that sometimes righteous people also
stumble in a sin - but this is only incidental, when his
impulse overpowers him. Moreover, the righteous
person's soul is bitter with him about the matter, and
he will be careful about it afterwards. However, the
person who thinks in his heart to remove the yoke of
one **negative** commandment from upon him anytime
he wants to transgress it, is called a heretic for one
thing. And we have already explained this earlier in
the first section of the Gates of Repentance. And they,
may their memory be blessed, said in the Talmud -
Regarding[444] all shepherds, we do not save them... as
they engage in such behavior. And the notion of the
shepherds is about people that would graze their
animals in the fields of others, removing the yoke of
the prohibition of theft from upon themselves. And
their category is the category of the heretic to eat
carcasses, or one of the other transgressions, out of
desire. But one who is a heretic to eat carcasses in
order to anger God is a full-fledged **Apikoros**
[heretic]. And the content of angering, is that he does
not sin out of a desire for desirable food. Rather even
if there is also slaughtered meat in front of him, he
will take from the carcass. For he is rebelling, and
does not accept upon himself to beware of the
prohibition of carcasses at all.

[444] Avodah Zarah 26a

Behold we have explained the matter of - But[445] the person whether citizen or stranger who acts defiantly reviles God that person shall be cut off from among the people. And our Rabbis, may their memory be blessed, said in the Talmud that - Because[446] he has spurned the word of the Lord and has breached His commandment, this is a reference to one who says - The Torah is not from Heaven... one who reveals the Torah inappropriately; one who spurns Torah scholars; and one who spurns the festivals. For even though he has Torah and good deeds in his hands, he has no share in the world to come.

And the explanation of one who **MAGALA PNEM** [reveals the Torah inappropriately], is a man who has the temerity to say things about the Torah which are not so - And he says that some of the verses or some of the recounting of things were written for nothing. And from his arrogance and his pride, he says in his heart that since he does not grasp how to get to the nature of the explanation of the things, thinking that there is nothing hidden to it. And it is stated - For[447] it is not an empty thing from you. And our Rabbis, may their memory be blessed, said in the Talmud - If[448] it is empty, it is from you. For you do not know to explain the reason for the thing. And likewise, one who leaves one of the words of the Torah and does not concede to it - this is certainly revealing the face

---

[445] Numbers 15:30
[446] Sanhedrin 99a
[447] Deuteronomy 32:47
[448] Yerushalmi Ketubot 51a

of the Torah - for example one who says - Of what benefit are the Torah scholars for us? If they become wise, they become wise for themselves, and do not bequeath anything to us. And behold they have contradicted that which is written in the Torah - And[449] I will raise spare the whole place for their sake.

And the content of one who spurns the festivals, is that he does work on the intermediate days of the festival and spurns the punishment, because the prohibition of work on the intermediate days of the festival is not explicit in the Torah. And this is in the way of one who is a heretic for one thing, to anger - as we have explained, such that he has no share in the world to come. And our Rabbis, may their memory be blessed, said in the Talmud - That[450] one who comes to convert and says - Behold, I accept all of the Torah except for one matter from the words of the Sages. We do not accept him. And they, may their memory be blessed, said in the Talmud - One[451] who spurns the holidays is like one who worships idolatry as it is stated - You[452] shall observe the Feast of Unleavened Bread; and adjacent to it is - You[453] shall observe the Feast of Unleavened Bread for on this very day I brought your ranks out of the land of Egypt you shall observe this day throughout the ages as an institution for all time. explained in the Talmud[454] -

449 Genesis 18:26
450 Bekhorot 30b
451 Makkot 23a
452 Exodus 34:18
453 Exodus 34:17
454 Chagigah 18a

You[455] shall observe the Feast of Unleavened Bread for on this very day I brought your ranks out of the land of Egypt you shall observe this day throughout the ages as an institution for all time. Observe it to not do work all of the Feast of Unleavened Bread. And we were warned with this about work on the intermediate days of the festival. And that which it is written - A[456] complete **Shabbaton** [rest] on the first day, and a complete rest on the eighth day. Is because there are many types of work that are permitted on the intermediate days of the festival, as is explained in their words, may they be blessed.

And that which they, may their memory be blessed, said that one who spurns Torah scholars, spurns the word of God and does not have a share in the world to come - this is something with a root in logic and a basis in analysis. And behold we find good reason and knowledge about this matter - King Solomon, peace be upon him, said - The[457] wise shall obtain honor, but disgrace uplifts dullards. And likewise - And[458] I am prayer. Means a man of prayer; and - You[459] dwell in the midst of deceit. Means in the midst of people of deceit. Hence its explanation is that a lowly and disgraceful person uplifts dullard; and he honors and praises them. For there are great benefits in the honoring of the wise and upright; and many large snares in the honoring of the dullards and evildoers, and in putting them on a pedestal. For when the wise

---

[455] Exodus 34:17
[456] Leviticus 23:39
[457] Proverbs 3:38
[458] Psalms 109:4
[459] Jeremiah 9:5

are lauded and put on a pedestal, their words are heard more, the whole nation accompanies them and their counsel appears right to them. Secondly, when people see their honor, they will learn a teaching, to offer honor and amplify knowledge. And they, may their memory be blessed, said in the Talmud - A[460] person should always engage in Torah study... even if not for its own sake as through Torah study not for its sake, he will come to [doing it] for its sake. Thirdly, many of those asleep at heart will be aroused from their sleep, when they see the splendorous honor of the Torah, will recognize its sublimity and the desire for it will enter their hearts. So, their involvement with it will be for God, may He be blessed, and to serve Him with a complete heart.

Behold these are honorable reasons - strong as a mirror of cast metal. But there is another honorable reason above them all - and we hinted to it in the introduction to our words about the matters of the evil groups mentioned: As it is known that among the ways to sanctify His name, may He be blessed, is to make known - with every expression of the lips, with every hint of the eyes and with every practice and movement of the hands - that the foundation of man's soul and his glorious adornment, and the good and the essence, and the purpose and the preciousness in it, is the service of God, may He be blessed, and fear of Him; as it is written - For[461] this is all of man. And this thing is the glory of God, may He be blessed. And the

---

[460] Pesachim 50b
[461] Ecclesiastes 12:13

ones that spurn Torah scholars and fear of Him are nullifying this knowledge and showing the opposite with their behavior. And it is as if they are saying, the service of God is not the essence; and the root of the matter is found somewhere besides the service of God, may He be blessed. So, they are profaning the Torah - therefore they shall be lost from among the congregation. And it will **Vayikhlu** [cease] in their mouths. It appears to me that it should say **Vayiratsu** [pleased] with their mouths - like the usage as - The[462] end of those pleased **Yirtsu** [pleased] with their mouths, which according to some commentators is an expression of speaking. Or maybe it should say -And they will be able to say **Vayokhlu Leimor** [finished to say] with their mouths - meaning to say that they will be able to say, by way of an excuse. On my opinion, it should say, express **Vayokhlu** [finished] with their mouths. As they are serving God without involvement in Torah study. Is it not a well-known thing that the service does not survive without those that study Torah, who meditate upon it day and night? For they instruct knowledge and bear understanding of the times, to know what the Israelites should do. And they hold up the Torah in Israel, so that it will not be forgotten from the mouth of their seed. And in a place where there is no one involved with Torah, the snares grow and there is no upright person. Therefore, the servants of God, may He be blessed, honor the sages of the Torah for the sake of God's honor; and to make known that only His service is the essence of existence. And since it has been clarified that God,

---

[462] Psalms 49:14

may He be blessed, created everything for His glory - a man is obligated to pay attention at all times, to honor God and sanctify Him with all of his words; to exult Him, to praise Him and to always bless Him, as it is stated - I[463] bless the Lord at all times; praise of Him is ever in my mouth. And whenever he stands among the people and speaks with his friends, he should reflect with understanding, be exacting and supervise everything that comes out of his mouth; to sanctify God with his words; to speak in praise of His service and in glorification of His fear; and to praise His works servants and those that fear Him. And through this, he will merit - with the meditation of his heart and with the expression of his lips, and without exertion or the actions of his hands - great merit that reach to the heavens. For this is from the essence of man's creation. And it is stated - For[464] silver the crucible for gold the furnace and a man is tested by his praise. And its explanation is that the virtues of a man are according to what he praises - If he praises good deeds, the sages and the righteous ones - know that you have tested that he is a good man and the root of justice is found within him. For he would not find it in his heart to praise the good and good people with all of his words - and to detest sins and spurn their masters - without being disgusted by evil and choosing the good. And even if it is possible that he has some hidden iniquities in his hand, he is nevertheless among the lovers of justice. So, his root is from the right choice and he is from the

---

[463] Psalms 34:2
[464] Proverbs 27:21

congregation of those that honor God. But one who praises detestable acts or praises evildoers is a complete evildoer and profanes the service of God.

King Solomon, peace be upon him, also said - Like[465] a muddied spring, a ruined fountain Is a righteous man fallen before a wicked one. It[466] is not good to eat much honey nor is it honorable to search for honor. For when a man muddies a spring with his foot, its waters are temporarily moved; afterwards the water is still and becomes clear, like at the beginning. So is the righteous person - When he is fallen before an evildoer, his level is not lowered and he is not diminished because of it. And if he is temporarily murky - a righteous man falls seven times and rises and [then] returns to his strength and his glory. It is not good to eat much honey. But much perusing of the honor of the righteous is an honor for the peruser. For righteous ones are mentioned in the verse above; and the word **much**, also refers to **peruse honor** - as is its function in many places to refer to two phrases. But the snares found in the honor of evildoers are many and well known. For with their honor, there is a profanation of the Torah and the service of God; and it is a sin that destroys from the soul to the flesh.

Secondly, it is because many are pulled behind them and take hold of their actions.

And thirdly, because those that associate with them -

---

[465] Proverbs 25:26
[466] Proverbs 25:27

even if they do not do their deeds - receive punishment like them, as we have already mentioned. And fourthly, because they are bringing down the honor of people of truth, and nullifying their service. And there is no success in the honor of the righteous, except after the lowering of the [evildoers'] honor - as it is stated - The[467] house of the evildoers will be demolished, and the tent of the upright will flourish. And it is also stated - A[468] city is built up by the blessing of the upright, but it is torn down by the speech of the evildoers.

And our Rabbis, may their memory be blessed, also said in the Talmud - That[469] included in that which is written - He[470] spurned the word of the Lord, is one that speaks words of Torah in filthy alleys, anyone who has the possibility of being involved with Torah and is not so involved and one who reads the books of heretics; and that, that which it is written, **and he rescinds His commandment** - is regarding one who rescinds the covenant of the flesh circumcision.

And we also learned in the Talmud - All[471] of the Jewish people have a share in the world to come, as it is stated - And[472] your people all of them righteous Shall possess the land for all time They are the shoot that I planted My handiwork in which I glory. And

---

[467] Proverbs 14:11
[468] Proverbs 11:11
[469] Berakhot 24b
[470] Numbers 15:31
[471] Sanhedrin 90a
[472] Isaiah 60:21

these are the ones who have no share in the world to come - One who says that there is no resurrection of the dead derived from the Torah, and that the Torah is not from the Heavens, and an **Apikoros** [heretic]. And our Rabbis, may their memory be blessed, warned us in this statement to believe that faith in the resurrection of the dead is to be found in the Torah, and that it is one of its principles. And one of the places that resurrection of the dead is made explicit in the Torah is as it is stated - I[473] deal death and give life; I wounded and I will heal. And our Rabbis, may their memory be blessed, said in the Talmud - It[474] might be, death is with one person and bringing to life with another hence we learn - But[475] I will bring healing to you and cure you of your wounds declares God Though they called you Outcast That Zion whom no one seeks out.

And they, may their memory be blessed, explained about the matter of the **Apikoros** [heretic] in the Talmud - That[476] he is a man who does not act in a manner of awe and exaltation towards Torah scholars, even though he does not spurn them. For example, he spurns his fellow in front of a Torah scholar, and he does not pay attention to the honor of the sage's Torah status. For since the Torah is not exalted in his eyes - to act with honor towards it - he has no share in the world to come. For this one too will be considered as

---

[473] Deuteronomy 32:39
[474] Pesachim 68a
[475] Jeremiah 30:17
[476] Sanhedrin 99b

one of those that profane the Torah. Therefore, our Rabbis, may their memory be blessed, said in the Talmud - Fear[477] the Lord, your God - This[478] is to include Torah scholars.

And secondly, because awe of them contributes to fear of the Heavens. For when their words are obeyed by way of their awe, will they not teach and guide the people to fear the glorious and awesome God? And it is stated - And[479] the people stood in fear of the Lord and of Samuel. And also, in the category of **Apikoros** [heretic] is one who says - What have those studying benefited us with their study? Is there anything about which he can say - See, this is new? He has never permitted us any crow; and he has never forbidden us the young pigeons. And these people have also never heard or opened their ears to the benefits found in the occupation with Torah. And we have written some of these benefits in the Gate of the Torah, with God's help. That is so that the hearts will yearn for the Torah. And those that do not have the ability to study, will know the exalted honor of occupation with Torah, such that they will merit its knowledge and not lose their souls from the world to come.

And also, in the category of **Apikoros** [heretic] is one who calls his teacher by his name. And they said in the Talmud - That[480] the reason for which Gehazi was

---

[477] Pesachim 22b
[478] Deuteronomy 6:13
[479] Samuel-A 12:18
[480] Sanhedrin 100a

punished was because he called his teacher by his name, as it is stated - This[481] is the woman and this is her son whom Elisha revived.

And behold that the principle behind all of the punishments mentioned in this level is because of profaning the Torah. And our Rabbis, may their memory be blessed, said in the Talmud - that[482] the sin of profanation is bigger than all of the transgressions.

And it is not possible to atone for it with repentance and afflictions, as will be explained in the Gate of the Parts of Atonement. And our Rabbis, may their memory be blessed, said in the Talmud - There[483] is no deferral with the punishment for profaning God's name - whether one is inadvertent or volitional. And now stand and reflect upon our great obligation to sanctify His name: As the essence of that which God, may He be blessed, sanctified us with His Torah and His commandments and separated us to be a people for Him was to sanctify Him and to fear Him. Hence it is fit from the ones he sanctified to be holy - in that even the vessels used to serve in front of God, may He be blessed, need to be sanctified; as it is stated - You[484] shall not profane My holy name that I may be sanctified in the midst of the Israelite people I am the Lord who sanctified you. Note and understand that the matter that we said can be found explicitly in this

---

[481] Kings-B 8:5
[482] Yerushalmi Nedarim 3:14
[483] Kiddushin 40a
[484] Leviticus 22:32

verse - It is stated - He[485] ordered His covenant for all time; His name is holy and awesome. Its explanation is, because - He[486] sent redemption to His people He ordained His covenant for all time His name is holy and awesome. And commanded us with His commandments - to sanctify Him and to fear Him. Hence, it is written after it - The[487] beginning of wisdom is the fear of the LORD all who practice it gain sound understanding Praise of Him is everlasting. And through the holiness of the commandments - when we sanctify God, may He be blessed, we are associated with the supernal holy ones that sanctify and venerate Him, as it is stated - A[488] God greatly dreaded in the council of holy beings held in awe by all around Him.

There are other groups that do not have a share in the world to come: And they are the group of the enemies of the Lord, may He be blessed; the group of the destroyers of the vineyard of the Lord; and the group of the ones inflicting fear in the land of the living. Behold we will present their content and the proof of their punishment explicit in the Torah: For the group of the enemies of Lord will be lost from the world to come, as it is stated - But[489] who requites with destruction those who hate Him to his face never slow with those who hate Him, but requiting them to his face. Its explanation is that he repays the reward of

---

[485] Psalms 111:9
[486] Psalms 111:9
[487] Psalms 111:10
[488] Psalms 89:8
[489] Deuteronomy 7:10

the commandments fulfilled by those that hate Him, in this world - in order to destroy them from getting to] the world to come. And its **Targum** [translation by Onkelos] is - And He repays those that hate Him the good that they do in front of Him, in their lives, to destroy them. And King David said - But[490] the evildoers shall be lost and the enemies of the Lord shall be like heavy sheep completely consumed in smoke. And he mentioned the expression, **loss**, with the evildoers, as it is used for distress and exile - as the matter that is stated - And[491] in that day a great ram's horn shall be sounded and the strayed who are in the land of Assyria and the expelled who are in the land of Egypt shall come and worship GOD on the holy mount in Jerusalem. - My[492] people were lost sheep. And - I[493] have strayed like a lost sheep. And it is also used for death, as the matter that is stated - Were[494] not your teaching my delight I would have perished in my affliction. And - At[495] the loss of my kindred. And - And[496] I will cause that soul to be lost. Meaning excision from this world. For evildoers are punished with difficulties and afflictions or with death, and they are also punished with the judgement for their deeds in the world to come. But King David compared the enemies of the Lord to the meat of sheep, as it will become coals. Therefore, it will be

---

[490] Psalms 37:20
[491] Isaiah 27:13
[492] Jeremiah 50:6
[493] Psalms 119:176
[494] Psalms 119:92
[495] Esther 8:6
[496] Leviticus 23:30

completely consumed in smoke. Just like the fat of sheep is consumed in smoke, so too will the enemies of the Lord be consumed. For their souls will be consumed and lost from the world to come. And it is stated - Visiting[497] the guilt of the parents upon the children, upon the third and upon the fourth generations of those who hate Me.

And the matter of those that hate the Lord is sometimes found also among those that fulfill the commandments and are careful not to commit any transgression - in deed or in speech - if their soul is upset and it is difficult in their hearts when their fellows are involved in Torah. And it is bad in their eyes when people serve God and fear Him. It is like you say about a man who does not want people to honor the king and serve him, since he hates the king; all the more so if they carry their thoughts into action. As they dissuade people's hearts from occupation in Torah and from the commandments, for they hate the Lord. And likewise, people who are miserly about the honor of righteous and upright Torah students, and hate the glory of their crown; or if it is bad in their hearts when they come to them and become the leaders of the generation. And so is it written - For[498] it is not you that they have rejected it is Me they have rejected as their king. And all the more so, if they seek to embarrass their honor or to humiliate them. And likewise, if they love the honor of the evildoers and compare them to the proliferation of the dust - for

---

[497] Exodus 20:5
[498] Samuel-A 8:7

these really hate the Lord and they do not want His pure service. Nor do they want the elevation of His holy fear, or that His servants and those that fear Him greatly proliferate.

And likewise, the group of destroyers of the vineyard of the Lord - such as those that cause the masses to sin - are haters of the Lord. As you would say that people that destroy the cities of the king or his vineyards and orchards are haters of the king. And it is stated - For[499] the vineyard of the Lord of Hosts Is the House of Israel and the seedlings he lovingly tended are the men of Judah. And it is stated - They[500] plot craftily against Your people take counsel against Your treasured ones. And it is stated - Unanimous[501] in their counsel they have made an alliance against You. And it is stated - And[502] regents intrigue together against the Lord and against His anointed. Therefore, our Rabbis, may their memory be blessed, said in the Talmud - That[503] those that sinned and cause the masses to sin descend to Gehinnom and are judged there for generations and generations.

And Ezekiel, peace be upon him, spoke about the group of those inflicting fear in the land of the living - There[504] too is Elam and all her masses round about her tomb all of them slain fallen by the sword they

---

[499] Isaiah 5:7
[500] Psalms 83:4
[501] Psalms 83:6
[502] Psalms 2:2
[503] Rosh Hashanah 17a
[504] Ezekiel 32:24

who descended uncircumcised to the lowest part of the netherworld who struck terror in the land of the living now they bear their shame with those who have gone down to the Pit. They[505] made a bed for her among the slain with all her masses their graves are round about her They are all uncircumcised slain by the sword Though their terror was once spread over the land of the living they bear their shame with those who have gone into the Pit they are placed among the slain. Meshech[506] and Tubal and all their masses are there their graves are round about They are all uncircumcised pierced through by the sword they who once struck terror in the land of the living. And[507] they do not lie with the fallen uncircumcised warriors who went down to **Sheol** [Hell] with their battle gear who put their swords beneath their heads and their iniquities upon their bones for the terror of the warriors was upon the land of the living. We learned from this that death does not atone for them. Indeed, their iniquities are upon their bones forever. And our Rabbis, may their memory be blessed, said in the Talmud - But[508] the heretics and the informers and the **Apikoros** [heretic] and those who denied the Torah and those who denied the resurrection of the dead and those who separated from the ways of the Jewish community and refused to share the suffering and those who cast their fear over the land of the living and those who sinned and caused the masses to sin for

---

[505] Ezekiel 32:25
[506] Ezekiel 32:26
[507] Ezekiel 32:27
[508] Rosh Hashanah 17a

example Jeroboam son of Nebat and his company all of these people descend to Gehenna and are judged there for generations and generations, as it is stated - And[509] they shall go forth, and look upon the carcasses of the men that have rebelled against Me for their worm shall not die neither shall their fire be quenched and they shall be an abhorrence to all flesh.

And the punishment of those that inflict their fear in the land of the living is from five aspects - two are from himself and three are from the people - The two that are from the angle of himself - The first is that man is maggots and worms; and he is called this even when he is alive. Yet it is not enough for him that he does not bow and does not lower himself, but he also lords it over others, not for the sake of the Heavens? And even the thought of pride - without lording it - is destructive to a man, as it is stated - Every[510] haughty person is an abomination to the Lord.

And the second is that a man is obligated to always set up frameworks of the heart to enshrine dread and fear in his heart in front of God, may He be blessed. But it is stated about the evildoers - They[511] have not said in their hearts **Let us revere the Lord our God**. But the man who inflicts his fear in the land of the living, not for the sake of the Heavens, does not have dread in his heart in front of God and wants to impose his own fear upon His creatures. And instead of his

---

[509] Isaiah 66:24
[510] Proverbs 16:5
[511] Jeremiah 5:24

having to set up thoughts to enshrine the dread of God in his heart, he designs them to impose his own fear on the people of God, may He be blessed. And it is stated - He[512] who rules men justly He who rules in awe of God. The explanation of this is that it is fit for a righteous man who fears God to be a ruler of men. Since once he fears God, may He be blessed, it is fitting for people to fear him.

And the three that are from the aspect of the people: The first is that he distresses the public when he instills his fear upon them. And it is stated - Do[513] not wrong one another. And that is with regards to distress about things that we have already explained.

And the second is that several stumbling blocks come as a result of his instilling his fear - as our Rabbis, may their memory be blessed, said in the Talmud - A[514] person should never impose excessive fear within his household; as the husband of the concubine of Gibeah imposed excessive fear upon her and this caused the downfall of many tens of thousands of Jews.

And the third is that the holy people who are servants of God, may He be blessed, should not humble themselves to flesh and blood. So, it is not fitting that the fear of flesh and blood be upon them except for

---

[512] Samuel-B 23:3
[513] Leviticus 25:17
[514] Gittin 6b

the sake of the Heavens. As it is stated - For[515] it is to Me that the Israelites are servants. - They are My servants, and not the servants of servants. And it is stated - But[516] you shall be to Me a kingdom of priests and a holy nation. The expression, priests, is to mean masters and officers; and like this usage is - And[517] David's sons were priests. And the whole nation is called a kingdom, from the usage - There[518] is no nation or kingdom. For[519] the nation or the kingdom. The explanation in the Thora - Is[520] that you shall be a kingdom that is all officers, such that the yoke of flesh and blood shall not be upon you. And it is stated - What[521] ails you that you fear man who must die. And it is also stated - Fear[522] not the insults of men. And our Rabbis, may their memory be blessed, said in the Talmud - From[523] the time when those who say to evil good; and to good, evil, proliferated, they removed the yoke of the Heavens from upon themselves, and the yoke of flesh and blood was thrown upon them.

And King David, peace be upon him, said - Rise[524] O LORD Let not men have power let the nations be

---

[515] Leviticus 25:55
[516] Exodus 19:6
[517] Samuel-A 8:18
[518] Kings-B 18:10
[519] Isaiah 60:12
[520] Exodus 19:6
[521] Isaiah 51:12
[522] Isaiah 51:7
[523] Sotah 47b
[524] Psalms 9:20-21

judged in Your presence. Strike[525] fear into them O LORD let the nations know they are only men. Selah. We have learned from this that at a time when a man has power, he does not recognize that he is only a man. For dominion is not fitting for man, except for the sake of the Heavens.

And now we will explain the matter of the punishment of those that separate from the ways of the community, and that he is included in the punishments of the groups that we mentioned above: When the heads of the people and the holy communities gather to serve God, may He be blessed, and make agreements to place commandments upon themselves - they are surely sanctifying God, may He be magnified and sanctified, as it is stated - Then[526] He became King in Jeshurun when the heads of the people assembled the tribes of Israel together. And it is also stated - The[527] great of the peoples are gathered together the people of Abraham's God for the shields of the earth belong to God He is greatly exalted. Israel is called - **peoples**, because they are twelve tribes, like the matter that is stated - They[528] invite the peoples to the mountain. But they are one people to serve God; therefore, is it stated - **The people of Abraham's God**. And the kings and the officers are called - **shields**, from the usage - Grease[529] the shields. The explanation of Psalms is, the great of the peoples

---

[525] Psalms 9:20-21
[526] Deuteronomy 33:5
[527] Psalms 47:10
[528] Deuteronomy 33:19
[529] Isaiah 21:5

gathered together to serve God, may He be exalted, because their kings and their officers are for God - as they are His servants and his faithful, like the matter that is stated - Truly[530] our shield is of the Lord our King of the Holy One of Israel. **He is greatly exalted**, since the Holy One, blessed be He, is exalted and glorified in His world in their gathering together and in their service. And the man that separates from the ways of the community is like an opponent of the agreement about the service of God; and like one who exits from the aggregate that is sanctifying God. So, he shows himself to not want to be in their council, nor be written in their writings. Behold he is thus among those that profane the service and is included in the groups that we mentioned - that are scorning the word of God, and do not have a share in the world to come. And secondly, they dissuade the heart of the weak-minded by their separating from the ways of the community, and so are among those that cause the many to sin.

Now we will explain the matter of those that forsake God; and we shall say that they are people that do not have the yoke of the fear of the Heavens, so they fulfill the commandments in a rote fashion. So, when the impulse overpowers this man and the spirit [to sin] passes over him, and he transgresses and will be guilty - he does not sigh and he does not worry about his sin. He ate and wiped his mouth; but in his eyes, he is like one that did not do evil. It is like the matter

---

[530] Psalms 89:19

that is stated - What[531] transgression says to the wicked is within my heart the dread of God is not in front of his eyes.

And there are some from this evil group for which it is not enough that they do not wear trembling when they bypass the law and the testimonies, but they praise and bless themselves when they fulfill their desires. So, they bring anger and scorn before God, as it is stated - The[532] wicked crows about his unbridled lusts the grasping man reviles and scorns the Lord. And Isaiah, peace be upon him, spoke about the destruction of this group - as it is stated - But[533] rebels and sinners shall all be crushed, and those who forsake the Lord shall perish. And he compared the rebels and the sinners to a broken vessel that has a remnant; but he said that - **those that forsake God shall perish**. For they have no share in the world to come, as the matter is stated - And[534] leave of them neither stock nor boughs.

And the destruction of the groups mentioned is at a time when they have not repented. But if they repented from their evil ways, their souls escape destruction - like the matter that is stated - Repent[535] O rebellious children I will heal your afflictions.

Explanation of the words of iniquity of four groups -

---

[531] Psalms 36:2
[532] Psalms 10:3
[533] Isaiah 1:28
[534] Malachi 3:19
[535] Jeremiah 3:22

Our Rabbis, may their memory be blessed, said in the Talmud - Four[536] groups will not greet the Divine Presence - The group of scoffers, the group of liars, the group of flatterers, and the group of slanderers. The group of cynics, as it is written - He[537] draws His hand from cynics; the group of liars, as it is written - He[538] who speaks falsehood shall not dwell before My eyes; the group of flatterers, as it is written - That[539] a flatterer cannot come before Him; the group of slanderers, as it is written - For[540] You are not a God who has pleasure in wickedness, evil shall not sojourn with You.

Now we will speak about the nature of their contents and the nature of their aspects, so as to enlighten you with understanding about some of their depths; and we will divide them into sections. We will reveal the end of the weighty punishments of disgusting deeds, and acquire much benefit through the analyses of the sections. For perhaps you have never stood over our words, you have not properly examined the weightiness of the transgression of each part of the sections. So maybe you have never seen the sight of the weightiness of the punishment that is found in each one of them. And maybe you have seen its edge, but you have not seen all of it. And with each section that we organize, the first is worse than the second they will be in descending order. And from our words

[536] Sotah 42a
[537] Hosea 7:5
[538] Psalms 101:7
[539] Job 13:16
[540] Psalms 5:5

- even from the light parts - that we will mention, you will recognize the terror of darkness, and know that their ends are the ways of death. And maybe you have not yet opened your ears, and it appeared like a straight path in front of you. But now that we will write about their bitterness, their fear will come into your thoughts. Also, the correct teachings will come into the chambers of your spirit when you see that I will have trusted witnesses testify - intellect, verses, the words of the Sages and their wonderful riddles. And they will be for a witness and a sign, and the truth will thus be revealed to you; and a spirit of grace will pour itself upon you from above. And you will destroy the bad traits from within you, and pure things will support your heart from the usage - With[541] the pure You act in purity and with the perverse You are wily.

And this is the thing about the group of scoffers - scoffing is divided into four sections:

And the first section:
Is the man of the tongue that spreads the infamy of people, like the matter that is stated - You[542] are busy maligning your brother, defaming the son of your mother. And he is called a scoffer, as it is stated - The[543] proud, insolent man, scoffer is his name, acts in a frenzy of insolence. Its explanation is that two bad traits - which are insolence and pride - gathered and

---

[541] Samuel-B 22:27
[542] Psalms 50:20
[543] Proverbs 21:24

joined in the scoffing man. For without having a benefit from the thing, he causes great damage to his fellows, whose reputations he sullies in the eyes of people. And this is the goal of the scoffer, more than the thief or the extortionist - who does it to increase his money. And he is also arrogant - for when one who is lowly and submissive recognizes his own deficiencies and blemishes, he will not scoff at people. And our Rabbis, may their memory be blessed, said in the Talmud - In[544] the future, all the animals will gather together by the snake and say to him, A lion mauls its prey and eats; a wolf tears it and eats; but you, what pleasure do you have when you bite a person? He will say to them - If[545] the snake bites because no spell was uttered, no advantage is gained by the master of the tongue. And this section is also from the sections of the group of the slanderers.

The second section:
The one who mocks people because he disdains them in his heart for their lack of reaching virtues or temporal successes regarding honor or power; or he disdains them for their poverty or indigence. And it is pride that brought him to this trait; or much tranquility and pampering, like the matter that is stated - Long[546] enough have we endured the scorn of the complacent, the contempt of the haughty. And sometimes the scoffer will mock holy ones and

---

[544] Taanit 8a
[545] Ecclesiastes 10:11
[546] Psalms 123:4

prophets, like the matter that is stated - Everyone[547] jeers at me. And King Solomon, peace be upon him, said - He[548] who disdains his fellow is a sinner. It was also stated - He[549] who disdains his fellowman is devoid of sense. And it was stated - He[550] who mocks the poor affronts his Maker and he who rejoices over another's misfortune will not go unpunished. One who mocks the poor shows about himself that he imagines that successes are in the hands of people to surely achieve them with their wisdom - like the matter that is stated - My[551] own power and the might of my own hand have won this wealth for me. And it is stated - For[552] he thought - **By the might of my hand have I wrought it by my skill**. And because of this, he mocks the poor; for he says in his heart that he did not reach wealth from lack of intellect and from the lowliness of his work. And behold he affronts the One who makes the poor and the rich, because it is all from God, may He be blessed - like the matter that is stated - Rich[553] man and poor man meet the Lord made them both. And about - He[554] who mocks the poor affronts his Maker and he who rejoices over another's misfortune will not go unpunished. He said - Assuredly[555] the evil man will

---

547 Jeremiah 20:7
548 Proverbs 14:21
549 Proverbs 11:12
550 Proverbs 17:5
551 Deuteronomy 8:17
552 Isaiah 10:13
553 Proverbs 22:2
554 Proverbs 17:5
555 Proverbs 11:21

not escape but the offspring of the righteous will be safe. For even though he did not injure with an action or with speech - **man will not escape but the offspring**. However, the evil of the one that rejoices is not as great as the evil of the one who mocks. And because scoffing is caused by pride - which is the opposite of humility - King Solomon, peace be upon him, said - If[556] at scoffers, He scoffs but to the lowly He shows grace. Its explanation - **If at scoffers** - truly, God mocks scoffers who mock people, like the matter that is stated - He[557] who is enthroned in heaven laughs; the Lord mocks at them. And the expression, **if**, is to confirm the matter. And so is such a usage found in the Torah - Yet[558] if Kain be consumed. For[559] if you will have a future.

The third section:
One who always mocks things and actions, but he does not intend to disgrace those associated with them. Rather he pushes off things that should not be pushed off and pushes off the possibility of results from actions that have hope for results. And about this is it stated - He[560] who disdains a thing will be injured thereby. And they said Mishna - Do[561] not disdain any man and do not discriminate against anything for there is no man that has not his hour and there is no thing that has not its place. And what brought this

---

[556] Proverbs 3:34
[557] Psalms 2:4
[558] Numbers 24:22
[559] Proverbs 23:18
[560] Proverbs 13:13
[561] Avot 4:3

scoffer to this bad trait is his being wise in his own eyes. And sometimes this trait brings a person to heresy, to mock the commandments - like the matter that is stated - Though[562] the arrogant have cruelly mocked me I have not swerved from Your teaching. And this third section is a group that does not accept reprimand, as it is stated - Do[563] not reprimand a scoffer, for he will hate you. And it is also stated - To[564] rebuke a scoffer is to call down abuse on oneself. And it is further stated - Beat[565] the scoffer and the simple will become clever. And that which causes this group not to listen to reproof is that the trait that leads to this type of scoffing is that a person is wise in his own eyes. And this trait controls him so much until he scorns the intellect of anyone besides himself. And it is a trait that has no hope, as it is stated - If[566] you see a man who thinks himself wise, there is more hope for a dullard than for him.

And the fourth section:
One who always makes a habit for himself to engage in idle talk, and idle matters, like those who sit in the street corners. And there are two evils in the matter: The first is because all who proliferate words bring sin. And the second is that he is idle from speaking words of Torah. And the ways of death are found in this. For he does not remember or pay attention, that the time periods that he is wasting, he could use to

[562] Psalms 119:51
[563] Proverbs 9:8
[564] Proverbs 9:7
[565] Proverbs 19:25
[566] Proverbs 26:12

reach pleasantness, to acquire eternal life - if he were to set these available times for Torah when he is free, for the work of the Heavens which is upon him. Therefore, he will be punished to carry the yoke of afflictions - measure for measure - as it is stated - Now[567] therefore do not be scoffers lest your suffering be made strong. And they, may their memory be blessed, said in the Talmud - Anyone[568] who scoffs suffering will befall him as it is stated - Lest[569] your suffering be made strong. And the Sages would warn their students against scoffing even occasionally and by chance. And about this section they had to warn, since many have stumbled on it in an occasional way.

And this is the thing about the group of liars - the content of this group is divided into nine sections:

The first section:
The lying man that left the Torah and does evil and destroys with the response of his mouth - like one who contradicts his countryman about a deposit or a transfer or the wage of a wage-worker, as it is stated - You[570] shall not deal deceitfully or falsely a man towards his countryman. And likewise, one who bears false witness against his neighbor; and it is said - You[571] shall not bear false witness against your neighbor. And included in this section is deception and fraud in commerce and in partnerships; and it is

---

[567] Isaiah 28:22
[568] Avodah Zarah 18b
[569] Chronicles-B 12:7
[570] Leviticus 19:11
[571] Exodus 20:13

stated - You[572] shall not cheat, one man, his brother. And it is also stated - Fraud[573] and deceit never leave its square. And he is called a man of iniquity and a ruffian; and he is the heaviest with iniquity from the groups of the evildoers, as we have discussed in the Gates of Fear of Sin. And the characteristics of this man of iniquity are that he winks his eyes and rolls his fingers, as it is written - A[574] scoundrel, an evil man Lives by crooked speech. Winking[575] his eyes Shuffling his feet Pointing his finger.

The second section:
One who lies, but there is no damage or loss to his fellow from the actual lie; however he plans it in order to do the damage or the evil - like one who deceives his fellow to believe that he is his friend and trusted companion; and he plans that [the other] will trust him through this and not be on guard against him, so that he will be able to lead him to evil; like the matter that is stated - One[576] speaks peace to his fellow, but lays an ambush for him in his heart. And it is stated after it - Shall[577] I not punish them for such deeds says the Lord **shall I not bring retribution on such a nation as this**. And the punishment of these two sections is for two things - For the lie and for the damage that comes with it. For falsehood [even] without the angle of damage is an abomination to

---

[572] Leviticus 25:14
[573] Psalms 55:12
[574] Proverbs 6:12
[575] Proverbs 6:12
[576] Jeremiah 9:7
[577] Jeremiah 9:8

God, as it is stated - Six[578] things the LORD hates Seven are an abomination to Him. A[579] haughty bearing A lying tongue. Hands[580] that shed innocent blood. A[581] mind that hatches evil plots Feet quick to run to evil. And it is stated - I[582] have hated duplicity in speech. And it is stated - What[583] then of one loathsome and foul man who drinks wrongdoing like water. And to flesh and blood also is falsehood loathsome, as it is stated - Lying[584] lips are an abomination to the Lord. It appears to me that there is a printing error here, and it is supposed to say - And it is stated - I[585] have hated duplicity in speech. And it is stated - Lying[586] lips are an abomination to the Lord. And to flesh and blood also is falsehood loathsome, as it is stated - What[587] then of one loathsome and foul Man who drinks wrongdoing like water. And it means to say that the understanding of the language of the verse is that a man who drinks wrongdoing like water, is essentially loathsome and foul - for he is even loathsome and foul to flesh and blood.

And the third section:
One that comes with deception and deceptive words

---

[578] Proverbs 6:16
[579] Proverbs 6:17
[580] Proverbs 6:18
[581] Proverbs 6:19
[582] Proverbs 8:13
[583] Job 15:16
[584] Proverbs 12:22
[585] Proverbs 8:13
[586] Proverbs 12:22
[587] Job 15:16

to prevent good from someone and to bring the good to himself. It is not to rob his fellow of something that is his nor to extort him. Rather he puts his eye upon a good that will be coming to his fellow in the future, and ambushes it to bring it to himself by the falsehood of his words; or his lying words cause his fellow to give it to him as a gift. And the main punishment is for the lie. Indeed, the punishment of the lie is enlarged if it causes a loss to someone besides himself, even though the main part of the punishment is not for the loss here - for he did not cause him to lose something that he had acquired. It is like the matter that our Rabbis, may their memory be blessed, said in the Talmud - Anyone[588] who alters the truth in his speech it is as though he worships idols. As it is stated - Maybe[589] my father will feel me, and I shall seem to him a **Metatea** [deceiver]. And it is written there regarding idolatry - They[590] are vanity, the work of **Tatuim** [deception]. And our Rabbis, may their memory be blessed, said that it was as if **he worshipped idolatry here** - they brought it to the extreme and other and it appears to me that it needs to say, to the final extreme. For he is traded it needs to say, hidden - and it is from the usage of the verse - We[591] have hidden in falsehood - and so is it found in the Chapter on Falsehood in the Paths of the Righteous, the chapters of which are built upon the pearls of this holy book in falsehood and girded in

---

588 Sanhedrin 92a
589 Genesis 27:12
590 Jeremiah 10:15
591 Isaiah 28:15

vanity.

The fourth section:
One who lies in recounting things that he heard and alters some of them on purpose, yet he does not have any benefit from his lies, nor does he cause a loss to anyone else. Rather his characterization is that it is from his love of falsehood over just words, forever. And sometimes he will invent a whole story of words from his heart. And the punishment of this person will be lighter from one angle, since there was no loss to another person from his lies and from his wantonness. But his punishment will be very big due to his brazenness and his love of falsehood. And his punishment will be weighty, for he loved it without a benefit. And King Solomon, peace be upon him, said - He[592] breathes lies, a false witness. Its explanation is that if you see a man that breathes lies in his speech and in recounting his words - know that this trait will bring him to testify falsely against his brothers and testify that which is wrong against him, from his love of falsehood. And they permitted this section in order to fulfill a commandment and to seek good and peace. And they said in the Talmud - That[593] it is permissible to praise the bride in front of the groom and to say that she is fair and attractive, even though it is not so. And they said in the Talmud - That[594] it is permissible to alter the truth for matters of peace as it is stated -

---

[592] Proverbs 6:19
[593] Ketuvot 17a
[594] Yevamot 65b

So[595] they sent this message to Yosef Before his death your father left this instruction. So[596] shall you say to Yosef Forgive I urge you, the offense and guilt of your brothers who treated you so harshly Therefore please forgive the offense of the servants of the God of your father's house And Joseph was in tears as they spoke to him. And there are some people that change some of the things they have heard unintentionally, as they did not place it into their hearts to analyze it when they heard it. This too is a bad trait. And King Solomon, peace be upon him, said - But[597] one who really heard will speak forever. Its explanation is that a man who puts into his heart to listen and audit to the essence of the words that they speak into his ears - in order that he can tell them correctly to others, and not have a treacherous tongue in his mouth - **will speak forever**. For people will love to hear his words, and they will not say - Before they pray I will answer While they are still speaking I will respond.

The fifth section:

One who says to his fellow that he will benefit him and give him a gift; but as he is still speaking, he tells his heart that he will not give it. And it is stated - Guard[598] your tongue from evil your lips from deceitful speech. And our Rabbis, may their memory be blessed, explained it in the Talmud - As[599] saying that one should not speak one way with the mouth and

---

595 Genesis 50:16
596 Genesis 50:17
597 Proverbs 22:28
598 Psalms 34:14
599 Bava Metzia 49a

another way with the heart. And they also said in the Talmud - That[600] there are words that, if he goes back on them, are considered bad faith - but only if he says it with the mouth, and decides upon it with the mind. It appears to me to explain the words, and only **Oubilvad** as being in the place of the word, **rather**. And he means to say that the word of a man should only be in such a way that he says it with the mouth and decides upon it with the mind, which is the opposite of, one thing with the mouth and another with the heart.

The sixth section:
One who promises his fellow to benefit him, but falsifies his speech and makes his word worthless. Since after he said to benefit him upon with an expression of a promise, and his fellow's heart depended on it, he should not profane his promise - as this is the way of falsehood. And it is like a man who broke a covenant, as it is stated - The[601] remnant of Israel shall do no wrong, and speak no falsehood a deceitful tongue shall not be in their mouths. And likewise, one who says that he will give his fellow a small gift, even though he does not mention any expression of promise. And our Rabbis, may their memory be blessed, said in the Talmud - it[602] is because [there is] bad faith with this. As since the gift is small, his fellow counts on it; that he will surely give it. And if it is to a poor person, his evil is great

---

[600] Yerushalmi Bava Metzia 4:2
[601] Zephaniah 3:13
[602] Bava Metzia 49a

even if the gift was large - for he surely vowed it - **since charity is like a vow**. And it is stated - He[603] shall not profane his word. And likewise, one who glorifies himself in public by announcing that he will give a gift to someone. And see that he is like one who praises himself about his generosity with this. And this is surely like a promise, so it is not proper that he should go back on his words once he honored himself and boasted about the thing; like the matter that is stated - Like[604] clouds and wind but no rain is one who boasts of gifts not given. Its explanation is, just like people are distressed after signs of rain come, but rain does not come; so too is the matter of the man who boasts about a false gift. For that which he boasted about the thing is a sign about the fulfillment of the thing. Hence the man to whom he promised the gift will be distressed when his expectation is disappointed.

The seventh section:
One who fools his fellow, saying that he did him a favor or spoke favorably about him, but he did not do so. Our Rabbis, may their memory be blessed, said in the Talmud - That[605] it is forbidden to deceive **literally, steal the mind of** people. And note that this was more weighty among the Sages of Israel than theft. For lying lips is certainly a cause of great guilt. And we have been obligated about the fences of truth because [truth] is from the principles of the soul.

---

603 Numbers 30:3
604 Proverbs 25:14
605 Chullin 94a

The eighth section:

One who praises himself about virtues that are not found in him. King Solomon, peace be upon him, said - Lofty[606] words are not fitting for a villain; much less lying words for a great man. Its explanation is that a villain should not act proudly and raise himself up due to the virtues of his ancestors. For he said in the verse above this - And[607] the glory of children is their parents. Much less should a great man honor himself with lies and say, I did so, and spread and gave gifts. when he did not do so. And this is a disgrace for any person, but all the more so, a great man. And he disgraces the generosity that he has done; for he profaned his soul with what he did not do. For this will testify that all of the righteous deeds that he did were only for fame and praise. And our Rabbis, may their memory be blessed, said in the Talmud - That[608] one who is honored according to the level of one who knows two tractates, but knows only one, must tell them - **I know only one**. All the more so is it forbidden to lie and boast, saying - **I have learned many like these**.

The ninth section:

Children who do not lie in recounting things that they heard and telling over events, but switch the words according to the circumstances of their wishes, yet it is without hurting any person through it. However, they find a little benefit with their lies, even though

---

[606] Proverbs 17:7
[607] Proverbs 17:6
[608] Yerushalmi Shevit 10:3

they do not make money from it. And our Rabbis said in the Talmud - That[609] this is also forbidden, as it is stated - They[610] have trained their tongues to speak falsely. However, their punishment is not like those that lie about something that did not happen, the nature of which we discussed in the fourth section. Behold these are the sections of the group of liars; and we have already mentioned their centrality to you for the ways of faithful people, and that they are fundamental for the soul.

And this is the thing about the group of flatterers - the content of this group is divided into nine sections:

The first section:
The flatterer who recognizes or sees or knows that there is injustice in the hand of his fellow, and that he is holding fast to deception; or that he sinned to another person with evil speech or verbal abuse - and he blandishes him with improper speech, saying - Such[611] is the way of an adulteress She eats wipes her mouth and says I have done no wrong. The sin of one who refrains from reprimand - as it is stated - You[612] shall surely reprimand your countryman and not bear sin because of him - is too small for him; so, he increased the sin by saying - You did not sin. It is like the matter that is stated - They[613] encourage evildoers. And behold this is a criminal offense in the hand of

609 Yevamot 63a
610 Jeremiah 9:4
611 Proverbs 30:5
612 Leviticus 19:17
613 Jeremiah 23:14

the foolish flatterer, for he was not zealous against falsehood, but rather assisted the falsehood, and said about the bad, **Good**, and made darkness, light. He also placed a stumbling block in front of the sinner in two aspects. The first one is that he will not regret his evil. And the second is that he will repeat his evil on the next day. For the one who flatters the other one about his desire praises that evildoer. Besides that, he will carry the punishment for the damage that he caused to the one towards whom the sinner was guilty, by justifying the sinner; he will also be punished for the false words, as it is stated - You[614] doom those who speak lies. And it is stated - To[615] acquit the guilty and convict the innocent both are an abomination to the Lord. All the more so if the injustice in the hand of his fellow, the evildoer, is revealed to the public. For when he, the flatterer, said to him in front of people, **you are pure, without transgression** - he has profaned and disgraced the religion and the law.

And a person is obligated to give himself over to danger, and not to place guilt like this upon his soul. And our Rabbis said about the matter of Agrippa in the Talmud - That[616] when he read from the Torah and - Arrived at the verse - You[617] may not appoint a foreigner over you. tears flowed from his eyes. And they said to him, **you are our brother**. At that

---

[614] Psalms 5:7
[615] Proverbs 17:15
[616] Sotah 41a-b
[617] Deuteronomy 17:15

moment the enemies of the Jewish people a euphemism for the Jewish people were sentenced to destruction for flattering Agrippa. Especially should one who sits in judgement not fear mortal men, as it is stated - Fear[618] no man. And among the sections of the group of flatterers, there are some in which the flatterer is destroyed and lost just for the iniquity of flattery, as will be explained.

The second section:
The flatterer who praises the evildoer in front of people - whether in front of him or not in front of him - even though he does not justify him for his extortion or lie about his trial, but says about him that he is a good man. About this is it stated - Those[619] who forsake Torah praise the wicked. For had he not forsaken the Torah, he would not have praised one who transgressed its words and breached its commandments. Even if he only praises the evildoer for that which he finds that is good about him and he defends him to people to tell them of his righteousness, but he does not mention the bad - this too is a sore evil. For in his mentioning the good and not mentioning the bad and covering up all of his transgression, he will be thought of as a righteous man by those listening and they will give him honor and elevate him. And we have already mentioned [and] let you know the stumbling blocks and the destruction that is found in honoring evildoers. Hence it is incorrect to mention their righteousness without

[618] Deuteronomy 1:17
[619] Proverbs 28:4

mentioning their evil and foolishness as well, as it is stated - But[620] the fame of the wicked rots. And it is also stated - I[621] hereby pronounce judgment upon your deeds your deeds shall not help you. The explanation is that your good deeds will not help to save you from your evil when you will come to judgement and in My evaluation for eternity - since the matters of your iniquities finished off their merit. And it is like our Rabbis said in the Talmud - One[622] whose iniquities are greater than his merits are written and sealed for death. And evildoers are recognizable by their speech and behavior, as we discussed earlier with you, in the Gates of the Fear of Sin.

And behold the righteous abominate the evildoer, as it is stated - The[623] unjust man is an abomination to the righteous. And with one who is not in the counsel of the sages - if he does not surely abominate him, nor surely curse him; he should also surely not bless him.

And it is likely that the case of the one praising the evildoers is from foolishness. For the fool he intends to praise the good - whether it is about the truth, or whether it is the opposite. And without knowing, he is praising the dead. For our Rabbis said in the Talmud - That[624] evildoers are considered like wraiths, as it is stated - But[625] the dead know nothing. But this

---

[620] Proverbs 10:7
[621] Isaiah 57:12
[622] Rosh Hashanah 16b
[623] Proverbs 29:26
[624] Berakhot 18b
[625] Ecclesiastes 9:5

unintentional sin is considered wanton. For a master would not love a slave, if the slave loves the master's enemies and brings close those who he has distanced. Should they not know this from the intellect, that this is so? And it is stated - Disgrace[626] uplifts dullards.

The third section:
The flatterer who praises the evildoer to his face, yet his wisdom restrains him - for he does not praise him in front of other people, lest he be a stumbling block for them. The sin of this flatterer is also great, as he blandished him in his eyes; such that he will not repent from his evil path and not worry about his iniquities - for he is righteous in his eyes. And when they praise anyone who is not from the congregation of the righteous - he will say in his heart - Indeed, I knew that it was like this; like the matter that is stated - The[627] flatterer destroys his neighbor through speech but through knowledge the righteous is rescued. The explanation is that the flatterer destroys his neighbor with his mouth, because he will praise him and the neighbor will believe his words. So, he will harden his spirit and he will see himself with honor, and not understand that his soul is murky. And with this stumbling block in his hand, he will fall into the trap of his pride. So, behold, he surely destroyed him with his flattering lips. But through knowledge, the righteous is rescued - The righteous are saved from the damage of the flatterer through their knowledge. For if he flatters him, his heart will not be elevated as

---

[626] Proverbs 3:35
[627] Proverbs 11:9

a result, like our Rabbis said in the Talmud - Even[628] if all of the world says about you - **You are righteous** - be like an evildoer in your own eyes. And they also said in the Midrash - If[629] you have companions, some of whom praise you, and some of whom reprimand you - love the ones that reprimand you, and hate the ones that praise you. For these are bringing you to life eternal, and those, when they praise you, are gladdening you to your own detriment. And it is also possible to explain it as - The[630] impious man destroys his neighbor through speech but through their knowledge the righteous are rescued. their neighbors - as they will not flatter them; but will rather reprimand them and show them the path, when they err in the chaos that is not a path. And it is stated - And[631] a flattering mouth throws one down. This compares a flattering mouth with a crooked path; and it says that just like a man falls and is thrown down by walking on a crooked path - like the matter that is - Are[632] they so witless those evildoers who devour my people as they devour food and do not invoke God. There[633] they will be seized with fright never was there such a fright for God has scattered the bones of your besiegers you have put them to shame for God has rejected them. - so too does a man fall and get thrown down by a flattering mouth. And that is the mouth of the flatterer. And about the matter that we are

---

[628] Niddah 30b
[629] Avot D'Rabbi Natan 29
[630] Proverbs 11:9
[631] Proverbs 26:28
[632] Psalms 35:5
[633] Psalms 35:6

discussing, King David, peace be upon him, said - May[634] the Lord cut off all flattering lips, every tongue that speaks arrogance. He cursed a flattering mouth, since he destroys his neighbor with it; and a harsh tongue - which is the opposite of the smooth one, and that is evil speech. And among the flatterers, there are those that intend to flatter intimidating people, in order that they should honor them and promote them. And our Rabbis said in the Midrash - Anyone[635] that flatters his fellow for the sake of honor will in the end be removed from it in shame.

The fourth section:
One who attaches himself to an evildoer. It is not enough for him that he does not reprimand him with the rod of his mouth and surely distance him; but he rather brings him close like a friend. And it is stated - As[636] you have made a partnership, etc., the Lord will break up your work. Whereas the righteous are surely disgusted by the evildoer, as it is stated - A[637] contemptible man is disgusting in his eyes. And our Rabbis, may their memory be blessed, said in the Talmud - Not[638] for naught did the starling go to the raven, but because it is its kind. And it stated - All[639] fowl will live with its kind, and men with those like him. And they said in the Talmud - It[640] is prohibited

---

[634] Psalms 12:4
[635] Avot D'Rabbi Natan 29
[636] Chronicles-B 20:37
[637] Psalms 15:4
[638] Bava Kamma 92b
[639] Book of Ben Sira 13:17
[640] Megillah 28a

for a person to gaze at the likeness of a wicked man, as it is stated - Were[641] it not that I regard the presence of Jehoshaphat the king of Judea, I would not look toward you, nor see you. And they continued - Any one who gazes at the likeness of an evil man, his eyes become dim at the time of his old age, as it is stated - And[642] it came to pass that when Itzhak was old and his eyes were dim so that he could not see - because he gazed at the wicked Esau. And we have already discussed very well that there are many ways of death found by one who attaches himself to an evildoer.

And the fifth section:

A man whose words people trust, and everyone relies on his words; and he intends to boost one of the people or his redeeming relative, out of his love for him - and he says about him that he is wise, whereas he is not wise. And this will be a cause for faltering and a stone for stumbling; for they will rely upon his rulings - Every dispute will go according to his decision; he will twist every case and he will destroy the world. And likewise, if he says about a man, that he is trustworthy, but he does not know whether he is trustworthy or someone who cannot be trusted. So perhaps a listener will hear and appoint him over his house and give him everything that he has into his hand to watch; and he will deny it, saying - I never saw you. And the Rabbis said in the Talmud - Anyone[643] who appoints a judge who is not fit over the

---

[641] Kings-B 3:14
[642] Genesis 27:1
[643] Sanhedrin 7b

community is as though he plants **Ashera** [a tree-idol]; and in a place where there are Torah scholars, it is as though he planted the tree next to the altar. And in the early days, there was someone who appointed someone who was not fit to make rulings, as the head. And they read this verse about him - Ah[644] you who say - **Wake up** to wood **Awaken**, to inert stone; can that give an oracle; why, it is encased in gold and silver, but there is no breath inside it. And in the future, the Holy One, blessed be He, will repay the ones that appointed him, as it is stated - But[645] the Lord is in His holy Sanctuary let all the earth be silent before Him.

The sixth section:

One who has the ability to protest, but does not protest and has no words of reprimand in his mouth; and does not use the swords of his eyes and does not take responsibility for the deeds of sinners. So, he will not be a man of reprimand, whereas we were commanded to destroy the evil from within our nation - as it is stated - And[646] you shall destroy the evil within you. And our Rabbis said in the Talmud - Anyone[647] who is in a position to protest against the members of his household and does not protest, is apprehended for the members of his household; if he is in a position to protest against the people of his city, and does not protest, he is apprehended for the people

---

[644]   Habakkuk 2:19
[645]   Habakkuk 2:20
[646]   Deuteronomy 13:6
[647]   Shabbat 54b

of his city; if he is in a position to protest the whole world, and does not protest, he is apprehended for the whole world. And it is stated - A[648] man shall stumble over his brother. And they, may their memory be blessed, expounded in the Talmud - A[649] man over the iniquity of **his brother**. And they said that all of Israel is responsible for one another.

The seventh section:

One who sees the people of his place being a stiff-necked people, and says in his heart - Perhaps they will not listen if I speak words of integrity with them and fill my mouth with reprimands. Hence, he saves his mouth from speaking. Yet he surely bears his sin, for he did not try to reprimand and warn them - maybe if the city is pitied, they will awake from the slumber of their stupidity and their error will not continue to lay with them. And our Rabbis, may their memory be blessed, said in the Talmud - About[650] that which is written - And GOD said to him Pass through the city through Jerusalem and put a **Tav** [mark] on the foreheads of the persons who moan and groan because of all the abominations that are committed in it. The attribute of justice said - Even though these are full-fledged righteous people and keep the Torah, it was in their hands to protest, and they did not protest. The Holy One, blessed be He, said - It is revealed and known before Me that had they protested, they would not have accepted it from them. The attribute of

---

[648] Leviticus 26:37
[649] Sanhedrin 27b
[650] Shabbat 55a

justice said - Master of the Universe, if it is revealed before You, they did not know if the people would listen to their voice or ignore them. So afterwards God, may He be blessed, commanded - And[651] begin from My **Mikdash** [Temple] - and that is the **Mekudash** [dedicated] righteous ones. And it is stated - You[652] shall surely reprimand your countryman and not bear sin because of him. But if the matter is revealed to all, known, tested and analyzed that the sinner hates rebuke and will not listen to the voice of his teachers and will not bend his ear to his instructors - about this is it stated - Do[653] not rebuke a scoffer, for he will hate you. And they said in the Talmud - Just[654] as it is a commandment to say something that will be heard, so is it a commandment to not say something that will not be heard. And they said in the Talmud - It[655] is better that they be inadvertent, and not be intentional.

And the eighth section:
Someone who hears the words of the people saying evil speech, or hears every mouth speaking foully or sits among a group of jokers disgracing the Torah and the commandments - and he knows that they are stubborn and like thorns. So, if he would reprimand them, they will not listen to his words - hence he puts his hand to his mouth does not speak. This one will also be punished, since he did not answer fools about

---

[651]   Ezekiel 9:4
[652]   Leviticus 19:17
[653]   Proverbs 9:8
[654]   Yevamot 55b
[655]   Beitzah 30a

their foolishness - lest they say that he is like them and that he concedes to their words. Rather, he becomes obligated to answer and scold them, to give greatness to the Torah and the commandments which they disgraced and made light of. He should be zealous for the honor of the Clean and Righteous One about whom they are speaking.

This is one of the things for which a person becomes obligated to leave the group of evildoers. For he will be punished for hearing their evil words and being too listless to answer them. And this is something explicit in the words of Solomon, as it is stated - Do[656] not envy evil men Do not desire to be with them. For[657] their hearts talk violence and their lips speak mischief. And he meant to say it is because you will bear the iniquity when they sin. For you will constantly hear their evil words and you will be silent.

The ninth section:
One who honors evildoers in a way of peace. However, he does not speak well about the evildoer and does not act to honor him in a way in which people will think that he is honoring him because he is honorable and precious in his eyes. Rather he only shows him respect in the way that people honor the rich, in the way of dignification; and with the hope of benefit, since their path has been successful - and not because of the grace of his arrangement. Nevertheless, there is a sin and guilt in this thing. If it

---

[656] Proverbs 24:1
[657] Proverbs 24:2

is permitted to honor the rich, it is not so with the evildoers - as it is stated - Scatter[658] wide your raging anger See every proud man and bring him low. See[659] every proud man and humble him and bring them down where they stand. Nevertheless, this section is permitted in the case of worry about something - lest the evildoer injure him and cause him a loss, at the time when the evildoer is strong and his time is insolent; and we do not have the ability to humble him, and to put him down with our soldiers. Hence it is permitted to honor him in the way we honor very intimidating people out of fear and terror, by rising for them, noting them and that which is similar to these. However, one should not praise him, nor speak well about him to people. And likewise did our Rabbis, may their memory be blessed, say in the Talmud - It[660] is permissible to flatter evildoers in this world.

And this is the thing about the group of slanderers: Our Rabbis, may their memory be blessed, said in the Talmud - Anyone[661] who speaks evil speech is as though he denied a fundamental principle of faith, as it is stated - They[662] say by our tongues we shall prevail with lips such as ours who can be our master. Therefore, they considered him as if he denied a fundamental principle. For he causes and brings about great damage and much evil to his fellows by

---

[658] Job 40:11
[659] Job 40:12
[660] Sotah 41b
[661] Arakhin 15b
[662] Psalms 12:5

making them foul in the eyes of people or by other ways of causing them loss. And it is not likely that a man would prepare a mechanism of destruction and damage that is more bitter than death without it benefitting himself monetarily, unless it is to have his evil impulse honor himself and remove the yoke of the Heavens from upon him - to remove ethical constraints - as it is stated - When[663] the Ziphites came and told Saul. King David says - O[664] God arrogant men have risen against me a band of ruthless men seek my life they are not mindful of You. And our Rabbis, may their memory be blessed, explained Midrash - That[665] they intended that Saul would bless them, as he said to them - May[666] you be blessed of the Lord for the compassion you have shown me. But they did not place God in front of them - as it is written in His Torah - Cursed[667] be he who strikes down his neighbor in secret. And it is written - No[668] advantage is gained by the master of the tongue. And it is stated about Doeg - Your[669] tongue devises mischief like a sharpened razor that works treacherously. You[670] prefer evil to good the lie to speaking truthfully Selah. And they explained in Midrash - What[671] do you benefit and what do you

---

[663] Samuel-A 26:1
[664] Psalms 86:14
[665] Midrash Tehillim 54
[666] Samuel-A 23:21
[667] Deuteronomy 27:24
[668] Ecclesiastes 10:11
[669] Psalms 52:4
[670] Psalms 52:5
[671] Midrash Tehillim 52

gain when you say evil speech? Is it not that you did
not need money, for you had already become wealthy
- as it is stated about him - Saul's[672] chief herdsman. It
was only because you preferred the evil to the good,
and **the lie, to speaking truthfully** - as you have
removed His yoke. And it is stated - A[673] thief is not
held in contempt for stealing to fill his hunger; and it
is written after it - He[674] who commits adultery is
devoid of sense Only one who would destroy himself
does such a thing. This is meaning to say that he is
worse than a thief, for the former needs to **fill his
hunger**. Our Rabbis, may their memory be blessed,
said in the Midrash - That[675] one involved in evil
speech is worse than both of them. For he does a great
sin without benefit, as it is stated - What[676] can you
profit, what can you gain, O deceitful tongue.

And secondly, for this too is one who speaks evil
speech considered as if he denied a fundamental
principle - For he says in his heart that his lips are in
his own control; and because they do not do an action
and he is in charge of his tongue, he determined in his
heart that he should not restrain the spirit of his lips
from saying that which comes to his spirit; and that
only all the other limbs are not in his control to sin
with them - like the matter that is stated - They[677] say
with lips such as ours, who can be our master. And

672 Samuel-A 21:8
673 Proverbs 6:30
674 Proverbs 6:32
675 Midrash Tehillim 120
676 Psalms 120:3
677 Psalms 12:5

they do not say - Where is the God that made me, to whom all the movements of His creations are given - not one is lacking. They are all subjected to doing His will. Rather, it is no matter - the petitions about the lips are in our control. The evildoers that sin with other sins is not like this. For they know that their leaving God is bad and bitter, however they were pulled after their desire and their overpowering evil impulse; yet they are pained by this. And our Rabbis said in the Talmud - Evil[678] speech... corresponds to three transgressions and these are them - Idol worship, forbidden sexual relations and bloodshed.... With regard to idol worship, it is stated - Oh[679] this people have sinned a great sin. With regard to forbidden sexual relations, it is stated - How[680] can I do this great wickedness. With regard to bloodshed, it is stated - My[681] punishment is greater than I can bear. And with regard to evil speech, it is stated - May[682] the Lord cut off all flattering lips, the tongue that speaks great things.

And behold we must explain to you how it is possible that the iniquity of evil speech can be more than these three. Did our Rabbis, may their memory be blessed, not say about each one of them in the Talmud - Let[683] a man be killed and not transgress them? And they said that idolatry is weighty, for anyone that concedes

---

[678] Arakhin 15b
[679] Exodus 32:31
[680] Genesis 39:9
[681] Genesis 4:13
[682] Psalms 12:4
[683] Sanhedrin 74a

to it is like one who denies all of the Torah. And they also said in the Talmud - That[684] one who is an apostate only for idolatry is like one who is an apostate for all of the entire Torah. And when you put your heart to these statements of theirs, may their memory be blessed, you will find several roots to them and several aspects.

The first is because the one involved in evil speech repeats his stupidity - he will embarrass, sully and shame ten times a day. He will speak superfluously and strike in secret. So, who can measure his punishment? For one involved in evil speech does not put an end to his words. And even a light sin is very weighty when the stupidity is repeated many times - as we discussed earlier - all the more so, when it is a big sin and a grievous evil. And when our Rabbis, may their memory be blessed, said in the Talmud - Evil[685] speech... corresponds to three transgressions, they meant to say, corresponding to one who transgresses them at a time when his impulse attacks him - not corresponding to a habitual sinner or one who has left the congregation to transgress them all the time.

The second is because the repentance of one involved in evil speech is difficult, since he has taught his tongue to speak falsehood, and sent his mouth to evil. From so much habit, he does not control his spirit, and it is as if his mouth causes the thought - like the

---

[684] Chullin 5a
[685] Arakhin 15b

matter that is stated - Your[686] tongue devises mischief; and it is stated - But[687] a fool's lips will swallow him up; and it is stated - The[688] fool's speech is his **Mechitah** [ruin]. And **Mechitah** [ruin] is an expression of fear and trepidation. It means to say that the fool is afraid and in trepidation from the rage of his tongue, lest he be ensnared - like he fears from his enemy - as his lips are not in his control.

And the third is because the sin of the one involved in evil speech is light in his eyes - as he says it is only something of the lips, and he does not pay attention to its damaging the many. Hence, he does not repent from his evil path. And if he does repent, his repentance will not be complete - as he will not recognize the greatness of his sin. For complete repentance to be cleansed from such a great transgression is when a fire of anguish is surely lit and there is like a fire burning inside his soul.

King Solomon, peace be upon him, said - The[689] violent, proud man, scoffer is his name, acts in a frenzy of violence. The explanation is that the scoffer whose violence is great to strike with his tongue in his pride and his loftiness, his anger and his rage - do not say about him that he only strikes with his tongue, and not with a deed. For you should surely know that he **acts in a frenzy of violence**. He means to say that if

---

[686] Psalms 52:4
[687] Ecclesiastes 10:12
[688] Proverbs 18:7
[689] Proverbs 21:24

he could not strike his enemies with his tongue and he could strike them with a deed, he would strike them with a frenzy and have no pity. It is like our Rabbis, may their memory be blessed, said regarding Doeg in the Talmud - That[690] when Saul commanded that the priests be smitten but his people refused to strike them, he said to Doeg - You struck them with the tongue, you strike them with the sword, as it is stated - You[691] go and strike down the priests.

And the fourth is that if the one involved in evil speech does repent, he will need to request forgiveness from those upon whom he poured the fury of his tongue, but he will not remember all of them. As he generated much pain and saddened many souls - also more than he remembered that he sullied. And they did not know that he sent the evil to them, so he will be ashamed to inform them and open their ears to that which he did evil to them. For he strikes, but his strike is not known, like the matter that is stated - What[692] can you profit what can you gain O deceitful tongue. A[693] warrior's sharp arrows with hot coals of broom-wood. Therefore, evil speech is compared to an arrow - for many times, one who pulls the bow sends forth his arrows but does not know who he struck.

And it was also compared to an arrow for another

---

[690] Yerushalmi Sanhedrin 10:2
[691] Samuel-A 22:18
[692] Psalms 120:3-4
[693] Psalms 120:3-4

reason. For one who draws his sword can put it back in its sheath if he has mercy on someone who pleads with him. Not so is one who sends forth an arrow - he is not able to bring it back. Such is one involved in evil speech - once the word came out of his mouth, he is not able to repair it. And sometimes he will speak about a family blemish and injure all of the generations that come after [the one he insults]; and he cannot get forgiveness for this. Therefore, our Rabbis, may their memory be blessed, said in the Talmud - That[694] one who speaks about a family blemish does not ever have atonement. And behold one who sends out his tongue, also speaks about the holy ones in the land. For upon whom has his constant evil not expressed itself? And our Rabbis, may their memory be blessed, already said in the Talmud - That[695] one who disgraces the Torah scholars has no share in the world to come.

And the fifth is that evil speech brings one involved with it to put his mouth to speaking wrongly about God - and as it is stated - They[696] set their mouths against Heaven, and their tongues range over the earth. And there is none among all of the sins the punishment for which reaches the punishment for flinging accusations at God. And our Rabbis said in the Talmud - Our[697] ancestors tried the Holy One, Blessed be He with ten trials, but their sentence was

---

[694] Yerushalmi Bava Kamma 8
[695] Sanhedrin 90a
[696] Psalms 73:9
[697] Arakhin 15a

sealed only due to the evil speech. For it is stated -
Say[698] to them As I live says God I will do to you just
as you have urged Me. and it is stated - When[699] the
Lord heard your loud complaint He was angry and He
vowed. and it is stated - You[700] have wearied the Lord
with your talk. And King David, peace be upon him,
said - And[701] to the wicked God said Who are you to
recite My laws and mouth the terms of My covenant.
Seeing[702] that you spurn My discipline and brush My
words aside. When[703] you see a thief you fall in with
him and throw in your lot with adulterers. You[704]
devote your mouth to evil and yoke your tongue to
deceit. You[705] are busy maligning your brother
defaming the son of your mother. Behold you have
learned from this that Torah study does not protect
those involved with evil speech or one accustomed to
steal or to engage in forbidden sexual relations; and
that they are not fit to be involved with Torah. And
our Rabbis, may their memory be blessed, said in the
Talmud - That[706] because Doeg spoke evil speech, his
wisdom did not stand him in. And that which our
Rabbis, may their memory be blessed, said - Sin
extinguishes a commandment, but sin does not

---

[698] Numbers 14:28
[699] Deuteronomy 1:34
[700] Malachi 2:17
[701] Psalms 50:16
[702] Psalms 50:17
[703] Psalms 50:18
[704] Psalms 50:19
[705] Psalms 50:20
[706] Sotah 21a

extinguish Torah, as it is stated - For[707] the commandment is a lamp, and the Torah is a light. they said about someone who sins by chance, and not about one who removes the yoke of the warning of a sin from upon him.

And consider how great is the sin of a man who speaks evil speech: Is their sin that they have sealed their lips and quieted their tongues from speaking words of Torah not big enough for them; that they surely use them to destroy with evil speech? And King David, peace be upon him, said - Though[708] princes meet and speak against me your servant speaks out Your laws. The explanation is that they are still from speaking out Your laws and speak evil speech and speak against me, while I am still speaking out Your laws. And our Rabbis said in the Talmud - That[709] the cure for evil speech - to save oneself from it - is to be involved with the Torah; as its stated - A[710] healing tongue is a tree of life. And this is the meaning of what is stated - I[711] resolved I would watch my step lest I offend by my speech I would keep my mouth muzzled while the wicked man was in my presence. And our Rabbis, may their memory be blessed, explained in the Midrash - That[712] the muzzle is involvement with Torah. And our

---

[707] Proverbs 6:23
[708] Psalms 119:23
[709] Arakhin 15a
[710] Proverbs 15:4
[711] Psalms 39:2
[712] Midrash Tehillim 39

Rabbis said in the Midrash - The[713] Congregation of Israel is beloved by her voice and hated by her voice: She is beloved by her voice, as it is stated -Let[714] me hear your voice for your voice is sweet. And she is hated by her voice, as it is stated - She[715] raised her voice against Me therefore I have hated her. And this is the meaning of what is stated - Death[716] and life are in the power of the tongue those who love it will eat its fruit. And its explanation is - Those[717] who love it will eat its fruit. And one who loves the tongue, and that is a man that always wants to talk, for him the proper counsel is that he should, **eat its fruit**. That is, he should not speak idle words but rather words of Torah, wisdom and ethics and the bringing of peace between a man and his fellow; justify the actions of the masses; praise the good; disparage the evil; and be zealous about the truth. For there is no end to the merits that he can acquire for himself with his tongue. And it is as we discussed earlier, that life is in the tongue.

And behold this group of slanderers is divided into six sections:

And the first section:
When he attributes a blemish to a person and that person does not have the blemish. There are times that he will lie against beauty. And behold the heart of this

---

[713] Yalkut Shimoni on Nach 721
[714] Song of Songs 2:14
[715] Jeremiah 12:8
[716] Proverbs 18:21
[717] Proverbs 18:21

one gathers the evil of the traits of two bad groups - which are the group of the liars and the group of the slanderers. And behold we have been warned by the Torah not to accept evil speech - perhaps it is empty or a false matter - as it is stated - You[718] must not carry false rumors. And King Solomon, peace be upon him, said - An[719] evildoer listens to bad talk a lie gives ear to malicious words. Its explanation is - two groups accept evil speech - The first is a violent evildoing man - from the usage - For[720] all are ungodly and doing evil. For he suspects the innocent, and loves to find a blemish and guilt about his fellow and a disgrace to his honor. And it will be that when he hears someone saying evil speech about his companion, the violence in his heart brings him to believe that the things are true. And the second group is that of the lying man. He also listens and believes malicious talk. Since he does not distance himself from false words, he will not be concerned if he accepts a lie, or if he listens to a false rumor. Hence, he will be quick to accept evil speech. The meaning of - A[721] lie gives ear. is like a man of lies. And likewise - You[722] dwell in the midst of deceit, means in the midst of people of deceit; and also - And[723] I am prayer. Means a man of prayer.

And know that when the listener concedes to the evil speech, his lot and measured portion a scriptural

[718] Exodus 23:1
[719] Proverbs 17:4
[720] Isaiah 9:16
[721] Proverbs 17:4
[722] Jeremiah 9:5
[723] Psalms 109:4

expression - This[724] shall be your lot your measured portion. is with the one who speaks evil speech. For they will surely say - See, the listeners accepted the thing, and that is a sign that the thing is really true. Even if the listener tilted his ear and made himself appear to be listening and believing these words in front of people, this also helps the evil, causes a disgrace to the subject of the talk, and strengthens the hands of the one who brings his evil speech against people. And King Solomon, peace be upon him, said - A[725] north wind **Tehollel** [glory] rain, and a raging face, a hidden tongue. Its explanation is, just like a north wind scatters the clouds and prevents the rain, so does a raging face stop evil speech. For when the speaker sees the face of the listener enraged, he will stop the voice of his raining words. But if he sees that the listener is listening to him, he will not stop his mouth from his lies; and tomorrow will be like today. For he will repeat his stupidity, to always speak false speech; and his tongue will follow the rain of his falsehoods. **Tehollel** [glory] is from the expression **Challilah** [God forbid]. And likewise - He[726] shall not **Yechal** [annul] his word. And also - It[727] was then **Huchal** [began] to call. which means it was then prevented.

King Solomon, peace be upon him, also said - A[728] lying tongue does a **Dakav** [suppress it] hate. The

---

724 Jeremiah 13:25
725 Proverbs 25:23
726 Numbers 30:3
727 Genesis 4:26
728 Proverbs 26:28

258

explanation is that a humble, contrite and lowly person hates a lying tongue - he will not seek it nor listen to it. For a humble person desires people's worth, and is pained by their embarrassment and disgrace. The letter - **Vav** - ו, is in place of a hay in the root, like the **Vav**, in the word - **Anav** [humble] And some explain the verse as, someone with a lying tongue will hate those who make him contrite and reprimand him, so he will not bring them more evil slander against people. And behold we have been warned by that which is written - You[729] must not carry false rumors. not to believe in our hearts the telling of evil speech - to hold in our thoughts that the things are true, such as to demean in our eyes the one about whom it is spoken.

The second section:

The one who speaks evil speech, but distances himself from a false matter. And this is what they meant when they spoke of the group of slanderers, even though they are not from the group of liars. And behold, if someone mentions to his fellow - between the two of them - the bad deeds of his ancestors, he transgresses that which is written in the Torah - A[730] man may not abuse his countryman. For the verse is speaking about verbal abuse, as we mentioned earlier. And it is stated - A[731] child shall not bear the iniquity of a parent. And if he embarrasses him in front of others about the deeds of his ancestors - about this our

---

[729] Exodus 23:1
[730] Leviticus 25:17
[731] Ezekiel 18:20

Rabbis said in the Talmud - That[732] one who whitens the face of his fellow in public is from those that descend to Gehinnom and never ascend from it. And if he speaks about and makes known the abominations of his forefathers in front of people - but not in front of him - about this they said, this is the group of slanderers that does not receive the Divine Presence. And likewise, if the one he spoke about was a penitent, and he speaks about his earlier deeds.

And know that if a man sees that his fellow has transgressed against an item in the Torah privately, and the former reveals his sins at the public gate, he will surely be guilty about this. For maybe that sinner repented from his evil way and his anguish about it is in his thoughts. And the heart knows the bitterness of his soul. So, it is incorrect to reveal them, except to a discreet sage, who will not tell the rest of the masses. He will only distance himself from the sinner's company until he knows that he has repented from his evil way. And if the sinner is a Torah scholar and a man who fears sin, it is fitting to think that he has already truly repented. And if his evil impulse attacked him once, his soul causes him bitterness about it afterwards.

There are two things that the speaker of evil speech brings about: The damage and embarrassment that he causes his fellow; and his own decision to condemn and prosecute his fellows and his joy at their calamity.

[732] Bava Metzia 58b

And from one angle, the iniquity of the one who speaks evil speech about something true is greater than one who speaks about something false. For the people will believe his saying true things about his fellow, and that fellow will go up in flames in front of them. So, he will be disgraced in their eyes even after he regrets his evil and is forgiven for his sins.

And King Solomon, peace be upon him, said - Reparations[733] mediate between fools Between the upright, good will. The[734] heart alone knows its bitterness and no outsider can share in its joy. Its explanation is - the fool advocates guilt, since he searches for the blemishes of people and their guilt. So, he will attribute defects to them and never speak about their praise or about something good that is found with them. And the analogy for this is that flies always all land on dirty places. And his saying - Fools will advocate - literally, Fools advocates. in the singular is to address each and every one of the fools, like - Daughters[735] treads on the wall. And our Rabbis said in the Talmud - Anyone[736] who is of flawed lineage never speaks in praise of others and his way is to disqualify them with his own flaw. Reparations[737] mediate between fools between the upright good will. For it is the way of the just to cover over transgressions, and to praise a man when a good thing is found with him. And they spoke in ethics about a

---

[733] Proverbs 14:9
[734] Proverbs 14:10
[735] Genesis 49:22
[736] Kiddushin 70a
[737] Proverbs 14:9

simple man and a sage who were walking past a
carcass. The former said - That carcass is so rotten.
The sage said - How white are its teeth. And King
Solomon said after this - The[738] heart alone knows its
bitterness and no outsider can share in its joy. And
every sage knows that King Solomon did not bring
words that are not useful among his chosen teachings.
Rather the matter is coming with regard to the first
verse - to say that the evil of the fool that advocates
guilt is because it is probable that the sinner has
repented from his way. And no one knows the
bitterness of the soul of a person, and its joy, besides
him. And that lifts up the sin, for the essentials of
repentance are according to the bitterness of his soul.
Therefore, the fool that mentions his iniquity sins and
is guilty.

And you must know that the punishment of the fool
that advocates guilt is only when he attributes a defect
in a man who fears sin, and whose evil impulse seized
him and he sinned and was guilty - as his practice and
way is to regret his sins. And all the more so if the
matter that he repented is known. But regarding the
man whose path you have examined and he has no
fear of God in front of his eyes and is also stationed
on the bad path - it is a commandment to speak in his
disgrace and to reveal his sins, and to make the ones
involved with sin foul in the eyes of people, so that
the souls of the ones listening will be revolted from
bad deeds. And it is stated - The[739] unjust man is an

[738] Proverbs 14:10
[739] Proverbs 29:27

abomination to the righteous. And it is also stated - To[740] fear the Lord is to hate evil. And they said in the Talmud - It[741] is permissible to call an evildoer who is the son of a righteous man **an evildoer, son of an evildoer**; and it is permitted to call a righteous man who is the son of an evildoer, **a righteous man, son of a righteous man**. And behold when you see a man who is saying something or performing an act, and one can judge the thing as him being guilty or being innocent: If the man is one that fears God, you have been obligated to judge him favorably in truth - even if the thing is closer to, and makes more sense to be, understood unfavorably. And if he is from the [group] in-between, that are careful about sin, but sometimes stumble over it - you must incline the doubt towards judging favorably, as our Rabbis, may their memory be blessed, said in the Talmud - One[742] who judges another favorably is himself judged favorably. And it is a **positive** commandment from the Torah, as it is stated - You[743] shall judge your countryman **Betsedek** [justly] which can also be understood as favorably. And if the matter leans towards guilt - let the matter be a doubt to you, and do not decide it unfavorably. But if most of that man's actions are evil, or you have examined that he has no fear of God in his heart - judge his actions or his words unfavorably, as it is stated - The[744] Righteous One observes the house of

---

740 Proverbs 8:13
741 Sanhedrin 52a
742 Shabbat 127b
743 Leviticus 19:15
744 Proverbs 21:12

the wicked man; he subverts the wicked to their ruin."
And we have already discussed its explanation.

And King Solomon, peace be upon him, said - Do[745]
not say I will do to him what he did to me I will pay
the man what he deserves. I[746] passed by the field of a
lazy man by the vineyard of a man lacking sense. Its
explanation is - It is not necessary to warn, saying -
Do not be a false witness, but do say - Do not be a
vain witness. For if your companion stumbles upon a
sin, do not testify about it and do not reveal it in vain,
without punishment. For while it is true that if a man
stole or extorted his countryman, a witness is
obligated to testify so that if there are two witnesses
he will return the theft that he stole; and if there is
only one witness, there will be an oath between them;
but if he saw his fellow stumble in a matter of a sexual
prohibition or one of the sins [that do not involve
payment], it is not fitting that he should testify about
this in vain - meaning to say without punishment -
even if there is another witness with him to
authenticate the matter. And if the sinner was
someone who fears sin, it is fitting to speak to one's
heart, to say that he truly already repented. And also,
because he should fear to himself and say in his heart,
"Since this man fears the Heavens, maybe His merits
are more numerous than his iniquities; and our Rabbis
said in the Talmud - That[747] a man whose merits are
more numerous than his iniquities is surely from the

---

[745] Proverbs 24:29
[746] Proverbs 24:30
[747] Kiddushin 39a

congregation of the righteous. However, if the sinner is from the fools - the way of which is to repeat their foolishness - it is good that they tell the judges, in order to chastise him and separate him from sin. However, if he is one witness, it is not good for a man to be alone, testifying about his fellow. For his testimony is vain, since they cannot rely upon it, as it is stated - A[748] single witness may not validate against a person any guilt or sin. And therefore, he is considered a defamer. And the word - **Fitita** [mislead] is in a causative structure - it means to say that through your lips, you are grinding his face from the usage - You[749] shall break it into bits. when you reveal his hidden iniquity. And after this, he said - Do not say **I will do to him what he did to me**. For if he revealed your sins, do not take vengeance or bear a grudge to do to him like what he did to you. And this is a glorious teaching and from the essence of fear of God. But if the sinner is a man that does not fear in front of God - like someone who removes the yoke of the Heavenly kingdom, and is not careful about a commandment which all the rest of his people know is a sin - it is permissible to embarrass him and to speak about his disgrace. Thus did our Rabbis say in the Talmud - A[750] man shall not oppress his **Amito** [countryman]. Meaning, from his **Amo** [nation] - One[751] that is with you in observance of Torah and commandments he shall you not mistreat. But

---

[748] Deuteronomy 19:15
[749] Leviticus 2:6
[750] Baba Metzia 59a
[751] Leviticus 25:17

regarding one who did not put his heart to the word of the Lord, it is permissible to embarrass him with his actions, make his abominations known and pour forth disgrace upon him. And they also said in the Talmud - We[752] publicize the hypocrites due to the desecration of God's name. But if he stumbled on a sin by chance and it is his habit most of his days to be careful about iniquity, we should not reveal his sin - as we have explained. So, it would then be possible to explain - Do not be a vain witness against your companion - to testify about sins with which you have also fallen sick, like him. Hence, he is called his companion. And this is shown by its stating afterwards - Do not say **I will do to him what he did to me**. For even though it is a commandment to publicize the ones that sin to their core and the hypocrites; in the case of a sinner - if it is a man like him in his evil and like other people with his sins, we should not publicize his sin. For the first one's intention to reveal his secrets will not be for the good, but rather to rejoice in his calamity. Secondly, how will he not be embarrassed to mention the defect of these actions in someone else, when he holds on to them himself? And it is stated - I[753] will punish the House of Jehu for the bloody deeds at Jezreel - Behold even though he did a commandment in cutting off the House of Ahab, Jehu bore his sin. For he was also full of transgression.

---

[752] Yoma 86b
[753] Hosea 1:4

And our Rabbis said in the Talmud - That[754] we give lashes for rebellion to the one who testifies by himself against his fellow about the matter of a sin. However, he may reveal the matter privately to his teacher or to a man who keeps his secret, if he knows that they will believe his words like the words of two witnesses. And if there is a second witness with him, they should have the judges hear their words - in order to discipline the sinner privately, and not to whiten his face in public, as it is stated - You[755] shall surely reprimand your countryman and not bear sin because of him.

And know that regarding things between a man and his fellow - such as robbery, extortion, injury, pain, embarrassment and verbal abuse - one can tell the things to people. Even a single individual who saw it may speak, so as to help the person who was mistreated and to be zealous for the truth. And behold the Torah stated that a single witness should testify in court for a monetary claim, to obligate the defendant to take an oath. However, he should first reprimand the man.

The third section:
One who goes talebearing. And we were warned about this in the Torah, as it is stated - You[756] shall not go talebearing among your people. And this is also called evil speech. And he is included in the group of

---

[754] Pesachim 113b
[755] Leviticus 19:17
[756] Leviticus 19:16

slanderers - as our Rabbis, may their memory be blessed, mentioned about Doeg the Edomite that he was involved in evil speech because he told Saul, and said to him that David came to the house of Ahimelech. And there is no counting the damage of talebearing: For it increases hatred in the world and makes people stumble on that which is written in the Torah - You[757] shall not hate your brother in your heart. And behold the world stands upon peace in the Mishna - So[758] due to hatred, the world deteriorates, as we have discussed earlier. And many times, the talebearer puts a sword in the hand of his fellow to kill his companion, as it is written - Talebearing[759] men were in your midst intent on shedding blood. And it is also stated - They[760] are copper and iron - they are all stubbornly defiant; they go talebearing; all of them act corruptly. And our Rabbis in the Talmud called talebearing - Third[761] speech, because it kills three - The one who speaks it, the one who accepts it; and the one about whom it is said - as you know from the matter of Doeg, such that he was banished from the world to come on account of the talebearing; the priests were killed; and Saul was punished for accepting the talebearing.

And our Rabbis, may their memory be blessed, said about the matter of talebearing in the Talmud - That[762]

---

[757] Leviticus 19:17
[758] Avot 1:18
[759] Ezekiel 22:9
[760] Jeremiah 6:28
[761] Arakhin 15b
[762] Niddah 61a

even though it is forbidden to accept it and hate one's fellow as a result, yet one should not belittle the matter. Rather he should guard himself and be concerned about the matter. They, may their memory be blessed, said in the Talmud - That[763] the generation of Saul had informers like Doeg and the Ziphites. And as a result, they went to war and fell. But the generation of Ahab did not have informers - as you know from the matter of the prophets that hid from Jezebel, as it is written - I[764] am the only prophet of the Lord left. Yet Obadiah hid a hundred prophets, but no one revealed that there was a prophet besides Elijah. And as a result of this, they would go to war and be victorious - even though Ahab worshipped idolatry.

And one who causes disputes between brothers and friends and brings hatred between them is the most severe of all the sections of slander, as it is stated - And[765] one who incites brothers to quarrel. And our Rabbis said in the Midrash - The[766] seventh is the most severe of all. meaning the trait of inciting. Which is the seventh of what it says above - Six[767] things the Lord hates; the seventh is an abomination to Him. As we have mentioned to you before in the Gates of the Fear of Sin.

---

[763] Yerushalmi Peah 1:1
[764] Kings-A 18:22
[765] Proverbs 6:19
[766] Vayikra Rabbah 17:1
[767] Proverbs 6:16

A man is obligated to hide a secret that is revealed to him confidentially by his fellow, even though there is no matter of talebearing involved in revealing that secret. For there is damage to the holder of the secret simply by its being revealed, and it can cause him to abort his plan - as it is stated - Plans[768] are aborted without a secret. Secondly - because revealing a secret is even an aberration of the ways of modesty, as he surely violates the will of the holder of the secret. And King Solomon said - He[769] who gives away secrets is a talebearer. He means to say, if you see a man who does not control his spirit, to guard his tongue from revealing a secret - even though there is no issue of talebearing between a man and his friend in revealing that secret - this trait will bring him to go talebearing, which is from the four bad groups, given that his lips are not in his control to guard. He also said - A[770] talebearer will reveal secrets. He means to say, do not confide a secret to someone who goes talebearing. For since he does not guard his lips from talebearing, do not trust him to hide your secret, even though you have given your words over to him in private and in confidentiality. And we have been warned by the Torah not to accept evil speech, as it is stated - Do[771] not accept a vain report. And it is stated - A[772] ruler who listens to lies, all his ministers will be evildoers. And our Rabbis, may their memory be

---

[768] Proverbs 15:22
[769] Proverbs 20:19
[770] Proverbs 11:13
[771] Exodus 23:1
[772] Proverbs 29:12

blessed, explained in the Midrash - That[773] when a ruler accepts evil speech and words of talebearing, his ministers will become evildoers and talebearers to find favor in the eyes of their master. And behold it is these three groups that we mentioned that they, may their memory be blessed, had in mind when they referred to the group of slanderers.

And the fourth section:

The dust of evil speech. Our Rabbis said in the Talmud - Most[774] of the world stumbles upon theft and a minority upon sexual prohibitions, but all of them stumble upon the dust of evil speech. And they said that the content of the dust of evil speech is when a person causes people to speak evil speech due to his words. And they said in the Talmud - A[775] person should never speak favorably of his fellow, as out of his praise comes his disgrace. And behold we need to explain this statement - for it is known that speaking the praises of the sages and the righteous is from the proper traits, as it is stated - But[776] it is honorable to peruse honor. And it is said about a fool that he does not speak the praises of the world. Rather this is the nature of this matter, that one should only speak favorably of a man face to face. That is to say, when a man speaks to his companion - and not to the larger community and in an audience of the masses, unless he knows that there is no one in that grouping who is

---

[773] Midrash Tehillim 54
[774] Bava Batra 165a
[775] Bava Batra 164b
[776] Proverbs 25:27

an enemy of that man whom he wants to praise or one who is jealous of him. And if he wants to praise a man who is already assumed by the people of his nation to be a proper man and no evil or guilt is found about him, he should be praised even in front of his enemy or one jealous - for they will not be able to disgrace him. And even if they do disgrace him, everyone will know that such a man's mouth spoke in vain, such that his mouth will be a trap for himself.

They, may their memory be blessed, also mentioned and said about the content of the dust of evil speech in the Talmud - That[777] if a woman asked her neighbor to light a fire from the hearth, and she answers and says - Where else is a fire of coals except at so-and-so's home, who is always roasting meat and eating. This and what is similar to it is the dust of evil speech. And it is stated - He[778] who greets his fellow loudly early in the morning shall have it reckoned to him as a curse. And our Rabbis explained in the Talmud - this[779] verse about someone who praises his fellow with a praise that brings a loss, to be about a guest who goes out to the town square and calls out in a loud voice and recounts how the householder did him good - since he prepared meat and made it for the guest that came to him. But it would be that when they hear the words of the guests, worthless people will assemble and turn aside to the home of the householder. And a person is obligated to guard his

---

[777] Arakhin 15b
[778] Proverbs 27:14
[779] Arakhin 16a

mouth and his tongue, such that he not be suspected about his words and that they not account him to be one involved in evil speech. And if he does bring such a suspicion about himself with this, he has surely destroyed his ethical standing, and it will be considered the dust of evil speech for him.

And contemplate this well to understand the principle of this matter - Behold we mentioned earlier that it is permissible to speak in disgrace of the sinner about the theft that is in his hands, if it is known that he has not left his path. For example, the robber and the extortionist, the damager and the harasser, the one who whitens the face of another, the one who makes others fowl and shameful and the one who speaks evil speech - if he has not returned the theft, or payed for his damage or requested from his fellow to remove his iniquity to forgive him. However, those that see their ways must surely first speak to the sinner - perhaps they will be able to help by way of a reprimand to have him repent from his evil way. And if he surely refuses, they may then inform the public about his ways and deeds. However, a person can be blamed from the deed of his fellow that was wanton against his fellow, when he recounts his deeds to people and reveals the obligations of the sinner and disgraces his acts with various claims - Behold, the recounter will be suspected about this and they will think him one engaged in evil speech. And they will surely say - Even if the thing was true, it would have been fitting to reveal it to the ear of the sinner as a reprimand first. And his listeners will suspect him about his not giving him a reprimand first, saying that he would not have said all of this in front of [the sinner] and he is flattering him - like the matter that is stated - Let[780] no man rebuke, let no man protest! And they will further say that he enjoys speaking about the guilt of the people, the iniquity of which brings him joy and the disgrace of which brings him honor when it is not front of them; and he is similar to someone involved in evil speech and is clinging to its dust. And people will also say - The things are not true and he made them up from his heart. And, however if not, why did he not reveal his iniquity in front of him first, but rather ignore him? Hence our Rabbis said in the Talmud - Any[781] statement that is said in the presence of its master, that is the subject of the statement is not in the way of evil speech. It means to say that if he previously gave an open reprimand to his fellow about his deed, and the latter did not pay attention to his words - he may afterwards inform people of that man's guilt and the evil of his conduct. And he will not be suspected of wanting to give his fellow a defect. And likewise, if the teller is assumed by the public not to seek the favor of any man and not to bend to a man; and everything he would say not in front of his fellow, he would also say in front of him and not be frightened by any man; and he also be assumed among his people to only speak the truth - he is not to be suspected when he speaks about the guilt of his fellow not in front of him. And so did they mention in their words, may their memory be blessed,

---

[780] Hosea 4:4
[781] Arakhin 15b

about this matter and say in the Talmud - Rabbi[782] Yose says from all of my days I have never said a word and turned around behind me. He meant to say - I have never said something about a person not in front of him but suppressed it when I was in front of him. They also said - Anything that is said in front of three is not in the way of evil speech. It means to say - since there were many people with him at the time that he told the thing, hence the thing will be known to his fellow. And behold it is as if he said the words in front of him.

And the fifth section:

Vulgar speech. Our Rabbis, may their memory be blessed, said in the Talmud - Anyone[783] who speaks vulgarly - even if he was sealed for a decree of seventy years of good, it will be reversed to bad. And Isaiah said - That[784] is why my Lord will not spare their youths, nor show compassion to their orphans and widows; for all are ungodly and wicked, and every mouth speaks vulgarity. And on account of this, one who speaks vulgarly has a heavy iniquity and is ungodly and wicked. For he has abandoned and left shame and modesty, which are the famous traits of the holy seed of Israel; and went to the paths of brazenness - which is the trait of the evil boors. Secondly - because he has profaned the Holy One of Israel, as it is stated and they will say - Surely[785] that

---

[782] Shabbat 118b
[783] Shabbat 33a
[784] Isaiah 9:16
[785] Deuteronomy 4:6

great nation is a wise and discerning people. But this one acted like the disgusting foolish ones that are distanced from the ways of the intellect, which is completely beautiful and also pleasant. And their foulness rises and their stink goes up, so every sage and understanding person surely despises and surely abominates them. And behold, he is profaning the tool of the intellect which is more precious than any beloved tool - as it is stated - But[786] wise speech is a precious tool. And the punishment of one who listens to vulgar speech is great, since he does not seal his ear and does not separate from the words of vulgarity. And about him is it said - The[787] mouth of a forbidden woman is a deep pit he who is doomed by the Lord falls into it.

And our Rabbis said in the Talmud - A[788] person should never put out a disgraceful matter from his mouth; as a verse was distorted by eight letters rather than have it put out a disgraceful matter, as it is stated - From[789] the pure animals and from the animals that are not pure. For at that time, the impure animals were permissible to eat but not pure for a sacrifice. Hence it is considered a disgraceful expression if one disgraces things that are for human food. And see that a man must be careful not to put out a disgraceful matter from his mouth - even if by his leaving it, it will bring him to speak at length and add to his

---

786 Proverbs 20:15
787 Proverbs 22:14
788 Pesachim 3a
789 Genesis 7:8

statements. And it is like a fence to be careful from vulgar speech - which is one of the weighty sins. And it is also a fence from speaking evil speech and the placing of defects upon the creatures - as our Rabbis, may their memory be blessed, have said about the distancing of disgraceful speech in the Talmud - The[790] verse did not even speak in disgrace of impure animals. And our Rabbis said in the Talmud that one of the priests said in front of Rabban Yochanan ben Zakkai - I[791] received for my portion, the size of a lizard's tail. They investigated his background, and they found a trace of disqualification about him. And our Rabbis also said in the Talmud - That[792] a person must choose an honorable phrase instead of using a dishonorable phrase - even if it is not disgraceful - whether it is in words of Torah or in speaking about matters of the world. And this is so long as he does not speak at length for its sake when speaking words of Torah. For a person is obligated to teach his students in a terse fashion. And the matter of honorable phrases is the path of words and speech that was tread upon by those of clean intellect and those that speak with clarity. And they weigh and know which phrase is honorable and which is its opposite, as it is stated - And[793] you choose the language of the crafty. And it is stated - And[794] that which my lips know they shall speak sincerely. And

---

[790] Bava Batra 123a
[791] Pesachim 3b
[792] Pesachim 3a
[793] Job 15:5
[794] Job 33:3

it is stated - The[795] tongue of a righteous man is choice silver.

And the sixth section:

The complainer - King Solomon, peace be upon him, said - The[796] words of the complainer are like **Mitlahamim** [quarreling] and they enter the innards of one's belly. Its explanation is that a complainer is a man whose way and whose nature is to always complain, get angry and find pretexts about this fellow, regarding his actions and his words - even though his fellow is innocent towards him, and did him no harm in anything. And he judges everything unfavorably, and not favorably; and anything inadvertent he makes volitional. And he surely makes himself like the oppressed and beaten, and as if the sin of his fellow is heavy upon him; whereas he is the hitter and the beater, as his words - Enter the innards of one's belly. For the one who places complaints in front of his fellow when he did not touch him and only did good to him brings a storm to the heart. And behold he is like one who throws darts that - Enter the innards of one's belly. The word **Mitlahamim** [quarreling] is spelled inverted, and is as if it were **Mithalmim** [they are beating]; and like the inversion of **Simlah** and **Salmah**. And it is like the usage it in - They[797] **Halamuni** [beat me] but I was unaware. And it is as if he was saying - It is like the words of the complainer, they are beating me. And his saying -

---

795 Proverbs 1:20
796 Proverbs 18:8
797 Proverbs 23:35

They are beating. In the plural, is because the complainer includes all complainers like - The[798] sacral flesh will pass away from you. which is in singular, but refers to the many; and - Triumph[799] sprout. King Solomon, peace be upon him, also said - And[800] a complainer separates his friend. He means to say that he separates his friend and his companion from himself, as they cannot endure his friendship. And our Rabbis said in the Midrash - Do[801] not proliferate complaints, so that you will not come to sin. And many times, the complainer will be ungrateful for the good and will even consider it bad, so he will return the good with bad. And it is stated - He[802] who repays good with evil will not have evil leave his home. And sometimes he will think about God's kindnesses, that they are for vengeance and retribution - like that matter that is stated - You[803] sulked in your tents and said It is out of hatred for us that God brought us out of the land of Egypt to hand us over to the Amorites to wipe us out. Hence, distance yourself from the path of the complainers, for they have twisted their paths - anyone who walks in it will not know peace. Rather teach your tongue to judge favorably, and justice will be the girdle of your loins.

---

[798] Jeremiah 11:15
[799] Isaiah 45:8
[800] Proverbs 16:28
[801] Derekh Eretz Zuta 9
[802] Proverbs 17:13
[803] Deuteronomy 1:27

Sha'arei Teshuvah

Gates of Repentance

Rabbeinu Yonah

Chapter Four

The differences in atonement

The differences in atonement in the same way as the body has sicknesses and ailments, so too does the soul. And the ailments of the soul and its diseases are its evil traits and its sins. But when an evildoer repents from his evil path, God, may He be blessed, heals the soul of the sinner as it is stated - O[1] Lord, have mercy on me, heal my soul, for I have sinned against You. And it is also stated - And[2] repent and save itself. And in the way that it is sometimes found with the sicknesses of the body that the sickness lightens itself from upon one, as does the length of most of the ailments, but the body is not cleansed of it without drinking a bitter drink and suffering further by afflicting his soul from eating all desirable food; so too is it with the soul sick from great iniquity: And even though most of the sickness is healed, and most parts of the punishment are removed after the

---

[1] Psalms 41:5
[2] Isaiah 6:10

repentance - and God, may He be blessed, has gone away from His anger - the soul will not yet be cleansed from the sickness and its sin will not be atoned until the sinner is made to suffer with afflictions, purified with pain and with bad and difficult things that happen to him. This is like the matter that is stated - Cain[3] said to God My punishment is too great to bear. Since[4] You have banished me this day from the soil and I must avoid Your presence and become a restless wanderer on earth anyone who meets me may kill me. However, through repentance, most of his iniquity was forgiven, the main part of his punishment was removed and he was rescued from death - as it is stated - And[5] the Lord put a mark on Cain lest anyone who met him should kill him. But the punishment of exile remained for him, as it is stated - And[6] I shall be a fugitive and a wanderer in the earth. Yet he had mentioned his migration with a double expression fugitive and wanderer; whereas after the repentance, it is only stated - And[7] he dwelt in the land of wandering.

And this matter is further clarified from that which is written in the Torah - If[8] any person from among the populace unwittingly incurs guilt by doing any of the things which by God's commandments ought not to

---

[3] Genesis 4:13
[4] Genesis 4:14
[5] Genesis 4:15
[6] Genesis 4:12
[7] Genesis 4:16
[8] Leviticus 4:27

be done, and realizes guilt. Or[9] the sin of which one is guilty is made known that person shall bring a female goat without blemish as an offering for the sin of which that one is guilty. And our Rabbis, may their memory be blessed, said that a sin offering comes for being inadvertent about something for which volition would bring excision. And on account of a sin that brings excision - due to its significance - the atonement of the sinner will not be complete until he brings a sin-offering, even though he confessed his sin. For without the confession and repentance, his iniquity will not be atoned by the sin-offering, as it is stated - The[10] sacrifice of the wicked man is an abomination. But after the confession and the sacrifice, his iniquity is atoned, as it is stated - The[11] priest shall make expiation for them and they shall be forgiven. And you should understand from this how strong the punishment of the volitional one must be, if the inadvertent one is not pure after repentance until he brings a sacrifice. Indeed, his iniquity is atoned with afflictions, as it is stated - He[12] is reproved by pains on his bed and the trembling in his bones is constant. He[13] detests food Fine food is repulsive to him. His[14] flesh wastes away till it cannot be seen and his bones are rubbed away till they are invisible. He[15]

---

[9] Leviticus 4:28
[10] Proverbs 21:27
[11] Leviticus 4:20
[12] Job 33:19
[13] Job 33:20
[14] Job 33:21
[15] Job 33:22

comes close to the Pit His life verges on death. If[16] he has a representative One advocate against a thousand to declare the man's uprightness. Then[17] He has mercy on him and decrees Redeem him from descending to the Pit for I have obtained his ransom. Let[18] his flesh be healthier than in his youth Let him return to his younger days. He[19] prays to God and is accepted by Him He enters His presence with shouts of joy For He requites a man for his righteousness. And it is stated - For[20] whom the Lord loves He rebukes, as a father the son whom he favors. But there is also advice and rectification for the sinner to protect himself from such pains - with good deeds, as will be explained.

And this matter is yet further clarified in the Torah, as it is stated - For[21] on this day atonement shall be made for you to purify you of all your sins; you shall be pure before God. Behold that Yom Kippur is required after the repentance - for the essence of Yom Kippur is that it be with repentance.

And there is an iniquity for which the soul cannot be cleansed; and it will not be accepted until death separates it from the body with which it sinned - just as there is a sickness from which the body will not be cleansed all of its days - And that is the sin of

---

[16] Job 33:23
[17] Job 33:24
[18] Job 33:25
[19] Job 33:26
[20] Proverbs 3:12
[21] Leviticus 16:30

profaning God's name, as it is stated - Instead[22] there was rejoicing and merriment Killing of cattle and slaughtering of sheep Eating of meat and drinking of wine Eat and drink for tomorrow we die. For they were not heeding the words of the prophets, nor trembling about them. Rather they were gathering with their friends with all types of mirth. And it is stated about this - This[23] iniquity shall not be atoned for until you die. And it is stated - But[24] they mocked the messengers of God and disdained His words and taunted His prophets until the wrath of the Lord against His people grew beyond remedy.

But even for this sickness - even though it does not have a remedy in the way of other iniquities - there is a remedy if God, may He be blessed, assists one to sanctify His Torah in front of people and to inform people of God's power and the glory of His majestic Kingship. And his iniquity is removed according to the greatness of the action's effect, which is the opposite of the effect of the action with which he was foolish and with which he sinned. This is like the statement of the physicians about the sickness of the body - that it is cured with its opposite, and its resuscitation comes about with its replacement. And King Solomon, peace be upon him, said - Iniquity[25] is atoned by kindness and truth. And we have explained this in the first Gate about repentance. And the

[22] Isaiah 22:13
[23] Isaiah 22:14
[24] Chronicles-B 36:16
[25] Proverbs 16:6

explanation of the matter of truth that he mentioned is that the sinner should prepare his heart to strengthen the truth, help those seeking faith and remove falsehood and error. For making the truth known and turning it back into a fortress is an aspect of the glorification of God - like the matter that is stated - He[26] upheld the rights of the poor and needy then all was well was not this to know Me. And it is stated - Through[27] deceit they refuse to know Me. And our Rabbis, may their memory be blessed, said about the matter of Herod - who killed the sages asking in the Talmud - Bava[28] ben Buta advice if he could heal him or cure him of his wound. And he said to him - You have extinguished the light of the world. Go and involve yourself in the light of the world and make efforts for the building of the Temple.

Our Rabbis, may their memory be blessed, said in the Talmud - Rabbi[29] Matya ben Charash asked Rabbi Elazar ben Azariah in Rome - Have you heard the four distinctions of atonement that Rabbi Yishmael would expound? He said to him - They are three, and repentance is necessary with each and every one - If one violates a **positive** commandment and repents, he is forgiven even before he moves, as it is stated - Turn[30] back O rebellious children I will heal your afflictions Here we are, we come to You for You O ETERNAL One are our God. I will heal your

---

[26] Jeremiah 22:16
[27] Jeremiah 9:5
[28] Bava Batra 4a
[29] Yoma 86a
[30] Jeremiah 3:22

backsliding. If one violates a **negative** commandment and repents, repentance suspends his punishment and Yom Kippur atones, as it is stated - For[31] on this day shall atonement be made for you, to purify you of all your sins you shall be pure before the Lord. If one transgresses a sin that warrants excision or a death penalty from the court and then repents, repentance and Yom Kippur suspend his punishment, and afflictions absolve, as it is stated - Then[32] will I visit their transgression with the rod, and their iniquity with plagues. But regarding one who has the iniquity of the profanation of God's name in his hands - his repentance has no power to suspend, nor does Yom Kippur have power to atone, nor do afflictions have the power to absolve. Rather, all these together suspend punishment, and death absolves - as it is stated - This[33] iniquity shall not be atoned for until you die. And our Rabbis, may their memory be blessed, said in the Talmud - That[34] a burnt-offering atones after the repentance - for one who transgressed a **positive** commandment. For while his iniquity was atoned by the repentance alone, the burnt-offering adds to his atonement and adds to his being accepted by God, may He be blessed.

They also said in the Talmud - A[35] burnt-offering atones for the meditations of the heart that come up in people's souls and the thought of sins. And

---

[31] Leviticus 16:30
[32] Psalms 89:33
[33] Isaiah 22:14
[34] Yoma 36a
[35] Yerushalmi Yoma 5:7

likewise, is it written - When[36] a round of feast days was over Job would send word to them to sanctify themselves and rising early in the morning he would make burnt offerings one for each of them for Job thought Perhaps my children have sinned and blasphemed God in their thoughts this is what Job always used to do.

And now that - due to our sins and due to the sins of our ancestors - we do not have sacrifices - If one sinned with the meditations of the heart or transgressed a **positive** commandment, he should read the section of the burnt-offering at the beginning of Parashat Vayikra and at the beginning of Parashat Tsav et Aharon. For the reading of the section of the sacrifice is in place of the bringing of a sacrifice for us - whether we read it from the written text or whether we read it by heart. It is like our Rabbis, may their memory be blessed, said in the Talmud - Anyone[37] involved with the section of the burnt-offering is as if he brought a burnt-offering; with the section of the sin-offering is as if he brought a sin-offering; with the section of the guilt-offering is as if he brought a guilt-offering. And if a person transgressed a **negative** commandment and repented, he should worry about his iniquity and long for and anticipate getting to Yom Kippur in order that he will be accepted by God, may He be blessed. For His desire is for the life of the soul and the body, and the

---

[36] Job 1:5
[37] Menachot 110a

life of all that has been created as it is stated - Life[38] is in His will. And therefore, our Rabbis, may their memory be blessed, said in the Talmud - Anyone[39] who fixes his meal on the eve of Yom Kippur is as if he had been commanded to fast on the ninth and the Tenth of **Tishrei** and fasted on them. For he has shown joy at the arrival of the time of his atonement; and it will be testimony for him, about his worry about his guilt and about his despondence about his iniquities.

Secondly - because on other holidays, we establish a meal for the joy of the commandment. For the reward for joy over the commandment increases and grows, as it is stated - Now[40] Your people, who are present here - I saw them joyously making freewill offerings. And it is stated - Because[41] you would not serve the Lord your God in joy and gladness. But since the fast is on Yom Kippur, they were obligated to fix the meal over the joy of the commandment, on the eve of Yom Kippur.

Thirdly - in order that we be strengthened to increase our prayer and supplications on Yom Kippur and think of strategies for ourselves regarding repentance and its main principles.

And if a person transgressed a sin that warrants

---

[38] Psalms 30:6
[39] Rosh Hashanah 9a
[40] Chronicles-A 29:17
[41] Deuteronomy 28:47

excision or a death penalty from the court and he repents - Since his iniquity is not absolved without afflictions given that repentance suspends the punishment, but afflictions absolve he should prepare his heart to do the commandments that protect him from the afflictions, such as the commandment of charity. For it also saves from death, as it is stated - But[42] **Tsedekah** [righteousness] which can also mean charity saves from death. And one who does not have money to give charity, should speak well about the poor person, so that he will be a spokesman for him, such that others do well by him. And our Rabbis, may their memory be blessed, said in the Talmud - Greater[43] is the one who causes a commandment to be done than one who does it. And likewise, should he involve himself with deeds of loving-kindness, to help his fellow with his counsel and his efforts. And [it is] like our Rabbis, may their memory be blessed, said in the Talmud - Acts[44] of kindness are superior to charity... Charity can be performed only with one's money, while acts of kindness can be performed both with his person and with his money. Charity is given to the poor, while acts of kindness are performed both for the poor and for the rich. And likewise, should he speak to the heart of the poor person and honor him and console him from his distress, like the matter that is stated - And[45] you offer your compassion to the hungry. And our Rabbis, may their memory be

---

[42] Proverbs 10:2
[43] Bava Batra 9a
[44] Sukkah 49b
[45] Isaiah 58:10

blessed, said in the Talmud - That[46] one who appeases his fellow with words is greater than one who gives him charity. And likewise, should he be involved in the commandments of visiting the sick, burying the dead, consoling the mourners and rejoicing the groom and bride. For all of these are from the ways of kindness.

And corresponding to all of them is the commandment of Torah study for the sake of the Heavens. And all of the counsel that we have mentioned is included in that which King Solomon, peace be upon him, said - Iniquity[47] is atoned by kindness and truth. For the acquisition of Torah knowledge is called the acquisition of truth, as it is stated - Acquire[48] the truth and do not sell it. And it is stated - And[49] Your Torah is truth. And our Rabbis, may their memory be blessed, said in the Midrash - It[50] is a tree of life to those who grasp it - If a person transgressed a sin that warrants excision or a death penalty from the court - If he was accustomed to reading one chapter of Mishnah a day, he should read two chapters; if he was accustomed to reading one section of Torah, he should read two sections. And Torah study protects him from afflictions from two angles - The first is because our Sages, may their memory be blessed, said in the Talmud - Torah[51]

---

46 Bava Batra 9b
47 Proverbs 16:6
48 Proverbs 23:23
49 Psalms 119:142
50 Vayikra Rabbah 25:1
51 Shabbat 127b

study corresponds to all of the other commandments combined. And the second is that when he toils in Torah, exerts himself upon it and pushes away the sleep from his eyes it is counted in place of afflictions. It is as our Rabbis, may their memory be blessed, said in the Talmud - All[52] bodies are born for toil - Happy is one whose exertion is for Torah. And they said in the Talmud - Why[53] is the Torah called **Tushiyya** [wisdom]? Because it **Mateshet** [weakens] the strength of a person.

And likewise, should he put fasts, tears and abstaining himself from delights in the place of afflictions - as it is stated - My[54] knees give way from fasting my flesh is lean has lost its fat. And it is stated - Turn[55] back to Me with all your hearts and with fasting weeping, and lamenting. And he should always sigh from the bitterness of his heart, as we mentioned in the first Gate about repentance. And he will place the abundance of bitterness in the place of afflictions, as it is stated - A[56] man's spirit can **Yekhalkel** [sustain] him through illness but low spirits who can bear them? The explanation is that when the body becomes sick, the soul will sustain it during its sickness - from the usage - But[57] who can **Mekhalkel** [bear] the day of his coming? Here it means to say help the body and sustain it by speaking to its heart and comforting it to

[52] Sanhedrin 99b
[53] Sanhedrin 26b
[54] Psalms 109:24
[55] Joel 2:12
[56] Proverbs 18:14
[57] Malachi 3:2

accept difficulties and to carry them. But when the soul is sick and low from grief and worry, who will console the soul, and who will hold it up and sustain it? Behold, worry and bitterness of the heart are heavier than sickness of the body - for the soul sustains the body in its sickness; whereas when the soul is sick and low from its grief, the body will not sustain it. So, if you find the sinner suffering, with troubles happening to him, justifying his judgement and accepting the rebuke with love - this will be a shield for him from the many afflictions that would be fit to come upon him. It is as it is stated - The[58] rage of men shall acknowledge You when You gird on the remnant of fury. Its explanation is, when the pain of a man acknowledges You - meaning that a man acknowledges You at the time of his pain. It is from the usage - If[59] my anger were surely weighed. The meaning of anger, like rage in **Tehillim** - The[60] fiercest of men shall acknowledge You when You gird on the last bit of fury. is pain - **The remnant of fury** that had been opened to come upon the man - like the content of - Let[61] not him who girds on his sword boast like him who opens it. Gird and hold them back and do not bring them upon him. And this is by way of a comparison to one who opens his sword, but then returns it to its sheath. And it is stated - Although[62] You were wroth with me your wrath has turned back and You comfort me. And likewise,

---

[58] Psalms 76:11
[59] Job 6:2
[60] Psalms 76:11
[61] Kings-A 20:11
[62] Isaiah 12:1

about the matter of acknowledgement for the good, it is stated - I[63] praise You forever for You have acted I will hope in Your name for it is good in the presence of Your faithful ones. Its explanation is - I will praise You for the good that You have done with me; and because of this, I will hope for the constancy of Your goodness. And it is stated - I[64] raise the cup of deliverance and invoke the name of the LORD. The[65] bonds of death encompassed me the torments of **Sheol** [hell] overtook me I came upon trouble and sorrow. And[66] I invoked the name of the LORD O LORD save my life. And our Rabbis, may their memory be blessed, said in the Midrash - About[67] the matter of that which is written - A[68] song of David when he fled. Justice[69] done is a joy to the righteous. The trait of the righteous is to pay their debts and to sing to the Holy One, blessed be He. There is a relevant parable about a householder that had a sharecropper, and that sharecropper was in debt to him. That sharecropper then made a threshing floor from his produce, gathered it together and made a pile. The householder came and took the pile, and the sharecropper entered his house empty-handed. But he was happy that he entered empty-handed. They said to him - You left your threshing floor with your hands on your head empty, and you are happy? He said to

---

[63] Psalms 52:11
[64] Psalms 116:13
[65] Psalms 116:3-4
[66] Psalms 116:3-4
[67] Midrash Tehillim 79
[68] Psalms 3:1
[69] Proverbs 21:15

them - Even so, the bill is now cancelled; I have paid my debt.

And a person is obligated to reflect and know that the troubles that find him and the afflictions that come upon him are not according to the greatness of his iniquity and the multitude of his sins. Rather God, may He be blessed - in His pity upon him - afflicts him in the way of the rebuke of a father upon his son, as it is stated - And[70] you shall know in your heart that, as a man chastens his son so the Lord your God chastens you. And our Rabbis, may their memory be blessed, explained in the Midrash - Your[71] heart knows the deeds you have done and the afflictions I have brought upon you that it is not according to your deeds that I have afflicted you. And it is stated - And[72] know that God has overlooked for you some of your iniquity. And it is stated - Though[73] You our God have been forbearing punishing us less than our iniquity. But when reproof comes upon the enemies of the Lord, may He be blessed, they are finished with one iniquity - for the punishment comes all at once, as it is stated - One[74] misfortune is the deathblow of the wicked. So, the rest of their iniquities remain upon their souls, as it is stated - And[75] their iniquities shall be upon their bones. However, when reproof comes to the righteous, it comes little by little, until the

---

[70] Deuteronomy 8:5
[71] Yalkut Shimoni on Torah 350
[72] Job 11:6
[73] Ezra 9:13
[74] Psalms 34:22
[75] Ezekiel 32:27

termination of their iniquities, as it is stated - You[76] alone have I known from all the families of the earth that is why I will call you to account for all your iniquities. And our Rabbis, may their memory be blessed, explained in the Talmud - It[77] is comparable to a person who lends money to two people, one of whom is his friend, and the other one is his enemy. In the case of his friend, he collects from him little by little; whereas in the case of his enemy, he collects from him all at once. And it is stated - Seven[78] times the righteous man falls and gets up while the wicked are tripped by one misfortune. Its explanation is that they stumble upon one misfortune and are finished. And it is stated - Chastise[79] me O Lord but only in judgement not in Your wrath lest You reduce me to naught. Its explanation is - **but only in judgement** - with the trait of mercy and the property of Your kindness. This is from the usage in - The[80] meal offerings and libations for the bulls rams and lambs in the quantities prescribed. In their count according to their judgement, which means according to their property - Who[81] conducts his affairs in justice. means with measure. And they compared it to another parable regarding this matter and said in the Midrash - One[82] who does not know how to hit will hit his son in his eyes and in his face; whereas one who knows

76 Amos 3:2
77 Avodah Zarah 4a
78 Proverbs 24:16
79 Jeremiah 10:24
80 Numbers 29:18
81 Psalms 112:5
82 Midrash Tehillim 18

[how] to hit will hit his son in such a way that it will not cause him damage. And likewise, is it written - The[83] Lord surely chastised me, but He did not give me over to death. And it is stated - But[84] only spare his life. And He only brings vengeful afflictions upon the evildoers. But probing afflictions only come upon the righteous; for they accept them with love and they increase the refinement of their actions. So, these afflictions are for their good and their benefit, and the increase of their reward, as it is stated - The[85] Lord probes the righteous one. And our Rabbis, may their memory be blessed, compared it to a parable regarding this and said in the Midrash - When[86] the owner of the flax knows that the flax is strong, he hits it much in order to make it soft and good.

And behold we are going back to the matter about which we were talking regarding the order of atonements; and we shall say that if a person unintentionally transgressed a sin that warrants excision or a death penalty from the court, he is obligated to confess, to seek supplications for his forgiveness, to sigh bitter-heartedly, to worry and be afraid. For these are the main catalysts of the various atoments. And he should constantly be involved with the Torah section about the sin-offering - and it will be considered as if he brought a sin-offering. I mean

---

[83]   Psalms 118:18
[84]   Job 2:6
[85]   Psalms 11:5
[86]   Bereishit Rabbah 58:32

to say, it will be very effective in the matter and atone
for him, similar to the sin-offering.

And know that the inadvertent sinner will certainly be
punished, as we have already explained; and all the
more so, the transgressor - meaning one who is
inadvertent about something that most people are
careful about - so he should worry and be afraid
because of his sin. And our Rabbis, may their
memory be blessed, said in the Midrash - In[87]
explanation of that which is written - Beautiful[88] for
situation, the joy of the whole earth Mount Zion the
sides of the north the city of the great King. That at a
time when a person was an inadvertent sinner, his
heart would be worried and he would tremble with
fear about his sin until he would go up to Jerusalem
and offer his sin-offering. And then he was
completely happy. About this was it stated -
Beautiful for situation the joy of the whole earth.
And that which it states - **The sides of the north**, is
speaking about the altar. As - **The sides of the north**,
were - **The joy of the whole world**, since the sin-
offering was slaughtered on the northern side. And
our Rabbis, may their memory be blessed, said in the
Midrash - When[89] a person commits a transgression
and constantly goes back and forth in his heart
concerning the matter of his sin that he sinned, and
trembles and fears about it - the Holy One, blessed be
He, forgives him. But when he removes the

---

[87] Midrash Tehillim 48
[88] Psalms 48:3
[89] Midrash Tehillim 51

transgression from in front of his eyes and it is little and light in his eyes, his case is similar to one who is bitten by a scorpion, but makes light of the bite. So, he presses his foot on the ground to remove the poison. But those who see him say to him, Do you not know that it will go up from the sole of your foot, even up to your skull?

Now let us speak about one who has the sin of the profaning of God's name in his hands, the iniquity of which is not atoned by afflictions. And behold we have mentioned above that he has a healing cure if he constantly sanctifies God's name, may He be blessed. You can find another atonement in his constantly meditating upon the Torah and his efforts in its study. This is as our Rabbis, may their memory be blessed, said in the Talmud - It[90] will not be purged with sacrifice nor offering forever. With[91] sacrifice or offering it is not atoned but it can be atoned through Torah study. And even though the sin of Eli's house was with the profanation of the commandment of sanctified foods, as it is stated - In[92] that he knew that his sons brought a curse upon themselves. And see that it is because Torah study is a cure for every very painful wound. Therefore, is it written - A[93] healing tongue is a tree of life.

And about that which they, may their memory be

---

90 Rosh Hashanah 18a
91 Samuel-A 3:14
92 Samuel-A 3:13
93 Proverbs 15:4

blessed, said in the Talmud - About[94] sins that warrant excision or a death penalty from the court, repentance and Yom Kippur suspend the punishment, and afflictions absolve. There is a question - And is it not written - For[95] on this day atonement shall be made for you to purify you of all your sins you shall be pure before God. And the answer to this is that, that which is stated - **You shall be pure before the God,** is a **positive** commandment to repent that we search our ways and investigate them and return to the Lord on Yom Kippur. And even though we have been obligated about this at all times, this obligation is added on Yom Kippur. And the purification that is in our hands is repentance and refinement of our - deeds. But that which is written earlier - For on this day shall atonement be made for you, to purify you. Which is written about the purification that God, may He be blessed, is to purify us from iniquity and atone for us with a complete atonement on Yom Kippur without afflictions - is stated about simple **negative** commandments. But regarding sins that warrant excision or a death penalty from the court, repentance and Yom Kippur only suspend the punishment, and afflictions absolve.

And our Rabbis, may their memory be blessed, said in the Talmud - Of[96] all your sins - **you shall be pure before the Lord** - Yom Kippur atones for transgressions between a person and the

---

94 Yoma 86a
95 Leviticus 16:30
96 Yoma 85b

Omnipresent. Yom Kippur does not atone for transgressions between a person and his fellow until he appeases his fellow. Hence one who has robbed his fellow must return the theft and confess afterwards. But if he confesses first, his confession is ineffective. This is as our Rabbis, may their memory be blessed, said in the Talmud - Concerning[97] a robber or one who swears falsely about his debt who is obligated to pay the principal and a fifth, and to bring a guilt-offering - that one who brings his theft before he has brought his guilt-offering has fulfilled his obligation; his guilt-offering before he has brought his theft has not fulfilled his obligation. For it is stated concerning the robber of a convert that has no heirs, such that the robber must give the repayments to a priest - Then[98] the guilt shall be to the Lord for the priest; besides the ram of atonement with which atonement is made on his behalf. Its explanation: The guilt that is mentioned in this verse is referring to the repayment - from the usage - And[99] he shall give it to whom he is guilty. And he brings the repayment first - **Besides the ram of atonement with which atonement is made on his behalf** afterwards.

And our Rabbis, may their memory be blessed, said in the Talmud - One[100] who angers his friend, verbally must appease him. And it is not even necessary to say this if he spoke evil speech about him, for that is from

---

[97] Bava Kamma 110a
[98] Numbers 5:8
[99] Numbers 5:7
[100] Yoma 87a

the more severe transgressions. And if his fellow does not forgive him, he is obligated to come to him with a group of three people. And if he does not forgive him [again], he comes in front of him a second time with a different group. And so must he do a third time. And Elihu said - He[101] should then assemble **Yashor** [honest] a row of men and say I have sinned and perverted that which was right **Yashor** [honest] and it was not **Shavah** [fitting] for me. The explanation is, I have perverted a just man - from the usage - Blameless[102] and just man **Yashor** [honest]. For I did not see the merit of the just man, but rather made him into one crooked and twisted. But it was not level **Shavah** [fitting] and just for me, from the usage - Is[103] it not if he leveled **Shavah** [fitting] its surface. And in - To[104] the level **Shavah** [fitting] valley meaning straight and level. And since he disparaged just ones in front of people, he must humble himself and confess in front of the many. Hence Elihu spoke about this sin in particular, for it is one of the weighty sins that destroys the soul. And our Rabbis, may their memory be blessed, said in the Talmud - Anyone[105] who disparages Torah scholars cannot be healed from his wound. For they profaned the Torah - as it is stated - But[106] they mocked the messengers of God and disdained His words and taunted His prophets until

---

[101] Job 33:27
[102] Job 1:1
[103] Isaiah 28:25
[104] Genesis 14:17
[105] Shabbat 119b
[106] Chronicles-B 36:16

the wrath of the LORD against His people grew beyond remedy. It could not be healed.

And that which our Rabbis, may their memory be blessed, said in the Talmud - Regarding one who has [the iniquity of the] profanation of God's name in his hands - Repentance[107] Yom Kippur and afflictions suspend the punishment but death absolves. It is because death absolves any sin for which repentance is effective. And if he is killed - but confessed before his death when the fear of death fell upon him - he receives atonement; and his killer is considered like someone who spills the blood of someone pure and pious - as it is stated - The[108] flesh of Your faithful for the wild beasts. And our Rabbis, may their memory be blessed, said in the Midrash - That[109] this is also stated about the evildoers among them; as it is stated about them - They[110] were well-fed, lusty stallions. For they were considered like pious ones, because the judgement was meted out upon them. As it is written - And[111] your brother be degraded before your eyes. Once he was lashed, he is certainly like your brother.

And our Rabbis, may their memory be blessed, said in the Talmud - Transgressions[112] that one confessed on this Yom Kippur, he should repeat and confess on

---

107   Yoma 86b
108   Psalms 79:2
109   Shemot Rabbah 53:2
110   Jeremiah 5:8
111   Deuteronomy 25:3
112   Yoma 86b

another Yom Kippur, as it is stated - And[113] my sin is ever before me. Rabbi Eliezer ben Yaakov says - He should not confess them on another Yom Kippur. But in the Midrash - They[114] warned a great deal not to repeat and confess them on another Yom Kippur. And they warned about this from three angles. The first is that he shows himself to be from those with little trust and as if he does not trust the greatness of God's forgiveness, may He be blessed - that He lifts off the iniquity and passes over the transgression. And they mentioned about this - Let[115] lying lips be stilled. And the second is because if he only mentions the earlier iniquities, he will appear like one whose only worry is about the earlier ones. And has he not sinned afterwards? And if so, he appears as one who does not search and examine his ways; and this is a very bad sickness. For those that supervise their souls always see matters of iniquity in it or its ailments; or that it is falling short in attaining levels of fear of God; or that it is falling short in divine service and involvement in Torah study - as there are great punishments for these. And also, since transgressions of the tongue are common. And our Rabbis, may their memory be blessed, said in the Talmud - There[116] are three things from which a person is not spared each day - Sinful thoughts, the dust of evil speech and that they are not focusing their hearts in prayer many times. And the third is because it appears as if he is boasting through

---

[113] Psalms 51:5
[114] Shemot Rabbah 53:2
[115] Psalms 31:19
[116] Bava Batra 164b

his confession that is only upon the earlier ones, as he did not sin afterwards. And in the Midrash, they said - Is it because you do not have from the new, that you are confessing about the earlier ones? And they explained in the Midrash that, that which it is written **and my sin is ever before me,** is to mean that they should be in front of his eyes and remembered in his heart, but not that he should mention them with his mouth. They also explained in the in the Talmud - That[117] they should not be in your eyes as if you did not do them; but rather as if you did them and they were forgiven. And we have already mentioned this in the Gates of the Fundamentals of Repentance. Nevertheless, he should seek mercy all the days of his life for forgiveness of his iniquities, both old and new; and be afraid and scared that maybe he has not completed the measure of the fundamentals of repentance. Secondly because the sins that warrant excision are absolved by afflictions, as we mentioned. King David, peace be upon him, also said - Do[118] not remember my youthful sins and transgressions. However, he did not mention the earlier ones individually, since he already repented for them and confessed them on Yom Kippur. So, he already fulfilled the commandment of confession and can trust that his confession was already accepted for that which confession is fitting to atone. However, he should pray for the forgiveness of his iniquities all of his days, as we mentioned. Yet it is not from the obligation of prayer to specify his sins; only from the

---

[117] Talmud Yerushalmi Yoma 8:7
[118] Psalms 25:7

obligation of confession. And there is yet another reason to pray about the iniquities of earlier days - because maybe he has iniquities and sins that he did not contemplate; and did not remember and confess, like the matter that is stated - Clear[119] me of unperceived guilt.

And the order of the confession is - We have sinned, we have been iniquitous, we have transgressed - **Chatanu** [We have sinned] **Avinu** [our wickedness] **Pashanu** [We have sinned]. And sin includes inadvertent sin and **Peshiyah**. And the meaning of - **Peshiyah** [crime] according to the Sages of Israel, is when one is not careful about a matter about which it is the way of most people to be careful, as we have already mentioned. And iniquities **Avonot** [maliciousness] are volitional sins. And transgressions - **Peshayim** [criminals] are acts of rebellion, from the usage in - The[120] king of Moab has rebelled **Pasha** [crime] against me. And - according to His great Kindness, God, may He be blessed, forgives even those who rebel against Him, when they repent to Him with all of their hearts. And it is stated - To[121] the Lord, our God belong mercy and forgiveness for we rebelled **Pashanu** [We have sinned] against Him. And it is stated - For[122] the sake of Your name O Lord pardon my iniquity **Avoni** [my sin] though it be great. And it is stated - All[123] manner

[119] Psalms 19:13
[120] Kings-B 3:7
[121] Daniel 9:9
[122] Psalms 25:11
[123] Psalms 65:4

of iniquities overwhelms me; it is You who forgives our transgressions **Peshaeinu** [our crime].